The Broken Eagle

*The Politics of Austrian Literature
from Empire to Anschluss*

The Broken Eagle

*The Politics of Austrian Literature
from Empire to Anschluss*

C. E. WILLIAMS

BARNES & NOBLE
BOOKS
10 East 53d St. New York 10022
(a division of Harper & Row Publishers, Inc.)

For Pam

Published in the U.S.A. 1974 by
HARPER & ROW PUBLISHERS INC.
BARNES & NOBLE IMPORT DIVISION

First published by Paul Elek Ltd, London 1974

ISBN 06-497713-7

Printed in Great Britain

Contents

List of Illustrations

Preface

Most books dealing with an 'Austrian' theme begin by trying to define what they mean by the term: this one, alas, is no exception. But instead of launching into a list of dates and constitutional changes, I would simply note that in my title the word 'Austrian' is used to describe writers who were born within the territory of the late nineteenth-century Habsburg Monarchy and whose language was German. There are those who claim Rilke, Kafka and Werfel for Czechoslovakia. Certainly, these writers are not Viennese Austrians—but then neither are they Czechs or Germans. By applying the epithet 'Austrian' to Werfel, for example, I am not attempting to annexe him to a particular national literature but merely using a convenient term of cultural history. For the purpose of this study it is, I believe, meaningful to associate him with his Viennese contemporaries. Where I wish to distinguish between the German-speaking and the Slavonic or Magyar citizens of the Monarchy, or between the Habsburg Germans and the Germans of the Reich, I have used the word 'Austro-German'. The Habsburg Monarchy, the Dual Monarchy, Austria-Hungary and the Habsburg Empire are here adopted as interchangeable terms. Historically speaking, the names denote the Habsburg dominions at different stages in their constitutional development but I do not feel that my laxity in this respect affects the arguments of the book.

I have not restricted myself to any particular method of approach to these writers. Certain chapters cover a limited period or single works in some detail; others range widely over three or four decades and a life's work. Some concentrate on work written before 1918; others on work written between the Wars. The shape of each individual chapter was determined by the nature of the material, although I have always tried to bear certain central themes in mind. The chapters are arranged in their present order not on grounds of chronology or importance but in order to show the gradual development of certain themes and variations. The book begins with Hofmannsthal, the most traditional of these writers in his response to politics, and ends with Kraus, the most radical.

In order to make my arguments readily accessible to the non-specialist, I have quoted illustrative material in translation. Unless otherwise indicated, the translations are my own. In each case the specialist reader will find a reference to the original source. The Notes consist largely of bibliographical references and have therefore been placed together at the end of the book. Anything of material relevance to the text has been included in the form of conventional footnotes.

In the Appendix I have included an outline of the political history of the period. It is meant as a guide to help English readers find their bearings in relatively unfamiliar terrain. It is no substitute for proper historical narratives such as are listed in the brief Bibliography.

Finally, a word about 'ideology'. I am aware that in a study of this sort one's own political sympathies are likely to colour the evaluation of the material. Given the nature of the problem and the historical circumstances in which it is defined, this could scarcely be otherwise. The notion of the detached intellectual free from all ideological contamination and hovering like the Spirit over the turbulent waters of political debate is itself an ideological concept to which I cannot subscribe. If my point of view distorts my evaluation, I have failed in my critical task. If it challenges some preconceptions and provokes debate, so much the better.

Acknowledgements

My thanks are due to Peter Stern for his pertinent criticism and patient advice. For his guidance and encouragement I am deeply grateful. I also owe a debt of gratitude to Robert Bolgar whose interest in this project stimulated my own enthusiasm and led to many enlightening discussions. To Edward Timms and James Joll who read the manuscript at an earlier stage; to the staff of the War Archives in Vienna and the Austrian Institute in London who helped me find material; to Roger Williams and David Charlton who placed their knowledge of Viennese music at my disposal; to Elisabeth Pablé, Elisabeth Stengel, Franz Kuna and Peter Flinn whose comments on my subject did not go unheeded, my thanks for their assistance or suggestions. I am indebted to the Editors of the *Journal of European Studies, German Life and Letters* and *Forum for Modern Language Studies* for permission to reprint material which first appeared in their periodicals; and to Messrs Alfred A. Knopf, Inc. for permission to quote passages from Doderer's *The Demons*, translated by Richard and Clara Winston (New York, 1961).

Introduction

These studies attempt to illustrate and analyse the reactions of several major Austrian writers to the political upheavals of the years 1914 to 1938—the First World War and its aftermath— thereby offering a contribution to the literary and intellectual history of Austria during this period. I have drawn on the work of Hugo von Hofmannsthal, Hermann Bahr, Arthur Schnitzler, Joseph Roth, Franz Werfel, Stefan Zweig, Heimito von Doderer, Robert Musil and Karl Kraus. I have traced the way in which certain political themes and problems are mirrored in both the creative work and, where they were available to me, the private papers of these writers. The enquiry relates their ideas to the wider field of Austrian politics, while at the same time examining the relevance of the literary tradition within which they wrote to their treatment of political issues.

The writers upon whom I have concentrated are as representative a selection as this particular situation can offer. They include established figures such as Schnitzler or Bahr whose important work already lay behind them by 1914; writers like Hofmannsthal and Kraus who were at the height of their careers at the outbreak of the War; others such as Zweig or Musil or Werfel whose work was still in the early formative stage; and Joseph Roth and Doderer whose literary careers had not yet begun. Many of these are Viennese either by birth or by adoption, though Bahr and Roth in their different ways represent the Austrian provinces, while Werfel is rooted in the German-Jewish culture of Prague. With the exception of Roth they all stem from well-to-do middle class homes, the sons of merchants, manufacturers and professional men. Their restricted social background clearly limits the significance of my study for the historian, but it is inherent in the literary situation of the time. I have chosen to omit the two most important and familiar Austrian writers of this age, Kafka and Rilke, because their work has no direct

bearing on my theme. Others such as Hermann Broch and Anton
Wildgans have been excluded or introduced only marginally because they do not appear to add substantially to the spectrum of
political opinion exhibited by writers already included.

The interest and significance of the Austrian situation in the
first decades of the present century lie in the fact that here certain
strains and conflicts were greatly intensified. Social and political
tensions were more evident in Austria-Hungary than in Wilhelminian Germany, owing to the fragility of the Habsburg framework. The rapid and far-reaching changes wrought by the War,
and the invidious circumstances which attended the First Republic's struggle for survival, contributed to the urgency of the
political pressures in postwar Austria. Yet the Viennese writers of
the time offered a determined resistance to these pressures. The
cultural sensibility of the Viennese educated classes appeared to
reinforce the 'non-political' tendency of the German intellectual
tradition. It is particularly instructive to examine the relationship between literature and politics in an exaggerated situation
of this kind.

My aim has been to ascertain how far politics impinged upon
the literature of the period and to investigate the way in which
political issues were transmuted into creative form. I have drawn
on literary works which themselves raise an expectation of political relevance. The political analysis thus represents an essential
part of the aesthetic interpretation of such works. One of my
themes is the impact of the War on Austrian literature. There
is no counterpart in Austria to the group of English writers
(Graves, Sassoon, Owen, Blunden, Jones, Rosenberg and
Manning) who tried to come to terms with their first-hand experience of war through the medium of literature. In a wider
sense, however, Austrian literature plainly bears the imprint of
the moral and political upheavals caused by the War. Yet this
subject has not received much attention hitherto.[1] A second
major theme of my book is the image of the Habsburg Monarchy
in literature after its collapse in 1918. Though some of my conclusions agree with the arguments advanced in the appropriate
chapters of Claudio Magris's *Der Habsburgische Mythos in der
österreichischen Literatur* (Salzburg, 1966), my interpretation of
the work of Zweig, Werfel, Doderer and Kraus differs materially
from Magris's analysis of these writers.[2] Where Magris is content
to identify and document the theme of 'supranationalism' as an

element of what he calls the Habsburg myth, I have tried to go a stage further by examining its objective foundation. More recently, a weighty study of *The Austrian Mind: An Intellectual and Social History 1848–1938* by William M. Johnston (Berkeley/Los Angeles/London, 1972) failed to come to grips with the issues that concern us here.

My task has not been confined to the study of a 'literature of commitment' in the sense of writing sustained by overt ideological principles, with its total demand on our allegiance, its simple moral schemes and predictable, reductive psychological portraiture. 'Committed' writing in this sense is rare in the Austrian literature of my period. Moreover the boundary between a 'literature of commitment' and political propaganda is fluid and ill-defined; at all events, that marginal area does not provide the most fertile ground for a study of the creative assimilation of political developments. There, form and language are determined solely by didactic needs. Rhetoric and allegory abound, while complexity, ambiguity, nuance and irony are ruled out by the desire to arouse the correct ideological response in the reader with the maximum clarity and effectiveness. There is a distinction between 'committed' writing which implies the projection of a closed ideological system, and literature which tries to explore and articulate the reality of political situations. The latter is primarily a literature of insight, not advocacy. The knowledge it affords has to do with the way men think and behave in political circumstances, the nature of their choices, the human consequences of political actions, the nature of leadership, the possibilities and limitations of power. It faces up to the relationship between ends and means and resists the facile equations of abstract theory. It deplores any divorce of politics and ethics, though it may well challenge and modify our conception of the relationship between them. It exposes lies and shams, it registers the disparity between words and deeds, it is sceptical and compassionate. The sort of writer I have in mind is not politically neutral. In the face of intense and urgent pressures he lends support to a particular party, principle or system of government, seeing in them the only practicable means of defending or realising certain moral and cultural values that are his chief concern. But that support is critical and lasts only as long as the crisis itself. In this sense, then, there is clearly a legitimate relationship between literature and politics, the more so when a

close rapport exists between a writer and his public. And this
brings me to my third theme. In the years 1914–1938 political
crises and public rapport were abundantly present in Austria.
Yet that legitimate relationship between literature and politics
was either ignored or viewed with deep misgivings by the majority
of writers. Their 'non-political' attitude involves indifference,
moral condemnation, aesthetic distaste or ingenuousness in the
face of political problems. At a deeper level, however, what such
attitudes frequently imply is an absence of creative interest in the
meaning and efficacy of political activity directed at practical
arrangements in the actual, and therefore imperfect, world. The
'non-political' disposition considers politics to be remote from the
authentic life of the individual and to be concerned only with
banal material aspects of existence. It argues that Art should be
concerned with fundamental questions of experience, with the
realm of the Spirit and the imagination. In its most extreme form,
aestheticism, it avers that Art has no purpose beyond creating
its own formal beauty. Among the authors examined here, Karl
Kraus is alone in affirming from the outset that (in Thomas
Mann's words) 'the political and social element constitutes an
essential area of the human situation, that it belongs to the totality
of the human problem, that it has its proper place in the sphere
of the mind and that this totality displays a dangerous breach
when the socio-political factor goes by the board'.[3]

In excluding politics from its rightful place the 'non-political'
mind not only neglects its social responsibility. It also exposes
itself to the threat of exploitation and self-delusion. In the highly
politicised atmosphere of a modern industrialised society, where
government affects everybody, the refusal to make an overt
political choice is itself a political decision—in favour of the
powers that be. Lack of political interest and experience may lead
to a fundamental misinterpretation of political events and possibilities. *Realpolitiker* have utilised the high-minded idealism of
the 'non-political' tradition to add a veneer of moral acceptability
to their ruthless ambitions. Sometimes, by hypostasising political
issues the idealists themselves have helped to intensify political
conflicts to a point where the clash of interests appears apocalyptic, reasoned debate futile and compromise a heinous betrayal.
Then only violence remains to restore their cosmic harmony.
Idealism turns into an unacknowledged ideology, a vortex of
abstractions that permits the real battle for power to proceed

unchecked. The history of Germany from Bismarck to Hitler provides ample evidence of what happens when the 'non-political' tradition is associated with an authoritarian or totalitarian regime. A more realistic relationship between art and politics does not necessarily produce quantifiable results. The pen rarely proves mightier than the sword in direct confrontation. But that is not the point. The task of political literature in our time is not to usurp the role of politicians and activists but to ensure that the voice of humanity, compassion, reason and integrity does not go unheard. Its function—the only function that can still be reconciled with its artistic conscience—is to challenge the presumptions of authority, to protest against the abuse of power and to disturb the complacency of the self-righteous, the indifferent, the ignorant. In short, it must seek to inhibit precisely that 'false consciousness' which is the product of the 'non-political' mind. At the last it will perhaps be able to say with Matthew Arnold :

> We have not won our political battles, we have not carried our main points, we have not stopped our adversaries' advance, we have not marched victoriously with the modern world; but we have told silently upon the mind of the country, we have prepared currents of feeling which sap our adversaries' position when it seems gained, we have kept up our own communications with the future. (*Culture and Anarchy*)

In itself the absence of political awareness or of a creative interest in the political world may be irrelevant to a writer's achievement. A great deal of literature is concerned not with the public or social area of our experience but with the inner self, the narrow circle of family and friends, the relationship between man and nature. We would not have it otherwise. Political indifference or ingenuousness in literature becomes aesthetically significant only when the historical circumstances in which it is written make a purely private response inappropriate; when the deliberate and arbitrary exclusion of political concerns gives rise to a perceptible element of constraint; when the desire to remain uninvolved impairs the artistic vision; when a work itself raises the expectation of political relevance, only to disappoint that expectation by evading or devaluing the political implications of its theme.

Many Austrian writers of this period echo the assumptions

upon which the 'non-political' tradition of German idealism rests
—the tradition of Kant, Fichte, Hegel, and what Fritz Stern has
called the *Vulgäridealismus* of the later nineteenth century. To
posit a causal relationship between this *German* tradition and
the response of *Austrian* writers to political events would take us
far beyond the limits of the present study. One would have to
take into consideration the differences between German and
Austrian attitudes to the State in the nineteenth century, and the
proverbial Austrian aversion to philosophical abstractions. There
are indeed close parallels with the reaction of German writers
to politics in this and earlier periods, but of more immediate
relevance perhaps is the history of political writing in Austria
itself during the previous century.

For almost two decades, from 1830 to 1848, political commitment was widespread among Austrian writers.[4] Before the revolu-
tions and risings of 1830 (in France, Poland and elsewhere) the
homeliness characteristic of *Biedermeier* Austria had encouraged
an acquiescence in political paternalism in reaction to the upheavals of the Napoleonic era. Gradually, however, Metternich's
'system' came under fire. The warning shot in the campaign was
loosed off by the novelist Charles Sealsfield (alias Karl Postl) in
his polemical travel journal *Austria as it is*, published in English
in 1828. For all his attacks on the narrow-mindedness, inefficiency
and treachery of the Austrian government, Sealsfield was no
Liberal and it was not until the appearance of Anastasius Grün's
Spaziergänge eines Wiener Poeten in 1831 that the battle was
joined in earnest. Grün's political poems were written in the spirit
of the Josephine enlightenment. They were anti-clerical, critical of
the government's fear of innovation, contemptuous of the
Austrian spy-system. They lashed out at the censorship and at
every form of reactionary behaviour. Immediately banned in
Austria, the *Spaziergänge* had a tremendous impact on a whole
generation of Liberal writers. The tone of protest slowly grew
more vehement. Younger writers such as Lenau, Meissner and
Hartmann abandoned any hope of a peaceful solution to Austria's
problems. By the second half of the 1840s, as the hold of the
regime weakened after the death of Emperor Francis II in 1835,
political protest had become so widespread among the Austrian
intelligentsia as to appear modish. Clandestine literature was
circulating freely. In 1845 the playwright Eduard von Bauernfeld
organised a notorious petition against censorship which was

signed by Grün, Grillparzer, Feuchtersleben, Halm, Hammer-
Purgstall, Saphir, Stelzhammer, Pyrker, Stifter and others. When
the Revolution came in 1848, Viennese intellectuals were very
much to the fore. The events of March in that year of hope and
disaster were inspired to a considerable extent by Liberal
ideology, and following the collapse of the regime in Vienna,
dramatists and poets sought to influence the course of history
amid a welter of pamphlets, newspaper articles and literary
works. One of the more significant commentaries on the Revolution is a series of political comedies from the satirical pen of
Johann Nestroy. In *Freiheit in Krähwinkel* (July 1848), *Lady
und Schneider* (February 1849), *Der alte Mann mit der jungen
Frau* (September 1849, withheld for fear of the restored reactionary censorship) and *Höllenangst* (November 1849), he conveys
his humane and undoctrinaire liberal values, while lampooning
the stupidity, extremism and corruption of politicians and intellectuals on both sides. Austrian writers also took a practical role
in the movement for reform. Grün and Bauernfeld negotiated
with the Court on 15 March 1848 for the granting of a Constitution and freedom of the Press; subsequently they were among
the four delegates chosen to represent Vienna at the Frankfurt
pre-parliament (though illness prevented Bauernfeld from attending). Adalbert Stifter, the foremost prose fiction writer of
nineteenth-century Austria, was a member of the electoral college
that nominated them.

With the restoration of Imperial authority and the renewal of
absolutism, political literature in Austria was almost stifled. In
any case many writers had been thoroughly shaken by the nightmare of mob rule glimpsed in the autumn of 1848, and were
driven either to observe a sceptical silence or to revise their own
political positions. The satirical *feuilletons* of Ferdinand Kürnberger, exiled in 1848 for his radicalism but allowed to return
to Vienna in 1856 to become the sardonic enemy of folly and
corruption in public life and of the vices of the Austrian
character, are exceptional in their commitment to political issues.
For many years politics remained more or less divorced from
literature, without being deliberately excluded from it. Towards
the end of the century, however, one observes an indifference
towards political issues which has more profound and far-reaching
implications.

Even during the two decades of Liberal agitation, Austrian

writers displayed a marked naivety in their approach to practical issues. (If anything, they displayed even less realism than their contemporaries in the Young Germany group.) When Karl Marx visited Vienna in August 1848 to address a newly-formed Workers' Association, nobody seemed to understand his economic analysis[5]—and small wonder. The one common feature in the writing of the Viennese opposition was anti-clericalism. Only two writers (Grün and Karl Beck) showed any awareness of the plight of the peasants. Apart from Beck, no critic showed any real understanding of the national problems within the Habsburg Empire. Initially several writers voiced a romantic sympathy with once independent nations such as the Poles, the Magyars and the Czechs, but all seemed to share the conviction that the answer to the problem of emergent nationalism lay in the wholesale embrace of German culture. In their naive enthusiasm the writers of the *Vormärz*, the pre-revolutionary period, hypostasised the struggle against the inefficiency, oppression and corruption of the Metternich regime into a mythical battle of good against evil. Practical, mundane problems of domestic and foreign policy were dismissed as trivial compared with the heroic proportions of the principles at stake.* We have here a clue to the débâcle of 1848 when the Liberals won power and proved incapable of using it. In short, a passionate commitment to politics was hampered by a failure to grasp the true realities of the political situation. This legacy of tutelage and inexperience will reappear in the period to which the present study is devoted.

To understand the background of the 'non-political' attitude of many Austrian writers in the first three decades of this present century, we have to examine more closely the relationship between art and politics in the Vienna of the *fin de siècle*. By the end of the nineteenth century the Viennese upper middle class was politically quiescent. In alliance with the aristocracy and the civil service it was pledged to maintain the status quo upon which its prosperity and influence depended. In an Austria threatened with disruption and haunted by an ever-increasing loss of power and prestige, the upper middle class was loyal to the Crown but displayed at the same time a notable apathy towards politics in

---

* In one of his few political statements, the poet Lenau ends the verse epic *Die Albigenser* (1842) by relating the modern political struggle to the religious conflicts of the late Middle Ages. The Liberals, like the Albigensians, are fighting for the true Spirit.

general. Memoirs of the time indicate that political passions were subordinated to cultural interests; the *feuilleton*, the cultural section of the newspapers which in Arthur Koestler's words was all too often 'a perverse blend of travelogue, essay and short story, bringing out the worst side of each', was far more real and of more immediate concern in well-to-do homes than the conferences of diplomats or the stormy, barren debates in the Reichsrat (Lower House). The Viennese have traditionally shown an intimate concern with the cultural affairs of their city but in this instance commentators are struck by the escapist aspect of such a cult at a time when the bourgeoisie was confronted with overwhelming political problems. Thus Ilsa Barea refers to a 'daunted professional class, clutching at its precarious cultural heritage' and to a new art which 'converted disenchantment and nervous tension into creative values'. She finds that on a less sophisticated level the lower middle class succumbed to a parallel temptation, treasuring 'a gluey pseudo-tradition of old Vienna revisited'.[6] Hermann Broch suggests that the withering away of political awareness leads to the cultivation of art as ornament rather than as a creative experience; art is thereby cheapened and vulgarised to the point where it becomes a form of hedonism —and he sees evidence of this in Vienna at the turn of the century. He too implicates most sections of Viennese society in this decline.[7] The point has been carefully argued by C. E. Schorske. Describing the exclusiveness of the inner circle of aristocratic society and the failure of the Austrian bourgeoisie to achieve social assimilation with the upper class, Schorske concludes that the only way in which the more influential sections of the bourgeoisie could attain the desired social standing was through the medium of culture, more precisely by imitating the traditional role of the nobility as patrons of the arts. Towards the end of the century a generation was growing up in an environment which paid exceptional deference to the arts and set great store by cultural refinement. As the political power of the bourgeoisie (which had always been limited) began to wane in the 1880s, the function and meaning of art changed : it became a refuge from political impotence.

Elsewhere in Europe art for art's sake implied the withdrawal of its devotees from a social class; in Vienna alone it claimed the allegiance of virtually a whole class, of which the artists were a part. The life of art became a substitute for the life of action. Indeed, art became almost a religion, the source of meaning and the food of the soul, as civic action proved increasingly futile.[8]

There is a temptation to argue that political failure *produces* the cultural efflorescence. What is certain is that both are related manifestations of the same fundamental malaise. An important element in the *bürgerlich* ethos—the liberal, moralising, social element—did not entirely disappear; at times, indeed, it conflicted with the new 'aesthetic' tendency, as bourgeois individualism was transformed into introversion and a preoccupation with the individual psyche. Viennese literature at the turn of the century could certainly display a muted moral and social concern, but it lacked an overt political awareness.

Schorske thus offers a sociological explanation for the 'non-political' attitude prevalent in *fin de siècle* Vienna. I suggest that such an attitude was encouraged, particularly among writers, by virtue of being invested with the authority of the classical tradition in Austrian literature. We have already seen how writers of the period leading up to 1848 became involved in political debate : what is equally important, and certainly more influential, is the reaction of two major Austrian writers of the nineteenth century, Franz Grillparzer and Adalbert Stifter, to the political events of their age. When twentieth-century writers, notably Hofmannsthal and Bahr, look to the Austrian literary tradition for ethical inspiration, it is to the work of Grillparzer and Stifter that they turn. There we find foreshadowed the attitudes adopted by many lesser figures of a later age.

In the *Vormärz* period Grillparzer earned the reputation of being at odds with the Imperial authorities. Though not a Liberal in the same sense as Bauernfeld or Grün, Grillparzer espoused the enlightened values of Emperor Joseph II sufficiently to be counted a member of the opposition in the Metternich era. He was bitterly critical of the censorship which harassed his literary career, and he was firmly anti-clerical. His public expressions of loyalty to the Imperial family were sometimes ambiguous; on one occasion he alluded fairly openly to the imbecility of the heir to the throne. In the 1830s, before his disgruntled withdrawal from social life, he was a regular member of the *Stammtisch* frequented by Grün and Bauernfeld. Thus in 1848 the Viennese Liberals generally looked to him for support. Yet

apart from a poem welcoming liberty but warning against radical
sedition ('Mein Vaterland'), he remained silent until the loyalist
tribute 'Feldmarschall Radetzky' of June 1848, which appeared
to endorse the ruthless suppression of the Italian rebels by the
Imperial armies and consequently inflamed Liberal opinion.
The important thing here is not Grillparzer's lack of revolutionary
enthusiasm or his fears that the Empire might disintegrate, but
his singular reluctance to explain his position and to bring his
influence to bear upon his fellow citizens in an attempt to
persuade them of the dangers they faced. There exist drafts of
open letters to the Viennese, indicating the achievements and the
perils of the moment—but they were never published.[9] The
notorious tribute to Radetzky was in fact misinterpreted by the
public, but Grillparzer refused to reveal his true motives for
writing it. (Fear of and contempt for anarchy and nationalism
determined his attitude far more than the merits of the Imperial
authorities.) He was as critical of the new absolutism after 1848
as he was suspicious of the Revolution, but he cloaked his doubts
and reserved his criticism, or obliged the regime with hollow
official tributes. In this context the dramas *Ein Bruderzwist in
Habsburg* and *Libussa* are less significant for their historical vision
than for the fact that they remained buried in Grillparzer's
writing desk until after his death. Again and again, Grillparzer
proved himself to be an astute political observer, with a far-seeing
understanding of the wider political trends of his age. Nevertheless, for one reason and another, he could or would not play the
constructive, albeit critical role in public life which he might
otherwise have done. He preferred evasiveness to open commitment, dissimulation or a brooding silence to the rough and tumble
of public affairs. The portrait of Emperor Rudolf II drawn by the
ageing dramatist is that of a kindred spirit; the two figures merge
in a poignant image of scepticism and fatalism, not without a
tragic grandeur.

The example set by Grillparzer's contemporary and admirer,
Adalbert Stifter, was of a somewhat different kind. After witnessing the horrors of revolution, Stifter embarked upon a career of
public education designed to forestall any future social and
political eruption. His novel *Der Nachsommer* (1857) embodies a
personal and social ethos which emphasises the control or sub-
limation of individual passion, the satisfactions of rural life, and
the importance of the family. The values informing the idyllic

world of Stifter's imagination are those of a paternalistic, pre-
industrial society, élitist and backward-turned, and by realistic
standards hopelessly irrelevant to the challenge of the post-
revolutionary years. Again, however, the specific values conveyed
are less significant for the present argument than the assumption
on which Stifter's enterprise rests—that personal morality is the
key to political and social harmony. As he wrote to his publisher
in March 1849, 'he who is morally free, can also be politically
free, indeed always is so.' Stifter took several practical steps in
the furtherance of the re-education of his compatriots, writing a
series of political essays in 1849 and devoting a good deal of
energy in the following years to the reform of the school system
in Upper Austria. What was never in dispute, however, was the
primacy of morality over political arrangements, and of Art and
Beauty over everyday conflict. Stifter shows a curious combination of political awareness and an aversion to political remedies,
which reappears in a later generation.

The First World War had as shattering an effect on the writers
rooted in the culture of *fin de siècle* Vienna as writers of an
earlier age had experienced in 1848. There was one major
difference. The Revolution had been preceded by more than a
decade of political literature which was virtually extinguished
in the bitter disenchantment and failure of that fateful year.
The events of August 1914, on the other hand, terminated the
divorce of literature and politics characteristic of Vienna at the
turn of the century. With the outbreak of war, Austrian writers
in general grew far more responsive to political developments.
Yet their reactions were frequently confounded by the legacy
of the 'non-political' attitude. The following study attempts an
analysis of the gradual (and sometimes only partial) transcending
of that attitude under the impact of the War and its aftermath.

I

Hugo von Hofmannsthal:
The Reluctant Witness

So dringt die Zeit, die wildverworrene, neue,
Durch hundert Wachen bis zu uns heran
Und zwingt zu schauen uns ihr greulich Antlitz.*
Grillparzer: *Ein Bruderzwist in Habsburg*

The world of politics held little interest for Hofmannsthal prior
to the outbreak of the First World War. His early lyrical poems
and dramas were steeped in the atmosphere of Viennese
décadence and at the same time informed by a dawning awareness of its ethical shortcomings. His fear of incipient nihilism in
the Nietzchean sense of collapse of all values led him through
various literary experiments to an espousal of the Austrian ethical
and theatrical tradition, especially in comedy. Prewar plays such
as *Cristinas Heimreise* (1910) or *Jedermann* (1911) embodied
general moral and social values intended to stave off the on-
slaught of egoism, materialism and spiritual despair. But they
stopped well short of specific and overt creative concern with
the problems facing the Dual Monarchy—the nationalism of its
constituent peoples, the spread of organised socialism and the
waning of Habsburg power and prestige in Europe. Even in his
correspondence one finds only passing references to political
conditions in the years leading up to 1914. The most significant
of these comments conveys a feeling of hopelessness and resignation in the face of what appeared to be insuperable difficulties.[1]
In another letter he pointed to the dearth of idealistic élan, the
disillusionment with the Imperial 'mission', and blamed the
aristocracy for failing to provide leadership and inspiration. He

* Thus press the wild confusions of the age
  Through serried ranks of sentries to confront us
  And force our gaze to dwell upon their dreadful features.

resented the shift in social balance in favour of the lower middle class and to the detriment of the traditional authorities.[2] There is a more profound reason for Hofmannsthal's pessimism than merely the dimensions of the problem : it is his enduring sense of the futility of political endeavour. During the earlier half of the War his scepticism towards political activity (though not towards the capabilities of professional politicians and civil servants) abated for a time. After being mobilised in August 1914 he was rapidly exempted from regimental duties so that he could devote himself to propaganda work and semi-official diplomatic missions to Poland, Belgium, Scandinavia and Switzerland. At one point he even had the ear of the Austrian Prime Minister, Graf Stürgkh. By the final year of the War, however, he had withdrawn from such activities. After 1918 his contribution to the attempt to reconstruct a ravaged Europe was directed at the individual conscience. He never again became enmeshed in the machinery of state or intervened directly in political affairs.

Initially the declaration of war left Hofmannsthal little time to reflect upon the wider implications of the impending conflict. In common with the majority of Austro-German intellectuals he was carried away by the tide of popular enthusiasm. Like Rilke he was infused with elation and a sense of national unity. His capacity for vital experience seemed to be heightened, personal cares fell away and he achieved a new insight into what he deemed to be the fundamental issues of the moment.[3] He condemned the treason of the Slav peoples of the Empire and expressed his belief that the structure of the Monarchy must be recast while it was still in a state of flux as a result of the outbreak of the War. He feared, however, that there was no Austrian politician with sufficient vision or power to take advantage of the opportunity. Hofmannsthal himself offered no concrete suggestion as to what might be done. These anti-Slav feelings of October 1914 echoed Austro-German public opinion and the prejudices of the Army commanders. It had been a commonplace of political thinking for some time that the loyalty of the Slav nationalities could not be relied upon in the event of war with Russia. Vienna feared the defection of the Slavs as much as the nationalists of the Wilhelminian Reich feared the pacifism of the German Socialists. Thus in the first days or weeks of the War, until it became clear that the Slav nationalities were responding to the Habsburg call, the Austro-Germans were keenly aware of the racial tie and political alliance upon which their future seemed to depend. In fact, despite enemy agitation and the activities of Slav nationalists in exile, instances of sedition, treason and desertion among the Habsburg peoples were relatively isolated until early 1918.[4] This did not prevent the Austro-Hungarian Army in 1914 from behaving like an occupying power in its own frontier areas along the Russian and Serbian borders. Hofmannsthal's initial patriotic outburst emphasised that Austria was a German state and conveyed an uncharacteristic mood of Pan-German feeling; all that mattered, he felt, was that Germany should gain its rightful place in the world.[5] Yet this aggressiveness proved shortlived. In the spring of 1915 he fell victim to bouts of depression which lasted with occasional fluctuations until 1917. For nearly three years from the beginning of the War his creative work was interrupted. He was disturbed by the course of military and political events, by evidence of shortsightedness, frivolity and a lack of probity in the administration, and failed to attain the level of detachment and concentration necessary to his literary work. Much of his time was taken up with publicistic activities. Moreover he seemed to feel that the realm of the literary imagination was inappropriate to a time of bloodshed and destruction. (So too Karl Kraus tried to rationalise his silence at the beginning of the War.) In September 1916 Hofmannsthal endeavoured to concentrate on a new comedy and recommenced work on the narrative version of *Die Frau ohne Schatten*, but he made little progress.

In the following summer, however, his faith in his function as a writer was restored. His confusion, pessimism and increasing sense of impotence disappeared and, writing to his friend Eberhard von Bodenhausen, he expressed in a breathless passage the transformation that he had undergone :

You summoned me, and it is so hard not to come when you call. But precisely because I am more alert now than I have been for a long time, indescribably alert, not apathetic and not despondent, for that very reason external events have a powerful impact on me, draw me wholly out of myself and my whole being vibrates at length. That is what these two weeks in Prague among the Czechs were like. I don't want to talk about it, it was almost too much for me. The determined hostility of this nation, their pride and presumption, the almost sacrilegious anticipation of a future which will never dawn as they dream it will—and

the way they muster all their resources in this struggle, everything united in one cause, their whole past, their Hussite deeds
and sufferings and sacrilege and holy relics, centuries of history
wheeling overhead—I returned home with such curious feelings,
they were so mixed, trepidation and anxiety and a degree of
fascination. You Germans in your monotonous existence, bereft
of history, have no idea what is now happening in this country
of ours. Nation set against nation in the midst of our common
plight, and the account rendered for a whole century and the
alliances and accusations of centuries are all present and
ready to demand a bloody reckoning. This, this is now the death
agony, the final death throes of the thousand year old Holy
Roman Empire of the German Nation and if from this cataclysm
nothing emerges and enters the new Reich of the future, enlarged by a few million Austro-Germans, nothing but a simple,
dull nation state—something the old Reich never was, it was
infinitely more, it was a holy Reich, the only institution which
stood on something more sublime than power and permanence
and self-assertion—then, as far as I am concerned, we will have
seen the last vestiges of that nimbus which still surrounded,
admittedly with no more than a wan and feeble glimmer, the
German image in the world. But from all this, from all this,
Eberhard, Beauty must again rise up, from this hell around us.[6]

Hofmannsthal acknowledged in this letter that the Austro-
Hungarian Empire could not survive the War, even in a modified
form. With this realisation came a renewed awareness of what he
felt to be the historical and cultural significance of the Monarchy,
and a keen appreciation of the loss which its destruction would
represent for Europe as a whole. His attitude was no longer
coloured by the nationalist and Pan-German prejudices of 1914 :
instead he drew a distinction between Germany and Austria and
emphasised the uniqueness of his homeland, a uniqueness stem-
ming from its close historic links with the other peoples of the
Habsburg Empire. His visit to Prague had brought home how
tradition could act as a living force, an experience which helped
to determine his approach to the problem of the spiritual regeneration of Austria in the following years. The sad resignation and
fascination with which he now viewed the Czech struggle for
independence contrasted sharply with his feelings in 1912 when
he had written of 'the Czechs lurking with a malevolent snarl'[7]
and with his bitter indictment of Czech treason in October 1914.
What also emerges from the passage is Hofmannsthal's tendency

to idealise the Holy Roman Empire, the values for which it stood, and the Habsburg Monarchy which was for him its spiritual and political heir. (We shall return to this point for it is a theme that occurs repeatedly in the writers with whom we are concerned.)

The apocalyptic days of October and November 1918, though long since anticipated, reverberated through the very fibre of his being. As the fabric of centuries collapsed about him, the political changes involved were less important to him than the final dissolution of a venerable and unique culture. He experienced a feeling of loss and desolation which he never really overcame, despite the energy with which he applied himself to the task of reconstruction. As late as 1928 he still revealed how profoundly he had been shaken by the disintegration of the Empire.[8]

At the end of the War Hofmannsthal's hopes for the immediate future were soon dashed. He expected the Christian Socialists to be returned in the elections of February 1919, he hoped that Trieste would become an international city, and that the new constitution would preserve the old *Kronländer* (the Austro-German provinces of Upper and Lower Austria, Styria, Carinthia, Salzburg, Vorarlberg and Tyrol) as autonomous cantons; he was opposed to a strong centralised machinery of government.[9] On all these points he was to a greater or lesser extent disappointed. Yet he called 1919 one of the most productive years of his life. In the following decade he strove to carry out the mission which he felt to be incumbent upon the writer—to purge reality of its impurities and complexities, to reveal the bare lineaments of existence, and to endow noumenal values with aesthetic form. Through the process of *Gestaltung* the literary imagination could overcome the apparent chaos and formless of the natural world. This spirituality informs almost all of Hofmannsthal's work in the postwar years, up to his death in 1929.

The themes of much of Hofmannsthal's later writing were anticipated in the lectures entitled 'Gesetz und Freiheit' and 'Die Idee Europa' which he delivered in 1916 in the course of a propaganda tour of Scandinavia. (Of his wartime essays and articles these speeches, of which the notes have been preserved, alone merit closer attention in the present context.) In both addresses Hofmannsthal dealt with the moral implications of suffering.

Witnessing the consequences of the War, he concluded that pain and grief could be transcended if they were seen as a necessary component of human experience and a condition of individual fulfilment.

The War had shown how men could overcome natural egoism, even the instinct of self-preservation, and accept suffering and death in an act of supreme self-denial. Hofmannsthal envisaged suffering as positive affirmation rather than as passive endurance; he spoke of 'pain and action in one', anticipating Eliot's 'action is suffering/And suffering is action'. It was a religious response characteristic of the idealist tradition in which Hofmannsthal wrote. He addressed himself to an élite, the happy few who commanded the spiritual resources required to sustain this vision. At the same time he hoped that the knowledge would then emanate in ever widening circles until it was diffused among all sections of the population. The interest of this argument lies in the tendency to confuse 'metaphysical' evil, divinely imposed and inexorable, with suffering of a more humble and ignoble order. Other Austrian writers—Schnitzler and above all Kraus—reject what to them appears to be an attitude of fatalistic acquiescence in social evils which can at best be eradicated or at worst mitigated. Pious submission to one's destiny becomes questionable when it is associated with the defence of an existing social structure (as happens in Hofmannsthal's postwar morality play *Das Salzburger grosse Welttheater*) or when it is used to justify a concrete political situation (as here the War). (Hofmannsthal was not unaware of the interests he was serving : he wrote of his plan to visit Scandinavia as a journey in aid of political propaganda.[10]) The attitude of resignation and acceptance was foreshadowed in Hofmannsthal's essay 'Der Dichter und diese Zeit' (1906/7) where he compared the true poet to a seismograph, registering the tremors shaking his culture. Removed from the literary context and applied to the life of action and decision, this passive sensibility may lead to the strength of the moral will being sapped by the curiosity of the aesthetic imagination. Robert Musil's novel *Die Verwirrungen des jungen Törless* and Thomas Mann's *Mario und der Zauberer* both illustrate this defective sensibility, the former uncritically, the latter in ironic awareness of its implications.

Hofmannsthal's position with regard to politics in the Scandinavian speeches and in subsequent essays was not without a certain piquant paradox. He remained disenchanted with politics, yet frequently dealt with what were essentially political problems, albeit in a highly idealistic manner. We have an example of this in his comments on the Habsburg Empire. In the 1916 addresses he referred to Austria's future, maintaining that there was a great deal of latent energy in his homeland which had to be tapped for the purpose of furthering international co-operation once peace had returned to Europe. He felt that Austria was in the unique position of being able to mediate between the Germanic-Roman world of Western Europe and the Slav cultures of the East. In the letter to Bodenhausen describing his impressions of Prague in 1917 he spoke of the Empire as having been founded on something more than purely political ambitions.* The notion occurred in another wartime essay ('Die Österreichische Idee' of 1917) in which he described Austria as the point from which waves of colonisation and civilisation spread eastwards, at the same time mingling with the opposing cultural current that flowed westwards to meet them. After the War he again took up this theme in a lecture delivered in 1926 to the Congress of Cultural Associations in Vienna, where he reiterated his conception of Austria-Hungary as heir to the supra-national ideal. This ideal, he claimed, remained alive almost up to the last days of the Monarchy and had a decisive impact upon Slav and Austro-German alike. Moreover, it exercised a beneficial effect over the whole area of German-speaking peoples beyond the frontiers of the Empire. The ideal of supranationalism was no longer embodied in the Habsburg Empire but it provided the motive force behind the various organisations working for European unity in the postwar world. In discussing the Habsburg ethos, particularly during the critical war years, Hofmannsthal was also contributing to a political debate—yet we notice how he avoids direct political statements. In discussing European co-operation, Hofmannsthal was again dealing with a political issue

---

* Hofmannsthal had already heard this argument from his old friend Leopold von Andrian, once a fellow aesthete and now a Habsburg diplomat. When in 1913 Hofmannsthal lamented the loss of idealistic impetus behind the Imperial idea, Andrian had replied that the Austrian idea was a given fact of history, 'an ideal which far transcends that of the simple nation-state ... the cooperation and partial fusion of the genii of all the peoples whose existence is only conceivable within a great empire.' Hofmannsthal twice visited his friend in Poland during the War.

—yet like so many well-meaning supporters of the European movement between the Wars (Stefan Zweig was another) he tried to bypass politics and speak directly to the individual conscience. They failed to recognise that to discuss political problems exclusively in terms of individual moral decisions or of cultural idealism inevitably amounted to whistling in the dark.

In the Scandinavian lectures as in several postwar essays Hofmannsthal turned away from the highly organised technological society of Germany and predicated the hitherto unexploited potential of the Austrian *Volk*, the untapped strength of an earlier phase of German culture which had been spared debilitating intellectual crises and had preserved its youthful innocence and vigour. There is a connection between this evoking of the ethical power of the people and his political disillusionment, inasmuch as the *Volk* is seen as the repository of the old and the new Austria, remote from the political débâcles of the nineteenth century. The notion that the *Volk* could supply the qualities whereby Austria might be revived was again anticipated in Hofmannsthal's prewar writing. The 'Briefe des Zurückgekehrten' (1907), with their criticism of the confusion, indecision, disunity, contradictions and fragmentation of modern German life, contrasted this desolate scene with that sense of the 'whole man', of a living community, of integration with the natural world which characterised the art of Dürer. Through art, whether that of Dürer or Van Gogh, the nullity of contemporary Germany could be transcended and a vision of harmony and coherence conveyed. But it was not through art alone that the healing vision could be attained : as a boy, the writer of the letters had associated Dürer's world with the peasant community of the Upper Austrian village where he spent his holidays, and the third letter of the series closed with the tentative hope that in Austria he might rediscover the wholeness that he sought. Significantly the Van Gogh paintings which reaffirm for him the concrete reality and inner 'connections' of the natural world depict rural scenes. Thereafter Hofmannsthal himself turned his attention to a revival of the Austrian cultural tradition through such works as *Der Rosenkavalier* (1911) and *Jedermann* (1911). In this stress on the *Volk*, on tradition, on the organic community (*Gemeinschaft*) lay the seeds of an ethos which would offer a remedy for the rootless, dispossessed nature of urban industrial civilisation in a return to the invigorating, devout, traditional way of life of the natural community in close contact with its hereditary soil. Hofmannsthal consciously supported this notion in the postwar period and we find that similar values were endorsed by Bahr and Roth. In sociological terms the cult of the *Volk*, in Austria as in Weimar Germany, represented an attempt to obscure the social and political transition from the nineteenth to the twentieth century. By 1919 the middle class had been reduced from a loyal and favoured pillar of the state to one class among others. At a time when the division of the body politic into parties and classes was more apparent than ever and the bourgeoisie had lost its traditional status, the idea of an 'undivided community' had an obvious appeal, even if it meant repudiating the liberal values on which the power of the bourgeoisie had originally been established.[11]

Hofmannsthal for his part believed that at its most complex level Austrian culture had taken a wrong turning when it severed its connection with the *Volk* and the popular tradition. Certainly, the link between (let us say) a literary drama directed at an educated élite, and a popular theatre offering dramatic entertainment to all classes of society, had survived far longer in Austria than in Germany, where it had been discredited by eighteenth-century aesthetics. By the end of the nineteenth century, however, the divorce of 'culture' and 'entertainment', of the intelligentsia and the people, was complete even in Austria, or so Hofmannsthal felt. The modern artist, sundered from his roots, was divided within himself and a prey to self-doubt. He was frustrated by anarchic licence and blinded to his true vocation. His art was full of nameless longings which remained unuttered and unfulfilled. Hofmannsthal pointed to the popular tradition as a rallying point in the hope that art and literature, renewed at this source of spiritual vitality, would proceed to influence the moral climate of the whole nation. He argued that it was this popular tradition which had given rise to the glories of the Baroque and the art of Mozart and Grillparzer. As we see from the following comment on Mozart, what he had in mind was primarily a certain ethos or ambience :

From the depths of the people the most profound and pure elements were translated into music; they were sounds of joy, they spoke with a holy, winged gracefulness, with no hint of frivolity; gladness at being alive; the abyss is sensed but without dread, the darkness illuminated by a warm glow; amidst all this there is gentle melancholy, to be sure—for the people are no strangers to melancholy—but scarcely any lacerating pain, never the petrifying awareness of solitude.[12]

Such qualities Hofmannsthal successfully embodied in his libretto for Richard Strauss's *Der Rosenkavalier*. In theory he advocated less a revival of 'folksy' literary forms than the idea which inspired Yeats's conception of a popular theatre, 'the making articulate of all the dumb classes each with its own knowledge of the world'. Nevertheless Hofmannsthal was *also* the author of two morality plays closely modelled on a medieval or Baroque tradition. He thereby succumbed to the mannerism that bedevils modern attempts to revive a 'popular' culture, as in the work of his fellow Austrians and contemporaries Richard von Kralik and Max Mell. (Brecht and Jaroslav Hašek, the creator of the Good Soldier Schweik, are among the few writers of our century who have forged a genuine link with the 'people'.) The archaic language of Hofmannsthal's morality plays, their *faux-naif* allegories, their attempts to meet the challenge of the modern world merely by reasserting the very values which history had called into question, convey less an authentic popular wisdom than a bid for popularity. Conversely the postwar society comedy *Der Schwierige*, for all its grace, lightness of touch and underlying seriousness, is far removed from the 'depths of the people' in its sophisticated intellectual theme. The abstruse symbolism of Hofmannsthal's story *Die Frau ohne Schatten* or the self-conscious high-mindedness of his 'mythical' tragedy *Der Turm* are likewise remote from the popular ambience he envisaged.

One of the best-known ways in which Hofmannsthal tried to encourage a renewal of the popular tradition was by helping to establish the Salzburg Festival together with the producer Max Reinhardt and others. This event he saw as a natural development of the South German theatrical tradition. To hold festivals of music and drama in Salzburg was, he maintained, to fulfil the basic urge of the Austro-Bavarian 'stock' and enable it to return to its true spiritual element.[13] But such references to *Stamm* and *Urtrieb* take us into that perilous marginal area where once again culture and politics meet.

In a notorious lecture Hofmannsthal announced to a Munich audience in 1927 :

* *

The process of which I speak is nothing less than a conservative revolution of unprecedented dimensions. The goal is Form, a new German reality in which the whole nation can participate.[14]

When Thomas Mann pointed out the political implications of this whole address, Hofmannsthal was embarrassed and non-committal.[15] Yet Mann's criticism was justified. Here Hofmannsthal defined and affirmed the yearning of contemporary intellectuals for union with their people and commended the liberty to be found at the heart of voluntary subjection to a higher ideal. The lecture dealt solely with the social and aesthetic responsibilities of the artist and the need for a spiritual underwriting of everyday life. Mann, however, saw a clear analogy between some of Hofmannsthal's phrases and the slogans of right-wing ideologies. There was, for instance, the argument

that it is impossible to live without faith in the whole [ohne geglaubte Gangheit]—that there is no life in half-faith, that to flee from life as the Romantics attempted is impossible, that life only becomes liveable through valid ties [gültige Bindungen].

—or the sentence

Never was a German struggle for freedom more fervid or more determined than this struggle, now being enacted in a thousand souls from among our nation, for true compulsion and the repudiation of the compulsion that is not sufficiently compelling.

The ultimate goal, we are told, is that

the Spirit should become life, and life become Spirit, in other words : the political expression of the spiritual and the spiritual of the political, to form a true nation.

Language is here driven to its limits and even beyond in order to express a vague spiritual malaise, a confused idealism that flirts with social reality without coming to grips with it. And Hofmannsthal goes on to describe the new generation of seekers after truth, the outsiders who tower over the intellectual ferment of Germany like lonely titans :

Who has not, more than once, met a figure who bears these marks and is surrounded by such an aura? The wandering man

of the spirit who emerges from chaos to lay claim to teacher-
ship and leadership—with even more audacious claims—with
the breath of genius on his noble brow, with the stigma of the
usurper in his sightless gaze or his dangerously formed ear?

Hofmannsthal was not, of course, referring to political leadership
but it is clear why Mann felt so uneasy.

The connection he perceived was not fortuitous. Despite
Hofmannsthal's distaste for politicking and the pursuit of power,
he was not devoid of political sympathies. Characteristically they
have usually to be inferred from his cultural or moral values; the
political support stems indirectly from purely idealistic motives.
For example, he professed to welcome the mingling of the metropolitan and the provincial in the Salzburg audiences. Yet the
grossstädtisch elements were unflatteringly typified in the shape of
American honeymooners and the international smart set, whereas the *ungrossstädtisch* [sic] public was plainly composed of the
pillars of society, land owners, monks, professors, country parsons,
magistrates and artisans. In the same context he alluded to 'the
restless isolated stratum of the metropolitan intelligentsia'[16]; it is a
matter of fact, even if he was too fastidious to say so, that the
majority of 'rootless urban intellectuals' were Viennese Jews.
Hofmannsthal praised Richard Billinger's *Perchtenspiel* as 'the
literary re-creation of peasant life' and as an authentic example
of the art of the people which exploited folk lore to good effect;
he even linked the play with Schiller's *Die Räuber* and Mozart's
Die Zauberflöte. The comparison was determined not merely by
the requirements of the festival programme for that year, but
also by what Hofmannsthal deemed to be the popular roots of
each of the three works. The point is that because of his cultural
predilections he could no longer distinguish between art and
artifact, between fantasy and the revival of an age-old paganism.
Hofmannsthal's commitment to grass-roots culture and to the life
of the provinces had strong political overtones in the highly
charged atmosphere of postwar Austria, where Vienna was a
bastion of socialist power.

In 1925 Hofmannsthal published an essay in a journal called
Europäische Revue; a year later he contributed an article on this
periodical to Vienna's leading daily, the *Neue Freie Presse*. He
wrote that the value of the journal lay in its resolution of the
tension between patriotism and a European consciousness. He

drew a distinction between 'pacifist internationalism' (presumably like that of Stefan Zweig) which attempts to suppress natural patriotic feeling, and the concept of supranationalism which embodies and transcends national loyalties.* The argument again places Hofmannsthal in the conservative camp, particularly when one considers the hidden implications of his praise for the *Europäische Revue*. Here and elsewhere he expressed his admiration for its editor, Karl Anton Prinz Rohan.[17] Now Rohan turned his periodical into a platform for the younger anti-democratic generation and proclaimed his respect for Italian fascism. His own essays spoke of the religious longing for a *Führer*, of the need for political reform, of a willingness for dedicated subordination. He attacked the Weimar Republic and the party system, urging that the country be ruled by a patriotic élite.[18] To what extent Hofmannsthal was aware of these sentiments and endorsed them, it is impossible to judge, since direct political statements lie beyond the scope of his essays. I would suggest, however, that they are at least compatible with his support for a social hierarchy, for regionalism, for patriotism and tradition —and with his antipathy towards a self-assertive proletariat. He was at least favourably impressed, again for moral and cultural reasons, by Italian fascism.[19]

We also know that in the mid twenties, while he was working on *Der Turm*, Hofmannsthal was favourably impressed by the writings of Carl Schmitt.[20] Schmitt, a polemical writer on constitutional affairs, had an enduring influence on many intellectuals of the period. He was a powerful critic of modern parliamentary democracy which he compared to a nineteenth-century model of what representative government should be like, in order to demonstrate the degenerated nature of the Weimar system. He believed that its defects were part of an inevitable decline, not temporary and fortuitous products of the historical difficulties facing postwar Germany. Parliamentary democracy had outlived its usefulness. What was now needed, Schmitt argued, was a strong and respected state under sovereign leadership that would transform the pluralistic anarchy of warring interest groups and mass parties into a coherent, unified order. Discussion and debate merely evaded the need for firm decisions: politics was a

---

* Thomas Mann's terms in *Betrachtungen eines Unpolitischen* (1918), a handbook of German conservatism, were 'international' or 'French' versus 'cosmopolitan' or 'German'. The distinction is identical.

matter of distinguishing between friend and foe. Schmitt's definition of the future was a dictatorship where rulers and ruled were identical and the political duty of the people would be 'acclamation', either assenting to or rejecting the decisions of the leadership.[21] It is arguable that there are parallels between some of Schmitt's ideas and the image of the political world presented in Hofmannsthal's *Der Turm*.

Hofmannsthal was one of those who coined the phrase 'conservative revolution' and it is indeed an appropriate description of where his loyalties lay. The values associated with it enlisted the support of several of his fellow Austrian writers, but it was also a European phenomenon which at various times claimed the allegiance of Chesterton, Belloc and Eliot; Bloy, Huysmans, Péguy, Barrès, and Maurras; Julius Langbehn, the Thomas Mann of *Betrachtungen eines Unpolitischen,* Moeller van den Bruck and the Juniklub. Such diverse figures do not, of course, subscribe to a single, clearly defined doctrine or programme. Their intentions and motives vary considerably. On the other hand, there is an area where their ideas overlap, forming a corpus of recognisable principles and feelings. The problem is to distinguish the 'conservative revolutionaries' from various other right-wing groups. Where Austria and Germany during the twenties and thirties are concerned, the 'conservative revolutionaries' can be differentiated from the reactionary parties on the one hand, who sought merely to restore a particular social and political system, and from the various fascist groups on the other, who were far more aggressive in their methods and more radical in their policies.

A comparison of Hofmannsthal and Eliot helps us to mark out in more detail the area with which we are concerned.

In October 1929 the *Criterion* carried a brief exhortation to its readers: 'Of your charity pray for the soul of Hugo von Hofmannsthal.' The affinities between the work of Eliot and Hofmannsthal have not gone unnoticed. Moreover, Curtius once likened the Austrian writer to Eliot and Maurras as a representative of the 'conservative revolution'. In fact, Maurras was primarily a political writer, concerned with practical political issues, whereas Hofmannsthal and Eliot were preoccupied with the defence and entrenchment of a traditional culture in its broadest sense. One can draw the further distinction that Eliot, unlike Hofmannsthal, was fully cognizant of the fact that a concern with culture has a legitimate and logical extension in the field of social and economic policies. He did not venture into that practical sphere, but he remained fully aware of the political implications of his cultural ideas. This political relevance Hofmannsthal preferred to ignore. Eliot—and for that matter Maurras—wrote for a nation which had already achieved its bourgeois revolution; their hierarchical notions were a rearguard action in a basically democratic society. Hofmannsthal's essays and dramas were addressed to a society in which political power and social influence still resided with a stratum of the population which was imbued with authoritarianism, a society where moreover the ideal of *Gemeinschaft* was far more tangible, given the predominance of the rural classes and the Roman Catholic Church. Hofmannsthal's cultural values therefore coincided to a far greater extent than Eliot's with the political values of the ruling classes. In view of this, in view too of the more prominent role of the intellectual in Viennese society, Hofmannsthal's ideas were likely to carry considerably greater political weight than Eliot's.

Eliot's most outspoken tribute to the ideals of the 'conservative revolution' found expression in *After Strange Gods* (1933). Here he defined the difference between 'conservative' and 'reactionary' in terms similar to those of Thomas Mann, acknowledging that it was misguided to 'aim to return to some previous condition which we imagine as having been capable of preservation in perpetuity, instead of aiming to stimulate the life which produced that condition in its time'.[22] His words aptly and succinctly summarised the common purpose of the 'conservative revolution'. Eliot went on to talk of a society 'worm-eaten with Liberalism', of blood kinship and the reciprocal influence of landscape and race one upon the other. He valued a homogeneous population, unity of religious background, the absence of disruptive social mobility and a proper balance of urban and rural communities. He also stressed the importance for the writer of being permeated by the aura of a living and central tradition. Eliot was to withdraw this particular essay and moderate his views; *After Strange Gods* remains an illuminating example of the way in which the 'conservative revolution' could veer in the direction of fascism, despite the real differences between them. Eliot's mature reflections on the subject of culture were published in *Notes towards the*

Definition of Culture (1948), which, though less contentious, remained faithful to the conservative-revolutionary ethos. He now argued that the disintegration of 'culture'—that is, of a peculiar way of thinking, feeling and behaving—into specialised, discrete areas of activity was a symptom of cultural decay, and he held that an organic interrelationship was necessary between the different levels of culture and between different facets of cultural activity at its more complex levels. He emphasised the importance of the family as the fundamental social unit and the basic channel for the transmission of cultural values; and he defined the family as a community of the living with generations that had passed and those as yet unborn. An organic social structure, combining class and a cultural élite, privilege and opportunity, was the best guarantee of social cohesion and continuity. By contrast the atomistic, competitive nature of modern reforms directed at an 'open society' was merely disruptive. He was firmly opposed to democratic egalitarianism, which to his mind bred barbarism, irresponsibility, egoism, uncontrolled conflict, and finally the decay of culture. He advocated regionalism in the conviction that local cultures could harmonise with and enrich those of neighbouring areas. Ultimately his cultural vision encompassed the unity of Christendom, a universal ethos composed of national cultures which themselves rested upon local regional cultures.

I have delineated Eliot's arguments because it seems to me that they paraphrase many of Hofmannsthal's random thoughts on the same theme. A belief in the intimate connection between culture and religion, in a paternalistic hierarchism, in the value of local, popular cultures, in *Gemeinschaft*, in the significance of tradition and the importance of language, in the unity of Christendom—this belief Eliot and Hofmannsthal share. On the other hand Hofmannsthal, living in a country where one-third of the population earned their living in farming and forestry and where the peasantry constituted a powerful political force, never overcame his preoccupation with a virile *Volk* in close contact with the natural world : but Eliot, even in *After Strange Gods*, could mock Hardy's 'period peasants pleasing to the metropolitan imagination'. It is precisely this self-conscious search for 'authenticity' which exudes from Hofmannsthal's Salzburg notices.[23]

The writers of the 'conservative revolution' responded severally to the particular circumstances of their respective nations. Maurras attacked republicanism, Rousseau, democracy, liberalism and centralisation. Eliot for his part described himself in 1928 as 'classicist in literature, royalist in politics, anglo-catholic in religion'. In Germany Moeller van den Bruck, author of *Das Recht der jungen Völker* (1919) and *Das Dritte Reich* (1923), attacked bourgeois materialism and mediocrity, proclaiming instead a moral Darwinism, the *Führerprinzip* and a form of national socialism which involved a corporate structure. He was hostile to the Weimar Republic and the party system. In general the 'conservative revolution' in post war Germany pivoted around the experience of the War and the social question. It had an urgent religious fervour about it and aimed at a rehabilitation of elemental laws and values that would link human society with Nature or God. Instead of egalitarianism it offered a hierarchy based on inner worth; instead of 'mechanical' election it offered 'organic' leadership; instead of bureaucratic compulsion, individual responsibility and self-discipline; instead of the happiness of the masses, the destiny of the *Volksgemeinschaft*. Its idealism aimed at a rebirth of the nation and ultimately a regenerated humanity. Yet as its chronicler Kurt Sontheimer notes, the ideology of the 'conservative revolution' was peculiarly remote from political realities.[24]

Characteristic of the Austrian representatives of the 'conservative revolution' such as Hofmannsthal and Roth is the Habsburg ethos mentioned earlier. They combined with their authoritarian hierarchism a paternal respect for the Imperial nationalities and for regional cultures. Their ideas were rooted in the reaction against the French Revolution and Napoleon, in the political writings of Romantic authors such as the Schlegel brothers, Novalis, Adam Müller and Josef von Hormayr.[25] Here was to be found that hostility towards the Reformation, the rationalist abstractions of the Enlightenment, the notion of a social contract and egalitarianism which characterised the thought of later conservative revolutionaries. Here too was to be found an emphasis on social harmony (the organic *Gemeinschaft*), on a corporative social structure based on medieval guilds, on an active Christianity and the power of a living tradition. Above all, it was here, in the face of the Napoleonic threat, that Austrian patriots started to define the Habsburg Monarchy as a supranational state with its own unique mission. Historically the agglomeration of peoples and territories had been due to the fortunes of war and wedlock. This mundane evolution was now stylised into an idealistic crusade. *Felix Austria* was presented as the bulwark of Western Christendom, a haven of tolerance during the Wars of Religion, and a commonwealth of nations united in the service of a noble cause. A widespread movement attributed to Austria the task of defending and liberating the German peoples from the foreign oppressor. Writers such as Hormayr, Caroline Pichler, Mattäus von Collin and Ladislaus Pyrker asserted that the Monarchy was a natural organism which fostered the interests of all the peoples of the Danube Basin by providing an opportunity for mutual benefit and friendly rivalry. The Romantic loyalists assumed that the Empire would always be governed by Germans and that German would remain the language of state (an assumption easily justified in the first decades of the nineteenth century). Nevertheless they valued local institutions and traditions and criticised the centralist policies of a previous emperor, Joseph II (1765–90). Behind their propaganda lay a genuine patriotic resistance to Napoleon which culminated in the dream of restoring the Holy Roman Empire which the French conqueror had finally destroyed. But it also reflected an aristocratic conservatism apprehensive of the social disruption emanating from France. The tendency to idealise the Imperial mission did not lapse with the defeat of Napoleon. In one form or another it remained the property of Habsburg loyalists who now strove to oppose the centrifugal forces of nationalism and to preserve German (and later Magyar) supremacy within the Monarchy. In the course of the nineteenth century the gulf between the 'ideological superstructure' and the defence of power and privilege grew ever wider, leading finally to the wartime apologetics of Hofmannsthal and a score of lesser propagandists.

The political significance of the 'conservative revolution' in Germany and Austria after 1918 was its contribution to antiliberal or anti-democratic thinking. It had different aspirations from the fascist groups proper : yet it frequently employed similar slogans, denounced the same enemies and displayed similar sympathies. The 'conservative revolution' helped to make the public intellectually and emotionally susceptible to the appeals of fascism. Sometimes it made a more direct contribution. The ideology of the *Ständestaat*, for instance, the corporate state which was adopted by the *Heimwehr*, the fascist Austrian militia, and by Dollfuss's more moderate Fatherland Front, owed much to the Catholic neo-romanticism of the Viennese sociologist Othmar Spann who conjured up a vision of the 'true' state where the individual counted only as part of the whole and where *Formaldemokratie* would give way to *ständische Demokratie.* Between 1933 and 1938 a number of Catholic writers, searching for an alternative to the pagan nationalism of Nazi Germany, dreamed of a new Austrian Reich in South East Europe, mildly reformist and based on the supranationalist tradition. By accepting the *Ständestaat* and the values associated with it these writers became allies of the 'Austro-Fascists' and played their part in bringing about the Anschluss.[26] As Kurt Sontheimer has pointed out, the notion of a feudal authoritarianism was impracticable in a modern industrialised society, once the masses had been mobilised and had become politically articulate. In practice the authoritarian state in our century degenerates into some form of totalitarianism. The way in which Hofmannsthal played a part in this general process will emerge from the analysis of his creative work during the postwar years that follows later in this chapter.

For Hofmannsthal the release of the ethical strength of the *Volk* and the renewal of the popular tradition particularly in literature were linked with a linguistic problem. Again the theme had its antecedents in his prewar work, notably in 'Ein Brief' (1902) and 'Der Dichter und diese Zeit' (1907). In his notes for the Scandinavian lecture 'Die Idee Europa' of 1916, Hofmannsthal's account of the decay of the prewar world included the observation that the sense of decline had been accompanied by a widespread scepticism with regard to the ability of language to apprehend the substance of reality. A despairing wave of linguistic criticism had spread throughout the world : for men had come to realise that the product of the scientific spirit was not truth but technology. Hofmannsthal perceived among his contemporaries an overwhelming awareness of the fluidity, complexity and relativity of the 'interpreted world'. The human mind, together with its instrument language, could no longer encompass the inner harmony and noumenal truth of experience (inevitably, so Nietzsche had asserted, since God and the Word were dead). Hofmannsthal felt that it was the vocation of the poet to transcend the ensuing fragmentation and incoherence. A writer might never again comprehend an ultimate synthesis and be able to communicate this sublime vision to his age : but poet and reader together might slowly draw near the truth. Maturity for a writer involved a recognition of and acquiescence in the limitations of language, such as Goethe had shown in passing from the titanism of his youth to the more moderate, restrained and communicable vision of his later years. (Hofmannsthal thereby overlooked the complex profundities and symbolism of Goethe's late work in which language constantly strove to extend its limits rather than accept conventional restrictions.)

During the War Hofmannsthal became increasingly conscious of the abuse of language at the hands of propagandists—though he himself was not entirely guiltless in this respect. After the War, as before it, he was aware of the vacuity of pseudo-philo-sophical clichés, the slackness of expression, the superficiality and confusion that had crept into everyday speech. He concluded that the language must be purged of its impurities and an attempt made to rediscover the fullness of meaning of ordinary words, to encourage a new sense of responsibility in the use of abstract concepts, and to bring about the revival of a truly communal language. True expressiveness—what he called 'the mimic element of speech'—had been neglected for the sake of imparting information, and linguistic fragmentation was one of the symp-toms of Austria's moral sickness. What Hofmannsthal desired was a literary or linguistic equivalent of the ideal of *Gemeinschaft*. He regretted that German lacked a natural middle language be-tween dialect on the one hand and the idiom of literature on the other, a transitional language which would be an organic growth, drawing nourishment from every section of the community and binding them all in a unified whole. The existing *Umgangssprache* (colloquial language) was a conglomeration of 'individual' languages in which separate words competed against one another instead of complementing each other within a wider harmony. The importance of language extended beyond the needs of the contemporary age, for Hofmannsthal regarded it as the timeless vessel of human experience, a medium through which the present generation could communicate with the past, contribute to the heritage of the centuries and impart their culture to future gener-ations. Thus he saw in language a mirror of human experience which reflected the moral condition of a society. For Hofmanns-thal, as somewhat earlier for Karl Kraus, linguistic decay was symptomatic of moral turpitude; for Freud language betrayed the secrets of the psyche; Wittgenstein attempted to describe an 'ideal language' which would be a repository of philosophical truth, and after abandoning that metaphysical quest, he still considered piecemeal *linguistic* analyses to be the only valid form of philosophical enquiry; for the Imperial peoples language was the gauge of patriotism—and therefore of integrity. In *fin de siècle* Vienna language constantly aspired to a symbolic dimension. Even Hitler was sensitive to the literary style of the *Neue Freie Presse* which he felt to be redolent of Jewish corruption. To reform one's use of language was for Hofmannsthal to transform the way in which one thought about reality and thus the nature and extent of one's experience. A corrupt use of language not only mirrored a corrupt mind, it could also help to create one. Hofmannsthal wished his fellow Austrians to be made aware of this vicious circle.

His vision of language was neither as intense nor as exclusive as that of Karl Kraus; more significantly, one seeks in vain in such major postwar essays as 'Das Schrifttum als geistiger Raum der Nation' or 'Beethoven' or 'Wert und Ehre deutscher Sprache' that exhaustive exploitation of the resources of the German language which characterised Kraus's œuvre. This is not to belittle Hofmannsthal's achievement in creating the splendidly dramatic language of *Der Rosenkavalier* or *Der Schwierige*. It is to suggest that by comparison with the density, lucidity, complex internal relationships and subtle overtones—in short with the *poetic* qualities of Kraus's language, the style of Hofmannsthal's later essays appears imprecise, loose and (for all its metaphysical allusiveness) shallow.

Hofmannsthal's response to the impact of the War and its aftermath is not, of course, confined to cultural essays. But these essays depict the background of ideas against which he formulates the major creative works of the postwar period, ideas which help to elucidate both the strength and the weakness of his mature writing.

The comedy *Der Schwierige* (1921) probably represents Hofmannsthal's greatest literary achievement in the decade after the War. It deals with many of the problems with which we are familiar : nostalgia for Imperial society, the decay of language, the value of tradition. It weaves these themes into the fabric of a subtle and delightful comedy. The plot, which is minimal, depicts the erratic course of an Austrian count through the hazards of Viennese high society into the arms of the woman he loves. In time-honoured fashion love finds a way to overcome all obstacles and hesitations, and behind the eventual union of the lovers there is a delicate suggestion that their personal happiness in marriage has its due place in the proper social order. Hofmannsthal conceived the plan to write a comedy as early as 1917, impelled partly by a desire to counteract the spiritual devastation of the War, and partly by a desire to perpetuate the memory of a society that was soon to vanish for ever. His depiction of Viennese high society in *Der Schwierige* is poetically rather than historically true. Although the play is set in the winter of 1918–19, social life still flourishes, oblivious of food shortages, civil disturbances, the disintegration of the Empire, and the threat of revolution and invasion. Even the Austrian equivalent of the House of Lords continues to meet when in fact it had disappeared along with all the other Imperial institutions. The War has played a major role in the hero's personal development, but unlike the general tendency of *Heimkehrer* literature—works such as Brecht's *Trommeln in der Nacht*, Werfel's *Barbara oder die Frömmigkeit* or Roth's *Hotel Savoy*, which deal with the situation of the returning soldier—the political and economic repercussions of the War are here ignored. The milieu presented to us is thus in one sense an idealised re-creation : nevertheless it remains instantly recognisable. The presence of Neuhoff, a North German aristocrat, brash, tactless, arrogant, a disciple of the Will and dynamic purposefulness, intimates Hofmannsthal's distaste for the boorish Prussianism to which Austria had so disastrously harnessed herself. Neuhoff may be an intruder and *indiskutabel*, but he has a necessary social role to play. The professor who, despite his vanity and snobbery, is ironically tolerated in an ostensibly exclusive *salon* because of his pretensions to scholarship, likewise affords a glimpse of the undermining of the Viennese aristocratic world. The hero's middle class secretary with his air of wounded pride, his envy and self-righteousness; the silly bluestocking who foreshadows Musil's Diotima; and the foppish, irresponsible nephew, Stani, all these suggest that Hofmannsthal is not unaware of the seeds of decay. But the awareness is mellow and urbane, and the muted criticism never permitted to obtrude upon the intricate charm of the comedy. *Der Schwierige* has some of the qualities of a subtle picture puzzle. One character's judgement of another is often an amalgam of truth and falsehood. Thus Neuhoff's verdict on Viennese society, like his criticism of the hero, is not entirely unjustified :

> All these people you meet here don't really exist any more. They are nothing but phantoms. No one who frequents these *salons* belongs to the real world in which the intellectual crises of the age are being decided.[27]

But coming from him, the statement requires qualification. The world of the comedy is indeed at one remove from the actual world. On the other hand, certain crises *are* present, only they are different from those with which Neuhoff and the outside world are familiar.

The hero, Count Hans Karl Bühl, is keenly aware of the limitations and inadequacies of language as a means of communication. He expresses his doubts in a variety of ways, not least by a remarkable degree of taciturnity. He avoids social functions and public speeches for fear of being misunderstood or of misunderstanding someone else's meaning. His withdrawal is not due to dislike of or contempt for his social companions—indeed he specifically denies this to his sister Crescence in Act I, Scene 3. It is prompted rather by his almost pathological distrust of the spoken word. He is convinced that the most important feelings and perceptions defy articulate expression. Clearly his fears are not without substance, for error, confusion and linguistic abuse provide much of the more obvious comedy in the play. But Hans Karl's distrust is so single-minded that its effect becomes comic. By despairing of language as a means of communication, he actively contributes to his dilemma. Again a picture puzzle quality emerges from the play, as the hero now commands our respect and sympathy, now arouses feelings of exasperation. Although he claims that words hinder understanding, many of the evening's complications spring from his own ineptitude or from his unwillingness to explain. For example, he embroils himself unnecessarily in further confusion by showing a curious insensitivity to the nuances of his own words *vis-à-vis* his former mistress Antoinette and her maid. There is no linguistic mystery here, merely tactlessness and excessive enthusiasm. The comedy is richly enhanced throughout by Hans Karl's inconsistencies. When his friend

Hechingen fails to understand what Hans Karl is trying to say, the hero complains that for some people everything is hopelessly complicated—thereby criticising unwittingly his own attitude. He finds conversation intolerable—but adores it in Helene, the woman he loves. For all his horror of indiscretion, he is himself indiscreet in trying to persuade Antoinette to return to her husband. On the other hand, it is only by the indiscreet betrayal of his true feelings to Helene that he ensures their lasting happiness. His problems over Helene are plainly due to his own psychological difficulties, rather than to the inability of language to convey his meaning. At two vital points in the action Helene insists that he should explain himself—before he relates his hallucinatory experience on the battlefield, and again when he returns to the soirée to find her—and on both occasions communication is shown to be possible. Hofmannsthal implies that although Hans Karl is right in criticising the abuse of language in modern society and in emphasising the difficulty of articulating anything meaningful, he is wrong to renounce language altogether. He should accept its limitations and avail himself of its resources, however meagre; then, with patience and good will, a true dialogue can take place. Mistakes, cross-purposes, self-delusion, all the ironies of life are factors one must learn to contend with. Hans Karl's ideal of perfect communication against which he implicitly measures the reality around him, is an absolute abstraction beyond the reach of ordinary men. Even if Hans Karl himself remains unconvinced (one of the last lines he speaks is, 'But this is the last *soirée* you'll ever see me attend'), the author at least strongly suggests the need for critical compromise by presenting at the core of his comedy the successful match between the lovers.

The hero's hesitation and fear of involvement are to a large extent overcome by the end of the play. He avoids the design, the calculation, the purposefulness that dictate the actions of so many other characters. Indeed whenever Hans Karl is motivated by preconceived intention, his plans go awry because he is incapable of sustaining it. Helene for her part has to beware of possessiveness since this would inhibit Hans Karl's response. The relationship between the lovers involves a spontaneous, unencumbered acquiescence in whatever the moment brings, and an ability to balance desire and respect, seriousness and serenity, love and patience.

At the end of *Der Schwierige* Crescence, in her brother's absence, embraces Helene's father in a traditional symbolic gesture, sealing the betrothal of the lovers. A similar, even more expressive rite seals the reconciliation of the lovers at the close of Hofmannsthal's libretto *Arabella*, when the maiden proffers a libation to her betrothed. Like the earlier comedy, the libretto (which appeared posthumously) tells of the tribulations of two people destined for one another. By the end of the opera the heroine and Mandryka have learned to cast aside suspicion and resentment, and to love each other unconditionally. The plot is trite, verging at times on farce, while the dialogue lacks the masterly stylisation of the Viennese vernacular which was such a distinctive feature of *Der Rosenkavalier* or *Der Schwierige*. The story of the lovers is marred by an obtrusive sententiousness. To the extent that Hofmannsthal points a personal and social moral, the libretto mirrors some of his cultural ideas. The original version of the story was a prose tale entitled *Lucidor* (1910). There the heroine was not Arabella but her sister. Their mother was a widow, Arabella herself had no suitor, and the character Mandryka was only vaguely foreshadowed in the form of a gentleman farmer from Tyrol. The action took place at the end of the 1870s. In the libretto, the most significant change—apart from the reversal in the importance of the sisters—centres on the creation of Mandryka. He has now become a loyal Croatian magnate who lives under the Hungarian Crown of St Stephen and who speaks the German slang of the Habsburg armies with a Slav intonation. His father, we learn, served in the Austrian provinces in Northern Italy. Hofmannsthal plainly intends Mandryka to be seen as a representative of the cultural and political synthesis of the Austro-Hungarian Empire. His hero is a feudal landlord with vast estates who lives among his peasants according to a tradition of mutual rights and obligations. Mandryka carries about him the aura of tall, silent forests, of deep, spontaneous emotion, of self-sufficiency and an uncorrupted natural order. In all this he is strongly contrasted with the decadent, frivolous, irresponsible atmosphere of Vienna—above all with Arabella's father (who did not exist in the original story). Mandryka's existence is rooted in the good earth of his hereditary lands; his occasional extravagance is committed with the blithe unconcern of an 'expenditure economy', paper money is unreal to him and has no place on his estates. Arabella's father, on the other hand, is an unpleasant city gent, a gambler whose whole life is devoted to the acquisition of money. In order to relieve his financial straits he is prepared to sell even his own daughter. Hofmannsthal's reason for bringing forward the action to the 1860s now becomes clear : the heroine's father is caught up in the financial fever of the *Gründerjahre*, the boom years of urban expansion and speculation which culminated in the crash of Black Friday, 1873. The libretto is thus clearly influenced by Hofmannsthal's postwar social preoccupations.

These concerns are central to the play *Das Salzburger grosse Welttheater*. The play was conceived in 1919 and Hofmannsthal soon came to envisage it as part of the Salzburg Festival in succession to the prewar *Jedermann*. It was at Salzburg that it had its première in 1922. Although it is based on a medieval morality play, its principal debt is to the treatment of this old theme by the Spanish dramatist Calderon. From the outset Hofmannsthal endowed his play with a modern social relevance; a note among his papers tells us that instead of the traditional passive Beggar he has created an active figure, representing a character of our time, the threat of chaos.[28] In other words, the Beggar epitomises the forces of social revolution. The drama opens with the summoning of three characters—the World, Curiosity and their constant companion, the Spirit of Denial—to stage a play before the throne of the Lord. The drama about to unfold is to be an allegory of the human condition; the roles are allocated to a Nun, a Rich Man (and Chancellor), a King, his Queen and a Beggar. These characters symbolise the five forces operative in human life, Wisdom, Wealth, Power, Beauty and Suffering. The first crisis occurs during the distribution of the parts, for the soul of the Beggar refuses to accept the role allocated to it, on the grounds that the part involves nothing but pain and suffering, with no glimmer of freedom, no opportunity for action which could lead to fame and fortune. Eventually, however, it accepts the part. But when the Beggar appears, dirty, ragged and starving, he immediately broaches the question of theodicy in its simplest and most personal terms. He has lost his wife in a border incident, his children have all died of famine or disease, and now he demands to know why. Meeting with no satisfactory answer, he resolves to seek justice and compensation by resorting to violence. At this and other points, Hofmannsthal undoubtedly had in mind the Communist regimes established for a time in Munich and Budapest after the end of the First World War, and the threat of revolution in Austria at that time. The Beggar's intentions bring him face to face with the Nun, whose piety, serenity and love so infuriate him that he raises his axe to murder her—only to have his hand stayed by some mysterious force from above. Then the true nature of human freedom and action is revealed to him. Freedom lies in liberating oneself from the thraldom of instinct, it is the freedom of the inner man, the capacity of the human spirit to triumph over material adversity. The Beggar's greatest deed lies in *not* accomplishing what he, in his blindness, had deemed his most decisive and positive action. He learns to acquiesce in the role allotted to him, no matter what it brings, and to abandon all thought of revolution.

In the *Welttheater* we find the same confusion or ambiguousness over the meaning of human suffering as emerged from the Scandinavian lectures of 1916. The play illustrates the political implications of this confusion. It is one thing to transcend suffering and doubt as an act of faith : it is quite a different thing to endorse fatalism in the context of social reform. The Beggar is told to pay less attention to the material world and to endure stoically everything that befalls him. What he is expected to suffer passively is the attacks of marauding brigands, greedy farmers and heartless financiers—social evils capable of being checked. Hofmannsthal, it is true, was primarily concerned to warn against revolutionary violence. At the same time, the play owes little to the Catholic movement for social reform in the tradition of the Austrian publicist Karl von Vogelsang and the encyclical *Rerum novarum* (1891). The lesson of the drama is unqualified acquiescence in the status quo, in the role allocated to each man by his Maker. Admittedly Dives receives his just deserts on the Day of Judgement, but here the vague moral of *memento mori* is less concretely related to social ills than in the gospel story of the rich man and Lazarus upon which the play seems to be based. Within the simplified framework of a morality play, Hofmannsthal reduces the complex forces of social revolution to a contravention of the Tenth Commandment. This considerable oversimplification means that the Beggar is invested with a weight of symbolic significance which an allegorical character of this kind is incapable of bearing. The point is that the drama is a partisan response to the threat of revolution. Hofmannsthal again allies himself with the forces of reaction—and again for idealistic reasons. Let us recall the occasion for which the play was written, and its setting in the baroque opulence of the *Kollegienkirche* in Salzburg. The festival audience in the early twenties would have comprised dignitaries of the Church, Catholic intellectuals, leading members of the main Government party, the Christian Socialists, visitors from the surrounding country areas of Salzburg, Upper Austria and Bavaria, and American and European tourists. A largely conservative audience witnessed the reiteration of a conservative social doctrine in the guise of religious edification.

The religious theme of the *Welttheater* was elaborated in Hofmannsthal's most ambitious postwar drama, *Der Turm* (1925/27). This tragedy attempts to convey in 'mnemonic' form —the term is Hofmannsthal's—the insights vouchsafed to the poet under the impact of the War and its aftermath. It tries to create a contemporary myth, a symbolic expression of the perils confronting the postwar world and of the ideals which might redeem it. *Der Turm* contains parallels with the story of Moses and Christ and with the Oedipal myth; there are also echoes of Kaspar Hauser, Boris Godunov, Schiller's *Don Carlos* and *Demetrius*, and many others. Among the themes of Hofmannsthal's tragedy are the perils of violence, the nature of human freedom, the need for social justice (an advance on the *Welttheater*), and the positive value of suffering. Sigismund, the hero, is the apotheosis of *la religion de la douleur* in Hofmannsthal's work. The plot centres on the relationship between King Basilius and his son Sigismund; the former, fearful of a prophecy that predicted his humiliation at the hands of his son, keeps Sigismund *incommunicado*, imprisoned in a tower, in the hope of averting the fulfilment of the prophecy. Basilius is persuaded to attempt a reconciliation with his son, but he thereby brings about the very catastrophe he has dreaded. When revolution breaks out, Sigismund dons the armour of righteousness and trounces the rebels in battle, while at the same time taking steps to allevi- ate the injustice and oppression which under the old regime had bred revolution. Although the dark forces symbolised by the revolutionary leader Olivier and his gipsy mistress succeed in assassinating Sigismund, his victory is guaranteed by the arrival of a messianic child-king who ushers in a new age of peace, justice and love. Such is the outline of the plot in the so-called book version of 1925. There is a second version of the drama, however, the so-called stage version of 1927, of which the final acts in particular diverge materially from the earlier text. In the later version Sigismund remains a passive victim of events. He refuses to countenance violence even in a just cause, and is murdered for his pains by a hireling of the revolutionaries. The tragedy now closes not with the *Kinderkönig* and the dawn of a new era, but with the revolutionaries apparently in control.

The endings seem at first sight contradictory. The earlier Sigismund is capable of achieving a political and military goal and does not shrink from violence in a righteous cause; despite his personal fate, his efforts are crowned with success. The later Sigismund does not accept that the end can justify the means; he refuses to play a political or military role; and in practical terms he achieves nothing by his death. However, the versions are not as different as is often assumed. The last scene of the stage version is not meant to strike a chord of futility and failure, but one of moral victory. By resisting the temptations of power and remaining unsullied by violence, the later Sigismund is in his own way as triumphant as his predecessor. Conversely the earlier hero achieves practical success only at the cost of moral compromise. In resorting to violence, he sacrifices his own integrity for the sake of his people, and his death is the ultimate atonement for his sin. Thereby the fruits of his labours are purified and hallowed, lest his people inherit the burden of guilt attaching to his victory. Sigismund is a transitional ruler between the corrupt regime of his father on the one hand, and the absolute purity of the child-king on the other. When the hero addresses his followers :

'Do not look askance, my friends. Have I been too harsh on you? —The iron has entered our soul for without it we cannot win battles.'[29]

he avers that violence can only be defeated by violence. Yet, as the play shows, 'woe to that man by whom the offence cometh'. There is clearly a connection between Hofmannsthal's attitude to power and the use of violence in both versions of his tragedy. In the earlier version the insufficiency of a mere political solution is manifested in the advent of the child-king. It is this metaphysical instance which is the ultimate sanction and guarantee of the political victory. The problem posed and the solution offered are on two different levels, the one realistic and political, the other metaphysical and individualist. The *deus ex machina* betokens the dramatist's doubts as to the feasibility or indeed the desirability of a political solution alone. The later Sigismund himself embodies the radical disavowal of political activity.

Hofmannsthal once indicated that there was a link between his tragedy and Goethe's *Egmont*. It must surely reside in the fact that both plays depict a moral victory being won in the teeth of physical destruction and practical failure. Moreover, although Goethe employs a political framework (the Netherlands under Spanish occupation) and presents his hero as a patriotic leader, *Egmont* remains a profoundly apolitical play.[30] Goethe's real interest lay elsewhere—in his hero's inner freedom, his 'daemonic' nature, his untrammelled drive for fullness of experience which is satisfied at the price of his political responsibility. The message of *Der Turm*, particularly in its stage version, is an even more forthright admonition that politics is of the Devil and that only the moral life of the individual is of any consequence.

It is equally illuminating to contrast *Der Turm* with a political tragedy written some seventy years earlier by Hofmannsthal's compatriot Franz Grillparzer. Emperor Rudolf II, the hero of *Ein Bruderzwist in Habsburg*, is torn between his duties as a ruler and his ethical misgivings about the nature and effectiveness of political action. Grillparzer's play is uncompromising on both the personal and the political level, thus avoiding the facile solution which both versions of *Der Turm* (in their different ways) put forward. Rudolf's condemnation of politics impairs his function as a ruler; his political duty can only be fulfilled if he is prepared to compromise his moral integrity. He is destroyed both as a monarch and as a moral being by the conflict between principle and expediency, for he cannot escape the obligations of either. That conflict is infinitely more realistic than Sigismund's privileged atonement (in the book version) or his unfeeling withdrawal (in the stage version). It commands our respect and compassion as Sigismund's spiritual triumph cannot do. For all its historical setting on the eve of the Thirty Years War, for all its medieval ideal of kingship, for all that it was written in the wake of the 1848 revolution to warn against the consequences of demanding Liberal reforms—Grillparzer's tragedy is closer to our modern political experience than Hofmannsthal's anachronistic sublimity.

Der Turm conveys Hofmannsthal's appraisal of and answer to the problems besetting Austria and the whole of Central Europe in the postwar years. It reflects the moral decay which he felt to be rampant, the consequences of materialism, and the social impact of inflation. It presents us with the spectacle of a selfish, opportunist, yet impotent nobility : Julian, the most energetic and enterprising of the aristocrats, devotes himself to the task of fomenting revolution among the lesser nobility and the populace in order to win personal power—but he is swallowed up by the monster he himself creates. (In several respects he is prophetic of the German conservatives who believed they could exploit Hitler for their own ends.) The bloody spectre of revolution recalls Berlin, Budapest and Munich, to say nothing of St Petersburg. The activity of the ruthless demagogue Olivier is matched by that of the Grand Almoner, who exemplifies the evils arising from the involvement of the Church in secular affairs. And in the figure of Basilius, we have a symbol of violence and power devoid of ethical responsibility. The King is a man of pride who is pre-pared to sacrifice his son in order to spare himself humiliation and to maintain his position. The conflict between Sigismund and his father can be seen from one point of view as a mythical pro-jection of the conflict between the generations, between the fathers who had urged war upon Europe, and the sons who had been sacrificed on the battlefields. (The theme recalls Wilfred Owen's poem 'The Parable of the Old Men and the Young'.) The scene in the book version in which Basilius is restored to power, expresses something of the disillusionment of those who had hoped for better things in the postwar world.

If we accept the stage version as Hofmannsthal's final political testimony—as I believe we must—the outlook for Central Europe is bleak indeed. The country is left in the hands of the revolu-tionaries, the masses are at their mercy, the King and the nobility have been liquidated as political forces. Hofmannsthal, it appears, sees no alternative to political extremism, to a violent conflict between Right and Left; he suggests that political power will eventually lie in the hands of the most unscrupulous type of revolutionary. By 1927, of course, politics had become brutalised both in Austria and Germany. In one respect Hofmannsthal's foreboding was only too justified. The disquieting aspect in all this is that he should have proclaimed his gloomy prognostication to be irrelevant, provided that the individual attained spiritual salvation. Schillerian sublimity here degenerates into moral isolationism. In the climate of the time, given the frailty of the democratic system and the intensification of authoritarianism, his judgement must have appeared to condemn as futile and misguided the efforts of those who were striving to make democracy work. And it must have confirmed the prejudices of those others who saw in the Social Democrats of today the rampaging mob of tomorrow.

There is little in Hofmannsthal's work prior to 1914 which is as directly relevant to the contemporary political situation as *Das Salzburger grosse Welttheater* or *Der Turm*. His prose essays from 1916 onwards—those concerned with the cultural renewal of his homeland—are suffused with a new urgency. His dilemma is that of a writer who, though compelled to take cognizance of political events, is hostile to politicking and all it involves, and is therefore obliged to seek solutions outside the political field. In the last analysis his sensibility was not attuned to the demands of the political situation in which he found himself. This led to a tension between his idealistic cultural and ethical preoccupations, and the political implications, unwitting or otherwise, of his statements. Like so many of his contemporaries, Hofmannsthal remained ensconced within the limitations of the literary and intellectual tradition in which he wrote.

Hermann Bahr: Phoenix Too Frequent

... this persistence of an insurance agent from the Phoenix who
guarantees resurrection in any shape or form ...

Karl Kraus

Hofmannsthal's activity during the First World War will always
be linked with an open letter from the Viennese critic and author,
Hermann Bahr, which Karl Kraus immortalised in the pages of
Die Fackel and *Die Letzten Tage der Menschheit*.[1] Kraus had already entertained a satirical opinion of the young Hofmannsthal's
precocious literary achievement, but when Hofmannsthal
directed his energies to helping the war effort, the satirist was
incensed. He exploited Bahr's letter in order to discomfit the
addressee, while at the same time pillorying Bahr himself, who for
years had been a familiar target of Kraus's satire. In Bahr, a
prolific reviewer, columnist, critic, novelist and playwright, Kraus
saw an intellectual buffoon and an unscrupulous poetaster whose
very influence and success indicted the would-be cultured public
which tolerated his antics.

The letter in question, 'Gruss an Hofmannsthal', was in fact
a newspaper article written on 16 August 1914. It purported to
be addressed to Hofmannsthal under arms 'somewhere in Poland'.
Evoking memories of past military service, the piece contained
stirring patriotic appeals and tributes to the mood of the hour.
It was reproduced in a volume entitled *Kriegssegen* which
appeared the following year. Bahr knew as well as Kraus that
Hofmannsthal was not in fact marching on Warsaw with the
Austro-Hungarian Army but was working in the Kriegsfürsorge-
amt (War Welfare Board) in Vienna. That deception apart, to
the satirist Bahr epitomised all those hypocritical propagandists
who whipped up spurious patriotic fervour and shrouded hard
facts in a miasma of uncritical emotionalism. If Bahr's wartime

writing consisted merely of such pieces, it would be of little interest to the literary or intellectual historian. However, his attitude subsequently underwent a significant fluctuation. His ideas were always shallow, frequently idiosyncratic, and sometimes fogged by religious obsessions; it is not as an original thinker but as a publicist attuned to the mood of the moment that Bahr deserves a measure of attention.

Bahr's concern with political developments did not commence with the events of July and August 1914. Scattered throughout the articles of previous years were sporadic references to the political scene. In 1909 he embodied his ideas on the subject of Austria in a travel book called *Dalmatinische Reise*. There he sought to show that the crux of the Austrian problem was the conflict between the abstract ideal of 'Austro-Hungarian' patriotism, which posited allegiance to a multi-national commonwealth, and the local loyalties of the Imperial nationalities. His realistic definition of the problem (which the Empire was never able to solve) goes back at least as far as the publicist Viktor Freiherr von Andrian-Werburg, who declared in 1842 :

> Austria is a purely imaginary name which does not denote any separate people, any country, any nation, a conventional tag for a complex of nationalities sharply divided one from another. There are Italians, Germans, Slavs and Magyars who together constitute the Austrian Empire, but there is no such thing as Austria or Austrians or an Austrian nationality, and such a thing has never existed if one excludes a tract of land around Vienna. No bonds of affection, no memories of a century-long harmony and greatness, no historic ties—Austria's history is altogether insignificant and poor in decisive events—bind the different peoples of one and the same state together, and none of them is so superior to the others in terms of size, intelligence, influence or wealth that it has the capacity gradually to absorb them.[2]

Sixty years later Bahr was pointing out that to the Viennese authorities the issue was one of 'either/or', whereas to the Imperial provinces it had to be one of 'both/and'. As in an earlier book, *Wien* (1907), Bahr attributed the abstract ideal to the legacy of 'liberalism' (although in fact it was rooted in the reaction against Napoleon). Bahr voiced the imperative need for a resolution of the problem that would be compatible with the continued existence of the Empire. He listed two practical reasons for nationalist discontent in Dalmatia : economic neglect by the central government, and the zeal with which a Vienna-oriented administration maintained the German hegemony. He held that Vienna had to prove itself worthy of loyalty before it could reasonably demand it, and he advocated economic development and cultural autonomy. The latter recommendation involved the right to employ the local language in official transactions, to have local universities, and to practise local traditions. But the cultural largesse which he bestowed with one hand was recovered by the other. Bahr's apparent respect for the cultures of the nationalities was belied by his conviction that it was the duty of the Austro-Germans to transmit their superior culture to their less fortunate neighbours, like missionaries among the heathen :

> And is it always just a question of language, is it not rather a question of German values and our national character? Is it not more important to instil the latter in the peoples of Southern and Eastern Europe? Let the spirit of Germany gain converts for us in the outside world! Whatever language it happens to speak, what does that matter provided that German culture [Deutsches Wesen] gives the lead to mankind![3]

Bahr's sympathy with oppressed Dalmatia was born of palliative expediency rather than of a commitment to federalist reform. In its insidious Pan-Germanism (*Stammesart*, and the echo of the infamous proverb 'Am deutschen Wesen soll die Welt genesen') the quotation anticipates his outbursts at the beginning of the War. In the early 1880s Bahr, then an unruly student, had been an openly extremist Pan-German who had dreamed of a Greater Germany including the Habsburg Monarchy. It took an unexpected rebuke from one of Bismarck's aides to convince him of the importance of an independent Austria-Hungary. From that moment Bahr liked to consider himself an Austrian patriot though that did not necessarily preclude a belief in natural German supremacy. (In short, he moved closer to the *Deutschnationalen*, the more moderate German nationalists who were loyal to the Habsburgs and whose political representatives joined with the remnants of the Austrian Liberals to form the Deutscher Nationalverband, from 1911 the strongest single group in the Austrian Reichsrat.)

A selection of what Bahr felt to be his more significant utterances on a variety of political subjects appeared in 1911 under the title *Austriaca*. In one piece dating from 1908 he recorded the enthusiasm with which the annexation of Bosnia and Herzegovina had been acclaimed all over Austria. His enthusiasm over what he took to be a sign of national resurrection was characteristically ill-considered. Three years later he looked back upon these events with a distinctly jaundiced eye for by then he had realised the international repercussions of the futile gesture, originally intended to balk Serbia, restore the conservative alliance with Russia and bring Austrian civilisation to the two neglected provinces. Hofmannsthal too, in one of his rare comments on the political scene before the War, expressed his admiration for the skill and judgement of Aehrenthal, the Austro-Hungarian Foreign Minister responsible for the annexation, and hopelessly misinterpreted the diplomatic consequences.[4]

Bahr was a supporter of Franz Ferdinand, the heir to the throne, and believed that the Archduke's accession would usher in a radical transformation of Habsburg policies. He admired Franz Ferdinand's personal qualities, his refusal to curry popularity, his discretion and his strength of will. This idealisation can only be explained by Bahr's antipathy towards the Viennese Establishment, which viewed the Archduke with apprehension and hostility. Bahr recommended some form of trialist solution for the constitutional difficulties of the Empire, a remedy which the Archduke was known to have considered and which, by restoring a Kingdom of Croatia, would have reduced the power and independence of the Magyar gentry. (In fact, as A. J. P. Taylor points out, such a scheme would have done nothing to solve the problem of the rivalry between the Germans and the Czechs in Bohemia.) As late as 1916 and 1917 Bahr penned further tributes to Franz Ferdinand, praising his sense of responsibility, his concern for the future of the Empire and his achievement in building up the Imperial Army.

The 'cultural imperialism' which Bahr displayed in the Dalmatian context found another outlet in his plan for non-violent Austrian expansion in the Balkans. In *Austriaca* he declared that by reforming the administration of her territories and pursuing a programme of industrialisation, Austria could provide an example of prosperity and enlightenment that would gradually woo the Slav peoples of the Balkans away from the Russian camp. At the back of his mind was probably the notion that this estrangement from Russia would be the first step towards some kind of voluntary association with Austria-Hungary.

From August 1914 to November 1918, Bahr's emotions ran the gamut of patriotic fervour, reappraisal, fluctuating enthusiasm and finally apathy. In common with so many of his compatriots he was taken by surprise by the developments of July and August 1914, but he adjusted to the new situation with considerable alacrity. The essays later collected in *Kriegssegen* were all written in the first two months of the War. Bahr, like Rilke, Hofmannsthal and Zweig, invoked the greatness of the hour. He proclaimed the sanctity of the German cause and the 'holy wrath' in every German heart. Germany, he cried, was waging not a war but a spiritual crusade and her heroes in uniform were 'sons of Light'. The whole of Germany's heritage from the *Nibelungenlied* to Richard Strauss sustained her in this hour of trial as she sought her promised destiny. *Kriegssegen* abounded in protests against English envy and French hatred, and in praise of German efficiency, planning, foresight and national unity. Bahr endorsed expansionist war aims and acclaimed the military dictatorship that had replaced civilian government.

One significant factor to emerge from *Kriegssegen* was the Pan-German feeling to which I referred earlier. It was of German, not of Austro-German culture that Bahr wrote; it was German, not Austrian security which he claimed to be threatened. There was only one specific allusion to Austria—when he stated gratuitously that the aesthetic revolution which he had helped to initiate in Vienna in the 1890s was the precursor of political regeneration. A similar Pan-German feeling informs the initial reactions of Hofmannsthal, Zweig and Musil. They too see no reason to distinguish between Germany and Austria in the first weeks of the War, and are keenly aware of common ties of kinship, language and culture. The phenomenon illustrates the inability of the Austro-Germans themselves to remain loyal to the abstract ideal of supranationalism in a time of crisis. Only when the emergency had passed did Hofmannsthal's Habsburg patriotism reassert itself. Similarly Bahr's German chauvinism gradually subsided, making way for an increasingly Austrian patriotism.

Regarded in some circles as a grand old man of Austrian letters, Bahr embarked upon lecture tours of Germany, in the course of which he appealed for a better understanding of Austria and her problems. The need for greater sympathy from the Reich was also recognised by Hofmannsthal, who edited a series called the 'Austrian Library' in an attempt to diffuse a closer

understanding and warmer appreciation of Austrian culture in
Germany. Hofmannsthal also tried to devise ways of persuading
the German press to give more sympathetic coverage to the
Habsburg Monarchy. The reason is that Austria-Hungary's
prestige was not high in the Reich. The prewar years had seen a
steady decline in her political influence and an increasing dependence on Germany. When war came the Austro-Hungarian
Army, designed originally as a defensive or police force, found
itself ill-equipped to launch offensive campaigns. Consequently
the German Army had constantly to be summoned to its aid. The
sterling Austrian resistance on the Italian Front was largely
ignored in Germany. And the Germans of the Reich had little
patience with Austria's constitutional difficulties.[5] Bahr accordingly appealed to his German audiences for a revaluation of
Austria, for an acknowledgement of her 'true' qualities which
were hidden behind the facade of 'gay Vienna'. The Austria of
which he spoke was not that of the operetta or the tourist trade
but the Austria of the working man and small farmer. If Austria
were to be regarded as just another German province and judged
by German standards, then of course she would be found wanting. But it was wrong, he argued, to apply German criteria to a
nation that was separate and unique with its own distinct
historical development. Bahr stressed the political regeneration
and unity brought about in the Dual Monarchy by the War: a
state once given up for lost was now vigorously and determinedly
pursuing a common purpose. The peoples who were once said to
be striving to break loose from one another were now of one
accord.

Bahr stated that Austria owed her historical evolution to the
mutual need of the various Imperial nationalities for aid and cooperation. By working together, or through healthy rivalry, the
member nations had benefited immeasurably from their contact
with each other and had by now become mutually indispensable.
Thus Bahr reiterated the traditional Habsburg ideology, in defiance of his more realistic analysis a few years earlier. He added
that the War had reinforced the supranational consciousness of
the Imperial peoples, a factor which allowed one to see in the
Dual Monarchy a model for the new supranational groupings
that would emerge after the War from the union of Germany,
Austria-Hungary, Turkey, Persia and the Balkan countries.[6]
Bahr's travesty of Austrian history was not made any more

palatable by the admixture of the *Mitteleuropa* concept, which
had been given fresh impetus with the appearance of Friedrich
Naumann's popular book of that name in 1915. Naumann had
discussed how the wartime alliance of the Central Powers and
their allies might be transformed into a peacetime economic
community. In effect this community was to be the vehicle of
German expansion in the Balkans and the Near East. Yet Bahr's
apologia was more than mere propaganda tailored to suit the
needs of a German public. His stylised view of history was due
to a genuine confusion of fact and fantasy; he was no longer
capable of distinguishing between Austria as she really was, and
Austria as she should be. It was wishful thinking in an hour of
dark doubt and suspicion. He was at least realistic enough to
voice the reservation that once the pressures of war were
removed, the unity of the Empire might again show disturbing
rifts; and in order to forestall this he called for a new attempt to
regulate the constitutional relationship between the different
nationalities. In an effort to reduce the fear, jealousy and hostility
which had characterised the politics of the Empire before 1914,
he urged that the rights and privileges of individual nations
should be guaranteed anew. Although he made no specific proposals, he was apparently moving towards the federalist idea
under wartime pressures.

That he should endorse the principle of federalism was consistent with the grass-roots provincialism which had been in
evidence in his prewar writing and which he continued to ex-
pound. He had been profoundly influenced in this by the French
writer Maurice Barrès, especially by the latter's novel *Les
Déracinés* (1897). In its simplest form the theory amounted to
a preference for the allegedly unspoilt life of the *Volk* as against
a degenerate urban 'civilisation', for the small rural community
or the ordinary working man as against the vanity and artificiality
of bourgeois society. Barrès taught that the youth of France
should be encouraged to serve their country in their native provinces, where their development would be fostered by ties of
kinship, education and tradition. In Austria the revival of
provincialism in literature was the work of Catholic writers and
part of the reaction against liberalism.[7] (There are obvious connections with Hofmannsthal here too.) The hero of one of Bahr's
novels declares :

'No, my lad shall not become a Viennese! He must be fully
formed and sure of himself and aware of his own capacities
before I'll even let him know that such a creature exists...
The War? Terrible! But it revealed the real Austria! Our
people in all their glory! All those anonymous, quietly resigned
men and women who sacrificed themselves uncomplainingly, as
though it had to happen that way... The people are always
there, in the countryside, in the factories, they toil silently day
after day, they create the life that we enjoy... My child shall
grow up in this secret Austria, amid reality, among woodcutters,
farmers, labourers who, smoking their favourite pipe on a bench
in front of their cottage of an evening, weary and brooding,
know more of the ultimate mysteries than any of us, and any
one of them is a better Austrian than the rest of us put
together!'⁸

Bahr was prepared to include the industrial proletariat in his
scheme, provided they led what he regarded as 'authentic' lives,
but his sympathy undoubtedly lay with the rural community. His
grass-roots idea was compounded of diverse elements—
Catholicism, disillusionment with the ruling classes, the civil
service and the political parties, a puritan distaste for the frivolity
of Vienna, pique against 'sophisticated' intellectuals such as Karl
Kraus, and a degree of exhibitionism. He enjoyed projecting a
'folksy' image, and had himself photographed well on in middle
age wearing *Lederhosen* and a waist-length beard; he would
write, for example, of his delight in sharing a railway compart-
ment with a group of raucous, beery, perspiring farm workers.
The literary precipitate was the deliberately homely language
of *Häusl* and *Pfeiferl*. The cult of the *Volk*, of the *Gemeinschaft*,
combined with his ostentatious Catholicism and his hostility
towards 'liberalism', placed Bahr within the orbit of the 'conservative revolution'. It also induced a degree of ambivalence over the
question of anti-semitism in his latter years.

The vision of Austria's future which Bahr evoked during the
war years revived the Romantic dream of a regenerated Holy
Roman Empire. Novalis and Richard von Kralik became his
mentors—representatives of both an older and a latter-day
political Catholicism. In reply to a critic who ironically asked him
in October 1918 if he realised that *his* Austria had disappeared
for good, Bahr wrote that the Austria which had just vanished
was never the one he had in mind. What he dreamed of was a

future Austria embracing Poland, Bohemia, Serbia, even Salonica, a strong but peaceful alliance of free nations uniting east and west.[9] In retrospect this sounds like a characteristically idealist gloss on monarchist plans for a 'Greater Austria' in the early postwar years; the royalists envisaged the restoration of a reduced Habsburg Empire to include Austria, Hungary and 'loyal' Croats, Slovaks and others. It should be added that as late as 1924 Bahr styled himself as one of the last 'vassals' of the late Emperor Karl.*

During the last two years of the War, Bahr associated himself with the liberal-conservatives Josef Redlich and Heinrich Lammasch. Lammasch was one of the few politicians who earned Karl Kraus's respect. In 1917–18 he delivered three major speeches in the Austrian Herrenhaus (Upper House) on the subject of a negotiated peace. His words aroused a storm of protest which led to his resignation. A devout Catholic, he was opposed to the *Mitteleuropa* concept and to the 'spirit of Potsdam', and was willing to grant concessions to the Austrian nationalities within the Imperial framework. Lammasch was first mentioned in Kraus's *Fackel* in January 1917, when he was implicitly compared with Hofmannsthal, much to the latter's detriment. He made his first outspoken appeal in the Upper House in June that year. A month later Bahr began referring to him in the weekly instalments of his Diary which appeared in the *Neues Wiener Journal*. In October 1917 followed Kraus's rebuff to Bahr for climbing aboard the peace 'band-waggon' : he confronted the sage of Salzburg with his 'Gruss an Hofmannsthal' of 1914. Bahr's relationship with Josef Redlich was more personal, as Redlich's political journal reveals. Redlich desired a reconciliation between Germans and Czechs, and some form of regional autonomy to replace the centralised administration of

---

* Even now the dream is not dead. When Dr Otto von Habsburg, son of the last Emperor, visited England recently, it was reported 'that Dr Habsburg would like to see Vienna as the eventual capital of a Europe stretching from the Atlantic to the Urals'. That unity is to be symbolised by the crown of the Holy Roman Empire. But the former Pretender has also apostrophised the Germans as the people of the Reich *par excellence* who for a thousand years have fulfilled their mission as standard-bearers of the Empire. Small wonder that such notions go hand in hand with a reliance on extreme right-wing circles inside Austria and with a strong anti-Russian bias. (See *The Times* (Diary), 20 January 1970 and Karl R. Stadler, *Austria*, London, 1971, p. 323.)

the existing Empire. (Both Lammasch and Redlich entered the last Imperial cabinet in the hope of making federalist reforms succeed : in fact all that remained for them to do was to supervise the dissolution of the Monarchy.)

Bahr began specifically to advocate federalism in 1917. In that same year constitutional government was restored, the censorship was relaxed, and there was open talk of the need for peace. His change of heart was thus attuned to the mood of his public. He was aware that the alternative to a new constitution along federalist lines was a dictated reorganisation in the context of a European peace conference. Yet although he supported the campaign for regional autonomy, he clung to the idea that one nation had to be *primus inter pares*; he no longer suggested that the dominant national group should be the Germans, but he plainly hoped that this would be the case. His concession to the increasing pressure from Slav nationalists was minimal. He invoked as a model the still-born Kremsier Constitution of 1849. In the Constitutional Assembly which had drawn up this document, the Czechs had dropped their demands for federalism in favour of a unitary state, while the Germans had acquiesced in a large measure of regional autonomy. Unfortunately the Hungarians had not been party to the negotiations. When Emperor Karl, the last reigning Habsburg, finally decreed federalist reforms in October 1918, they again—though for different reasons—applied only to the territories governed from Vienna, not to the areas under Hungarian administration.

From 1917 Bahr attacked chauvinism and imperialist expansionism. He censured the peculiarly German fusion of militarism and capitalism, and reprimanded the opponents of a negotiated peace. His erstwhile acclaim of military dictatorship was now replaced by an equally enthusiastic acclaim of the Emperor's amnesty for all those civilians imprisoned by courts martial. Moreover he now resented the increasing domination of his homeland by her powerful cousin and ally. The liberalisation of his ideas ensued from a growing awareness of the internal tensions within the Empire and from the realisation that a German victory was out of the question.[10] Bahr embraced his new standpoint with the same uncritical fervour that he displayed in every phase of his chequered career. He hailed the reign of the young Emperor Karl as a new Carolingian age, but in November 1918 all his high hopes finally came to naught. By then, however,

Bahr's interest in politics had waned. From October 1918 to April 1919 he held the post of dramatic adviser to the Vienna Burgtheater and his time was fully occupied with theatrical plans, productions and intrigues. In spite of his reply to the critic who mocked that 'his' Austria had disappeared, he seemed to suffer little sense of personal loss when the Empire collapsed (unlike Hofmannsthal).

After the War Bahr's diary continued to appear and contained along with other matters of current interest sporadic comments on political developments. These ranged from criticism of the Peace Treaty on the grounds that the Entente had exploited its power unfairly and given Europe not peace but war for the next fifty years, to a defence of the Social Democrats against a nationalist charge of having brought down the Austro-Hungarian Empire (the equivalent of the German 'stab in the back' legend). Bahr, like Roth after him, preferred to blame those who had clung far too long to a belief in Austro-German supremacy. He protested against the imprisonment and sentencing to death of Ernst Toller, the young Expressionist writer and revolutionary, by the forces of reaction in Bavaria—though the circumstances in which he registered this protest did him little credit.[11] He praised Rosa Luxemburg, a founding member of what was to become the German Communist Party who was murdered by right-wing thugs, as a 'pure character out of Stifter'—which showed how little he understood her as a political leader. The very mention of the Berlin Spartacist uprising of 1919 or the Hungarian Revolution of the same year struck horror into his heart.[12] The general sententiousness of his writing after 1918 was less a direct response to the social and political conflicts of the age than the expression of a religious zeal which had already been manifest before the War.

Towards the end of his life Bahr once again turned his attention to the Austrian problem. The novel *Österreich in Ewigkeit* depicts with a degree of prescience a state fighting for its existence. On the one hand we see the Nazis attempting to annexe the Republic; on the other hand we see monarchists and other patriots dedicated to Austria's survival. One character moots the idea of a union of Austria and Bavaria, which Bahr himself was prepared to accept if there was no hope of preserving Austrian independence, but another character points out that Prussia would never tolerate such a development. Bahr introduces into the novel the Austrian Chancellor, Ignaz Seipel, who in the course of an impossible nocturnal conversation with an ageing princess, discusses the political difficulties facing him. The princess reproaches Seipel for not being sufficiently authoritarian. Austria must be stronger and more determined, the aristocracy and bourgeoisie must resume their traditional role and function. The only man who fully realised the implications of this, she feels, was Franz Ferdinand. Seipel for his part outlines the 'Austrian mission' to provide a bulwark against the threatening hordes in the Balkans, reviving the notion of the defence of Christendom against heathen invasion; for Huns and Turks he substitutes nationalism and totalitarianism. The prelate complains that he lacks support in his own party and admits that in reality the hopes of achieving any meaningful purpose through Austria's continued independence are dim. He clings desperately to the thought that if Austria has survived for so long (since the death of Charles VI, to be precise) in spite of her questionable right to exist, then there is no reason to despair of her now. It is perhaps not simply fortuitous that Seipel resigned for the second and final time in 1929, the year which saw the publication of this novel. Bahr—understandably—leaves us with no clear idea of the future. At the end of the book a nebulous appeal to faith, hope and charity evades the realities of the political situation. Only one thing is clear, that salvation does not lie in democracy, in the horsetrading and hypocrisy of parliamentary politics. The call is for more authoritarianism, more determination, energy and courage, for a charismatic leader. But it is not suggested that Hitler is the *Führer* whom several characters desire. This may have been one reason—Bahr's clericalism, his Austrian patriotism and his Jewish wife were others—for the Nazis destroying all available copies of the last two volumes of Bahr's journal when they annexed Austria.

Unlike the majority of his fellow Austrian writers, Bahr was not apathetic towards politics; neither did he reject political solutions. In the ease with which he adapted himself to changing political situations, in his vague conservatism, in his search for a definition of Austria's political and cultural role, in his fluctuating interest in public affairs and—simultaneously—in his ability never to become too deeply and personally involved, Bahr was despite his eccentricities more representative of the educated bourgeoisie than several more genuinely creative writers of the period.

3

Arthur Schnitzler: The Astigmatic Vision

Schnitzler I would call a Viennese, not an Austrian.

Hugo von Hofmannsthal

In July and August 1914 Vienna resounded to a chorus of public acclaim for the War. Almost every Austrian writer, from Rilke and Hofmannsthal to Anton Wildgans and Franz Ginzkey, gave his literary blessing to the mood of the moment. But Arthur Schnitzler, the lucid chronicler of Viennese society at the turn of the century, remained silent. Karl Kraus, who had previously criticised Schnitzler's plays and stories for their apparent superficiality and triteness, paid tribute to his integrity in remaining detached from the popular enthusiasm.[1] Schnitzler's silence was not the result of indifference. He later rejected the charge that he had succeeded in preserving an aesthetic insularity above the turmoil of war, asserting that as always he had remained sensitive to even the slightest tremors in his social environment. In fact the work which he published during the war years revealed no overt concern with political developments;[2] but a series of notes discovered among his papers after his death in 1931 showed his attempts to grapple with the problem of war and peace.[3]

There we see that in the first weeks of the War Schnitzler was by no means impervious to the febrile mood of the country, though he allowed no trace of this to appear in print. At the outset he was moved by a sense of having witnessed a crucial moment in history. He felt that war had been inevitable. He employed a conventional patriotic vocabulary and accepted the need for suffering and destruction as the price of justice and peace. In October 1914 he believed German propaganda to the extent that he condemned Belgian atrocities, French hypocrisy and English perfidy. Yet his conviction that right lay on Germany's side was tempered by the realisation that the enemy

felt similarly about *their* cause, and he perceived the need for
tolerance and goodwill on all sides, once hostilities had ceased.
That literati such as Bahr or Wildgans or Csokor, who deliberately cultivated and exploited a close rapport with their public,
should have succumbed to the mood of national enthusiasm is
scarcely surprising : but that Rilke in his spiritual fastness, or
Freud* and Schnitzler with their realistic insight into human
motives, should also have shared the general sense of liberation,
betokens the strength of the feeling which gripped the nation.

Schnitzler's qualified assent to the War was shortlived, as was
the elation of Freud and Rilke. By December 1914 he was aware
of the paradox of his position, and his innate scepticism began to
reassert itself. He saw that he could no longer approve of certain
aspects of the War while at the same time disapproving of others,
and therefore came to deplore the whole adventure as an un-
mitigated evil. Reason and compassion, he felt, left him no
alternative. From January 1915 he began to retract (in his notes)
many of the notions he had earlier endorsed. He abjured patriotism and examined critically the causes of the War and the
prospects for peace. Again there was no public statement. The
only occasion on which he broke his silence was when, with the
help of Stefan Zweig and Romain Rolland, he published a letter
in the *Journal de Genève* in December 1914, protesting against
disparaging remarks imputed to him in the Russian press, where
he was alleged to have belittled the literary achievement of
Tolstoy, Anatole France and Maeterlinck. Schnitzler made no
attempt to embody his political observations in a creative work;
the draft of a story with a wartime setting betrays no connection
with the notes through which he tried to rationalise his attitude.[4]

He came to the conclusion that the War could have no meaning or justification. He thus rejected (by implication) the fatalistic
idea put forward by Hofmannsthal, that suffering brought out
the inherent nobility in human nature. Schnitzler pointed to the
singular lack of moral regeneration exhibited by the profiteers,
the diplomats, the newspaper columnists and the rulers of the
nations. He felt that those whom the War had apparently regenerated had already been righteous men before the War, and that

* In a letter to Karl Abraham on 26 July 1914, Freud wrote that
Austria's ultimatum to Serbia was a 'deliverance through a bold-spirited
deed' and that for the first time in thirty years he felt himself to be an
Austrian.

it scarcely required a European catastrophe to prove their worth.
In Karl Kraus's words :

> It was by no means necessary to demonstrate the virtues of the
> just, and impractical to do so in a way which allowed evil men
> to become even more evil.[5]

Schnitzler now revoked his earlier praise of heroism because he
saw in such an argument an excuse for incompetence, greed, sloth
and irresponsibility. Instead of finding fault with the Entente,
he wrote that all the nations involved in the conflict had to bear
their share of the blame.

On this question of 'war guilt', he apportioned (in 1915) much
of the blame among the respective governments, but he also
referred to 'the lack of imagination shown by the people'. To
the activity of a small minority in whose interest it lay to initiate
or prosecute the War, he added the callousness and indifference
of the majority to the sufferings of their fellow men. He maintained that the guilt of the ruling classes was shared by the
nations at large who had accepted war as a legitimate instrument
of policy. A similar argument was central to Karl Kraus's campaign against the press, the public and the politicians of the day.
Kraus was convinced that if his contemporaries had been capable
of experiencing in their imagination something of the reality
concealed behind their facile clichés, the War might never have
been declared. One may raise the same objection against both
Kraus and Schnitzler here : to stress the defects of the imagination is to concentrate on only one aspect of the problem of human
behaviour. In the moral and political sphere the quality of the
moral imagination is less important than the power of the will
to act, than the ability to translate moral insights into positive
action.[6] By emphasising what is essentially the aesthetic aspect of
the problem, Kraus and Schnitzler betray the influence of their
Viennese environment. The fact remains, however, that moral
insight was precisely what that environment lacked. The men
whom Kraus and Schnitzler attacked were the uncritical newspaper readers, the gullible voters, the artisans, business men and
industrialists whose only values were prosperity and security, the
war party who clamoured for Armageddon as a political and
spiritual tonic. Their society did not want for activity : what it
lacked was the moral lucidity needed to direct its energies into

constructive channels. Such was Nietzsche's prophetic insight into the Bismarckian Reich; hence the 'hollow silence' which greets the hero's query as to the ultimate meaning of effort and hard work in Thomas Mann's novel *Der Zauberberg*; hence too the futile search for a unifying purpose or 'idea' featured in Robert Musil's evocation of prewar Vienna. Kraus's satire implicitly provided the requisite moral lucidity, certitude and meaning. Schnitzler, on the other hand, was more adept at exploring the corruption and vacuity underlying conventional values than at offering a positive alternative.

Pursuing the problem of where the political responsibility for the War lay, Schnitzler wrote :

> The whole history of mankind is an intrigue of men in power against the consciousness and the imagination of *the individual, or rather, the masses*.[7] [my italics]

This simple, unproblematical transition from the individual to the body politic implies an exclusive concern with psychological factors; it suggests that the complex web of social, economic and political pressures, in which the individual is *also* enmeshed, is here of little consequence. Only in the combination of all these factors would Schnitzler have found a key to the contradiction he observed between the invidious penalties of war for the majority of people, and their enthusiastic acclaim for it. On the other hand, he ridiculed those starry-eyed idealists who dreamed of improving the lot of mankind simply by reforming the character of individuals. In 1916 Schnitzler claimed realistically that the only way to proceed was through the reform of social institutions, and that to achieve this, one had to appeal to enlightened self-interest rather than invoke some sublime ideal. He wrote that the self-righteousness of those highly moral thinkers who criticised politics from their ivory towers was worthless until it had been tested in the political arena. This observation did little to reduce his own sceptical attitude towards politics.

Hofmannsthal once remarked that he considered Schnitzler to be a Viennese, not an Austrian; what he had in mind was the insularity of the Viennese temperament and its indifference to the cultures of the Imperial peoples. Schnitzler was indeed pre-occupied with the Viennese psyche in one form or another and the Imperial hinterland beyond Vienna impinged little upon his work. Not even during the war years did his interest expand to encompass the peoples and problems of the Habsburg Monarchy. He evinced traces of an 'Austrian' consciousness only once when in a letter to Georg Brandes in August 1918 he wrote of the energy, resilience and talent still inherent in his homeland. Even here he places significant limitations upon his patriotism, drawing a distinction between a 'homeland' and a 'fatherland'.[8] In order to elucidate the difference we must look at Heinrich Bermann, one of the principal characters in the novel *Der Weg ins Freie* (1908) to whom Schnitzler attributes similar sentiments. In the novel the distinction is due to Heinrich's predicament as an assimilated Viennese Jew at a time when his 'assimilation' is increasingly being called into question by Gentile and fellow Jew alike. *Vaterland* has political overtones for Heinrich and implies a commitment to the State or to patriotic causes. This automatic allegiance he refuses to give. He prefers the word *Heimat* (like Schnitzler himself) which suggests a purely individual and voluntary cultural loyalty without any political strings. Elsewhere Schnitzler declares that he cannot feel solidarity with someone merely because the man happens to belong to the same nation, class, race or family as he himself; and he insists on being allowed to choose for himself those to whom he wishes to feel related. Again then we see his rejection of all irrational social pressures and claims on his person. *Vaterland* is something thrust upon one by an accident of birth, whereas *Heimat* one can create for oneself. Bermann feels no emotional bond with the proponents of Zionism who claim his support, for the concept of a Jewish national home means nothing to him. He 'belongs' not to Jewry but to the Austro-German culture of Vienna, and declines to acknowledge any political affiliation, Jewish or otherwise. His dissociation from vague, irrational and ill-considered political slogans is a sign of his proud integrity, an integrity shared by Schnitzler himself. But it also precludes total identification with the culture in which he is rooted.

However, the Jewish problem is of secondary importance in determining Schnitzler's indifference towards the Habsburg Empire as a political or cultural unit. After all, the Jewish bourgeoisie in Vienna and elsewhere was notably loyal to the Crown, even when patriotism was not regarded as a wholly effective means of achieving assimilation. Of greater significance is Schnitzler's assessment of the nature and value of political activity. Like so many of his fellow artists, he was unreservedly cynical about political life in Austria during the last years of the Empire. The politicians' search for personal power, their patent lack of dignity, intelligence, honesty and principle, inspired him with contempt. *Der Weg ins Freie* contains a veritable indictment of the political life of the day. Some of the observations (for example, 'People were inwardly indifferent and on the surface coarse') anticipate Musil's comment on the unreality and paradoxes of Austrian politics. Another stricture, 'the only genuine emotions here are malicious delight in the troubles of others, and hostility towards true talent', recalls Bahr's vendetta against public life in the Monarchy. Schnitzler's arraignment of the politicians on ethical grounds was accompanied by an intense intellectual antipathy towards the demands that party politics appeared to make upon the individual. He refused to make the *sacrificium intellectus* that ideological commitment entailed. But he not only repudiated ideology—he also avoided any constructively critical involvement in political debate. His political will was effectively paralysed by his ability to see the various sides of any given question. A realistic assessment of human motives, distrust of philosophical abstractions and scepticism towards the truth of any single faith or system left him unmoved by political conflicts. He was not misled into believing that the individual could somehow live his life outside politics. Yet he refused to play the political game according to the rules decreed by the age. Activism was totally alien to his disposition and his view of life.

In the recently published autobiography of his early years Schnitzler recalled that in a rare discussion about Austrian politics he was far more anxious to display his dialectical skill than to defend any political convictions. He went on to remark that it was the psychological aspect of the Jewish question which fascinated him, not the social or political dimension.[9] In other words, he was interested in how people behaved in a given situation rather than in the objective reasons for their dilemma or in the possible consequences for society at large. This psychological interest so characteristic of Schnitzler and his whole milieu proved an extremely limiting way of dealing with political problems. It meant, as he himself acknowledged, that society became a mere backcloth to personal dilemmas, the nation a mere administrative convenience, and history a remote arena where self-interested politicians indulged in sterile bickering. The litera-

ture of an age less privileged than that of late Victorian Vienna
was to turn increasingly away from 'psychology' in its attempt
to explore and articulate the nature of reality. The modernism of
the twenties abandoned the already disintegrating notion of the
self-determined individual in favour of myth, metaphysics, social
psychology and dialectical materialism.

Schnitzler's prewar writing did not completely ignore contemporary social and political problems. It might even be argued
that his plays and stories anticipated the final disaster of 1914,
insofar as they revealed the hollowness and futility of Viennese
society. In one sense this is true. Yet an impressionistic reflection
of the writer's milieu need not presuppose an analytical awareness of the consequences of the decay he seems to perceive. Time
and again, as critics have rightly concluded, Schnitzler stopped
short of the social and political implications of the individual
histories which supply his material. The play *Liebelei* (1896) is—
among other things—a social tragedy : not melodrama, not an
essay in social realism, but a poignant portrayal of the plight of
two characters trapped in a social situation which inevitably
gives rise to tragedy. Fritz, a young man-about-town, has an
affair with a girl from a lower social class. Despite her deep love
for him he never regards her as more than a temporary adjunct
to his life. He dies fighting a duel over a woman who means even
less to him than Christine. What drives her to despair is not the
manner of his death but his inability to respond to her passion
on any but the most superficial level, his failure to accord her the
basic dignity and respect to which her feelings entitle her. The
indictment of Fritz and of the class to which he belongs is
apparently clear. Yet as has been suggested Schnitzler concentrates on the personal consequences of social attitudes. The wider
implications of this tragedy for a society which condones Fritz's
attitude to his mistress are not delineated. Nor is the political
corollary of the behaviour of a Leutnant Gustl or a Georg von
Wergenthin ever adumbrated. Gustl, the protagonist of one of
Schnitzler's best-known stories, lives by a code of honour which
he lacks the courage to live up to. He is the epitome of a
redundant military caste, at heart demoralised and corrupted but
still seeking to justify its existence in blind fits of aggression. His
mixture of arrogance and cowardice is ruthlessly exposed as he
tries to summon up the resolve to commit suicide and thus
redeem his tarnished honour. Georg, the principal figure in *Der*

Weg ins Freie, is burdened by the dead weight of a barren heritage, crippled by doubt and knowingness, with no hope of finding a way out of his isolation through commitment to a binding human relationship. He is one of a host of drifting characters in Schnitzler's work who represent a class devoid of purpose, passion and the will to change their environment rather than succumb to it.[10] Yet the author himself does not place such figures in a wider historical context. There is no parallel in Schnitzler's prewar work to characters like Trofimov or Lopahin in *The Cherry Orchard* who imply a considerable degree of historical awareness on the part of Chekhov, even if they do not point an unambiguous moral.

It is surely no accident that in a play written after 1914 Schnitzler attempted to correct his defective vision. In *Komödie der Verführung* (1924) the emotional relationships between the characters—a kaleidoscope of flirtation, love and jealousy—remain as always his primary interest. But now the personal dilemmas carry faint political overtones. When one of the characters declares in exasperation,

'Is this the time for such—curious play-acting? There's no longer any fairy tale atmosphere in the air, believe me ...'[11]

—he sums up our impression of a civilisation under notice of dismissal. Characteristically, the dramatist conveys his insight in a tone of ironic constatation rather than of moral criticism. Engrossed with themselves, the figures in the 'comedy' are remote from the actual world of social conflict. Their affairs are fleeting, spiced with an intuition of transience; their eroticism is divorced from responsibility; and as their strangely ethereal gavotte culminates in suffering, loneliness, *Liebestod*, or pointless flight, the rumours of war which have all along punctuated their story become inescapable reality. Schnitzler uncovers the passion and violence suppressed beneath the mask of social convention and depicts the aimless drift of people who have given up any hope of directing or controlling their lives. The scene in Act I, a masked ball in a princely park, which closes with a silent deserted stage illuminated by the half-light of dawn, could have originated in one of the prewar plays—except that the park has been voluntarily handed over to the nation. The setting of the last act, however, a clear morning on a Danish beach on 1 August 1914, implies a historical awareness absent from the work of an earlier period. With the outbreak of hostilities, the process of self-discovery is hastened : the characters either try to flee from, or accept the claims of reality in both the private and public context. One couple escapes on a yacht, another pair of lovers seal their union in death, two others part for good, the girl to bear her child alone, the man to enlist.

Let us turn back to two prewar historical dramas which potentially at least offer Schnitzler the opportunity of coming to grips with political problems in a more direct fashion than in his 'social' works. Here his own choice of milieu and characters arouses certain expectations. *Der grüne Kakadu* (1899) is set in revolutionary Paris and ends with the murder of a duke and the appearance of a crowd shouting 'Freedom !' There is an integral connection between the historical background and the central theme of the bizarre intermingling of play-acting and reality, of truth and illusion.[12] In a sordid tavern groups of French aristocrats come to enjoy the spectacle of actors playing the parts of villains, ruffians and whores. Their surfeited palates are titillated afresh by this contact with an anti-social underworld which in reality they know to be a harmless fiction. Yet the actors and their audience are also opponents in the social world : the insults tolerated, even savoured by the aristocrats are in fact a safety valve through which real aggression is released. The underlying philosophical theme is again linked with the historical context by the fact that the nobility and the populace are depicted at a moment when they are no longer what they seem. The privileges of the ruling class and the repression of the people are being called into question even as the play proceeds, so that the traditional social roles which are ostensibly still maintained are in fact themselves becoming fictions. An effete nobility that views the whole of life as a spectacle for its own amusement fails to interpret the signs correctly when the tide turns against it. However, the new revolutionary reality is no more proof against delusion. Henri is hailed by the mob as a hero of the revolution when in fact he murdered the duke out of purely private motives of jealousy and despair. This supreme irony sets the stage for a new cast and a new audience who will be just as much prisoners of illusion and ambivalence as the *ancien régime*. As Martin Swales comments, the effect of this conclusion is to devalue the great historical and political event which serves as background to the play.[13]

In another historical play published a decade or so later the theme of the awakening of the hero to a sense of ethical responsibility is only perfunctorily linked with the political background. The setting of *Der junge Medardus* (1910) is Vienna under the Napoleonic occupation, and a main strand of the plot involves the conspiracies of exiled French royalists against the usurper. Not until the end of the play does Medardus himself see Napoleon as a political menace as well as a private enemy. Once again it is not his political activism which is the focus of interest but his reactions to the bewildering predicament in which he finds himself—his sense of honour and probity, his passion, his thirst for revenge, his moment of moral choice. The idealist Medardus dies rather than contemplate breaking his word in a patriotic cause. One of the best features of the play is the way Schnitzler exposes the almost total lack of political commitment on the part of the Viennese. With their fickleness, their love of spectacle, their frivolity and emotionalism, they show no political sense or enduring conviction. The Viennese have too little principle, Medardus too much for 'politics'. In short, the political scene is once more minimised and disparaged.

There are only two of Schnitzler's works where political problems occupy the forefront of the action. In both cases his attitude of scepticism or indifference precludes a successful treatment of the issues involved and thus impairs the literary achievement. The first half of the novel *Der Weg ins Freie* dwells at length upon the reactions of various Viennese Jews to their cultural situation. Their feelings of revolt, resignation, self-hatred or ironic detachment are explored with intelligence and subtlety— as is to a lesser extent the response which they elicit in Viennese society. The second half of the novel, however, is devoted largely to the social and moral dilemma of the hero, Georg von Wergenthin, in relation to his socially inferior mistress; and neither of *them* is Jewish. Schnitzler fails to integrate the two halves of his story. The most memorable writing in the novel occurs when he describes the birth and death of Georg's illegitimate child. By comparison, the discussions on the Jewish problem strike us as being detached and almost documentary interpolations. The novelist does not create a sustained narrative out of his study in the psychology of the Viennese Jews; thus the situation of Heinrich Bermann, for example, is far less vividly portrayed than that of Georg and his mistress. Schnitzler's creative imagination cannot encompass the political problem. The *malheur d'être juif* is amply affirmed, and various responses to it analysed, but it is not evoked with the full resources of Schnitzler's stylistic means. There is a tension between the collective, political nature of the problem, and Schnitzler's instinctive desire to treat it as an individual dilemma, as a legacy with which each individual Jew must come to terms according to his personality and circumstances. Georg, listening to yet another futile debate between his Jewish friends, asks himself : What is the point of political views unless one happens to make of politics a profession or an investment? Do such opinions have any influence at all on the way we live, on the shaping of our existence? Later a political discussion between Heinrich and Georg is described by the narrator as being about matters that are fundamentally of complete indifference.[14] The discussions of the Jewish problem are haunted by the author's awareness of their irrelevance, the conviction that if the crux of the matter is a purely individual dilemma, there is little point in talking about it as though it were a collective issue. And yet it is *also* a political problem which demands to be discussed in political terms.

Anti-semitism again appears to provide the theme of Schnitzler's play *Professor Bernhardi* (1912). But the real subject of the drama is the fate of the non-political man in an environment dominated by political considerations. Bernhardi, the director of a medical clinic, refuses to allow a priest to administer the extreme unction to one of his patients. He acts on humanitarian grounds, for the dying patient, a young girl, has entered a state of euphoria and believes that she is about to recover; the sight of a priest would betray the truth about her condition. Bernhardi is indicted, tried on a charge of insulting religion, and sentenced to two months' imprisonment. He refuses to appeal and duly serves his sentence. After his release, one of the chief prosecution witnesses confesses to having perjured herself in her account of Bernhardi's conduct towards the priest. He thus has a strong case for appealing for a free pardon and financial compensation. Again he refuses to vindicate himself, because he is more than ever sick of the whole affair.

Bernhardi is in many ways a projection of Schnitzler's own

apolitical attitude. In his relationship with his colleagues and acquaintances—with Cyprian, who counsels compromise for the sake of the clinic; with Ebenwald, who allows political considerations to outweigh personal merit; with Flint, the Minister, who is an unprincipled creature of expediency and the victim of his own rhetoric; with the priest, who is prepared to sacrifice his personal integrity for the long-term good of his Church—face to face with this politically-minded opposition, Bernhardi holds stubbornly to his refusal to compromise over what he regards as fundamental moral issues. He will not recant because he is convinced that he acted properly. Nor will he participate in the party-political intrigue which would enable him to avoid a shameful and unjust sentence. Least of all will he tolerate any attempt to influence his intellectual judgement by political considerations. He welcomes his prison sentence since it affords an escape from the political chess game which he cannot and will not play. To the end, he insists on preserving inviolate a small private sphere of thought and action in an area which others see as one of public concern. Inevitably his attitude brings him into conflict with his environment and great harm is done to his personal and professional interests. But conflict is precisely what the play lacks at any deeper level. It contains an unequivocal clash between the hero and his world and the opposing points of view are fully articulated. Yet there is no dialectic in the sense of collision of two equally valid principles. Schnitzler gives his unqualified assent to Bernhardi's uncompromising individualism. We feel that he has already weighed the arguments on the other side and found them wanting. The political men in the play, to a greater or lesser extent, bear the stigma of cowardice or dishonesty, weakness or self-interest, hypocrisy or opportunism, from the government minister Flint at one extreme to the priest at the other. So insidious is this emphasis that the reader may never think to examine more closely the very first link in the chain of events. It is always assumed that Bernhardi's initial action is noble and selfless, whatever we may think of his subsequent conduct. His protection of the hapless patient, however, raises the issue of faith versus agnosticism which is never spelled out. The young girl is deprived of the last rites of the Church because of Bernhardi's humanism. His decision has less to do with medical ethics or the defence of truth than with a purely subjective judgement about the importance of a brief moment of happiness in an otherwise unenviable existence. The fact that this act becomes a *Politikum*, a political issue, may be the fault of society : that it is a sentimental, even presumptuous gesture is surely Bernhardi's.

If the latent religious argument goes unheard, what of the arguments which Schnitzler does provide? Here again a vital point is glossed over to vindicate Bernhardi's intransigence. The basic political debate about the relationship between ends and means is too easily dismissed. What is the future of the clinic and Bernhardi's medical work worth? For that after all is what is at stake. The Professor's own answer is a straightforward '*not* my integrity!' Bernhardi is not troubled by such political niceties as the borderline between conciliatoriness and cowardice, between dishonesty and a realistic willingness to compromise. In the dramatist's view, the hero is undoubtedly right to preserve his integrity at any cost. From a more detached point of view, however, the elusion of such a fundamental political question casts a shadow of doubt on Bernhardi's decision. The arguments of the political characters, or at least of the more worthy representatives, Cyprian and the priest, assume a degree of importance which Schnitzler could scarcely have intended. That Bernhardi's stand proves of no avail to his patient (the dying girl was warned behind his back of the priest's arrival and was not spared the knowledge of her imminent death), causes his intransigence to appear strangely misplaced, even egoistic. His refusal to appeal against his sentence when new evidence comes to light, is explained merely by his contempt for the whole affair, an explanation which is psychologically and dramatically inadequate.[15] Schnitzler leaves us with the impression that he considers only Bernhardi's individual fate, not the price which is extorted from medical science, and ultimately from society, in order to preserve the hero's integrity. This is not to dismiss outright the validity of the individual moral protest : it is to suggest that Schnitzler has chosen the wrong situation in which to make that stand, and that his hero has never experienced the political pressures which his proud independence is meant to resist.

It might be objected that *Professor Bernhardi* is subtitled a 'comedy' and thus scarcely intended as a considered, definitive statement of opinion. The incompleteness and inconclusiveness of the play might be vindicated on the grounds of comic irony.[16] Bernhardi—the argument might run—is both right *and* foolishly stubborn, justified *and* irresponsible; the mouthpieces of society are meant to be seen as both eminently reasonable *and* cowardly. Only through this oscillation between sympathy and exasperation —it might be concluded—can Schnitzler do justice to the complexity of the issues involved, the conflict between the moral imperative of the individual and the inexorable demands of social involvement. One can only reply that such a reading is not consistent with the dramatic experience afforded by the play. In the first place it disregards the weighting of the dramatic scales mentioned earlier. Secondly, it suggests a characterisation of Bernhardi of a rather different order from the one Schnitzler provides. Northrop Frye once commented that an audience's assent to comedy takes the form not of a moral judgement but of a social one. The focus of attention is not the villainous but the absurd and any shift towards a moral comedy attenuates the humour. I believe it is just such a shift of emphasis which helps to explain the problematic nature of *Professor Bernhardi*. Schnitzler goes to great lengths to appeal to our moral sense where the hero's attitude is concerned, while at the same time evoking a situation which inevitably elicits a social response. To reconcile the two successfully would have meant creating a protagonist with all the inconsistencies and outré fervour of an Alceste who is morally in the right but socially impossible. This is not the sort of figure we see in Bernhardi. Moreover, to venture briefly into the field of extrinsic evidence, Bernhardi's defence of his integrity is entirely consistent with Schnitzler's own attitude. The need for personal uprightness and honesty was among his few deeply held convictions. It is unlikely that he would have chosen to treat it ironically and thereby give comfort to a politically minded world he despised.

The interpretation of the last scene between Bernhardi and Hofrat Winkler is clearly germane to our overall understanding of the play. Winkler accuses the Professor of making a stand when he was not cut out to be a reformer. It would have been better never to have become involved in the first place. Bernhardi protests that he was not trying to reform anything; he merely did what he thought was right in a particular case. That's just it, replies Winkler, if one spent a day doing always what was right, one would end up behind bars by nightfall. So far, so good— Winkler is a realist who sees that absolute moral standards are incompatible with social harmony. Is he therefore the belated

Before the deluge: the Imperial family at the wedding in 1911 of Archduke Karl (later to become the last Habsburg emperor) and Princess Zita. Next to the young couple stands the Emperor Franz Joseph. Archduke Franz Ferdinand can be seen in the middle of the group on the left

A scene typical of fin-de-siècle Vienna: the Café Griensteidl, frequented by writers such as Schnitzler, Bahr, the young Hofmannsthal and Karl Kraus (water colour by R. Völkel)

This postcard, purporting to depict the wartime execution of the Socialist Cesare Battisti, was used by Kraus as the frontispeice for *Die Letzen Tage der Menschheit*. It summed up for him the grinning inanity, callousness, self-satisfaction, moral corruption and barbarity of the Austrian ruling classes. The picture is in fact a propaganda montage

Hugo von Hofmannsthal in his villa at Rodaun, about 1904

Robert Musil

Arthur Schnitzler in 1915

Karl Kraus (water colour by Alfred Hagel)

The Proclamation of the First Republic; crowds assembled in front of the Parliament building in Vienna on 12 November 1918

raisonneur of the piece? Is Bernhardi's stance objectively qualified in the last lines of the play? What *is* clear is that Winkler is
incorrect in assuming that Bernhardi acted in some reformist
spirit. Furthermore the Professor assures him that for all Winkler's
air of sardonic superiority he would have done just the same in
Bernhardi's place. Possibly, retorts the Hofrat in the final twist
of the screw, 'But then I'd have behaved just as monstrously
as you.'* In other words, even though he criticises Bernhardi's
actions he admits that he could not have behaved any differently
himself. The 'political' attitude is a theoretical possibility embodied in secondary characters but scarcely a valid dramatic
alternative in the logic of the play.

Schnitzler belonged to a generation of disenchanted Viennese
intellectuals in the post-Liberal era. Bahr's disillusionment with
the Liberalism of his father's generation led him first to Pan-
Germanism, then to socialism, then to a revitalised Habsburg
Empire and finally to the authoritarian prelate Ignaz Seipel.
Schnitzler belongs to those other artists such as Leopold von
Andrian, the early Hofmannsthal and Stefan Zweig who turned
away from politics and sought a compensatory introversion and
preoccupation with the individual psyche. Schnitzler's writing after
the War was on the whole unremarkable. A major novel *Therese*
(1928) is still steeped in the mood of 1900. As in *Liebelei* or
Leutnant Gustl he refrains from pointing to any connection between the moral and emotional shortcomings of the hypocritical,
predatory society in which his heroine lives her unhappy life—
and the eventual destruction of that society which by now he
himself had witnessed. The incipient historical awareness of
Komödie der Verführung was not repeated. In December 1914
Schnitzler anticipated that his work thereafter would echo the
experience of the war years.[17] Such a task appears to have been
beyond his creative compass.

---

* 'Möglich.—Da wär ich halt,—entschuldigen schon, Herr Professor—, grad so ein Viech gewesen wie Sie.' It is impossible to convey
the force of the German *Viech* here: the word has overtones of animal
vulgarity, culpable stupidity, even indestructibility and eccentricity. By
comparison the English 'pig' is too forthright and unambiguous, but at
least it would convey the sudden change of stylistic level at this point, a
change dictated more by a desire for a shock curtain than by any inner
necessity of the plot.

4

Franz Werfel: Advocatus Domini

As soon as men understand that their participation in violence
is incompatible with the Christianity they profess, as soon as they
refuse to serve as soldiers, tax collectors, judges, jury, and police
agents, the violence from which the world suffers will disappear
forthwith.

Tolstoy : *The Law of Love and the Law of Violence*

When war broke out in 1914 Franz Werfel was working as a
publisher's reader for Kurt Wolff in Leipzig. He was already
well known among the younger literary generation, following the
appearance of his first volume of poetry, *Der Weltfreund*, in
1911. His verses had evoked enormous enthusiasm among those
of his contemporaries who, like himself, were disillusioned with
what they felt to be the rampant materialism of the age, its
hypocrisy, complacency and corruption. They hailed Werfel's
freshness and lack of sophistication, his frank outpouring of
emotion and his precocious pleas for goodwill among men. In
Werfel's work, the theme of the conflict between the generations,
so characteristic of German Expressionism, was enlarged into a
polemic against all authority, whether in the private, social or
religious sphere; the young poet viewed with apprehension the
ever-increasing organisation of modern society and the impersonal
State. As the preface to his play *Die Treoerinnen* (1914) showed,
he was sustained by the hope of an impending spiritual revolution. This drama has even been interpreted as a prophecy of the
impending catastrophe and as an anti-war protest : but while
it intimates a sense of disquiet, it is no more the work of a
politically-conscious writer than Musil's *Die Verwirrungen des
jungen Törless* (1906) or Schnitzler's *Leutnant Gustl.* Though
Werfel plainly felt compassion for the victims of war, his real
purpose lay in presenting a symbolic picture of the cruelty, irrationality and absurdity of life in general, and in depicting

Hecuba's moral victory over calamity as a preliminary to the re-awakening of religious faith. At this time he was deeply contemptuous of contemporary politics, of which he wrote shortly after the outbreak of the War :

Public life became a farce directed by a handful of newspaper editors; anyone who believed in peaceful human intercourse was disgusted by nothing so much as a parliament which betrayed the very idea for which it stood by squabbling over street names and by repeating basely the vile antics of the day; the new life that blossomed among the ruins wore the face of the stock-jobber or the smooth slickness of the gigolo who for selfish motives had concluded a business deal in which he himself was anything but the sleeping partner.[1]

(In view of the cordial relationship which then existed between Werfel and Karl Kraus, the stylistic echoes of *Die Fackel* may not be entirely fortuitous.) Werfel's antagonism towards politics arose both from frustration at the sterility and stagnation of political debate in Austria-Hungary before 1914, and from indignation at the dubious morality of public life. This moral condemnation, the charge of unrestrained egoism, figured prominently in his attitude to politics in the next few years.

Up to 1912 Werfel had lived in Prague, where his attention had been forcibly drawn to the problem of German-Czech relations. From the late eighteenth century—when the German literary revival reached Bohemia, and at the same time the foundations of a modern Czech culture were laid—up to the middle of the nineteenth century, German writers in the provinces constituting the present state of Czechoslovakia did not think of themselves first and foremost as Germans but as Bohemians or Moravians whose mother tongue happened to be German. This regional patriotism was encouraged by the German-speaking aristocracy in its struggle against the centripetal forces of Vienna and stimulated by the Romantic interest in folk cultures. After the first abortive resurgence of Czech nationalism in 1848 a new era in the history of German literature in Bohemia was ushered in by Josef Rank and his imitators. Even in the *Vormärz* period German writers had not in fact embraced a dual culture, German and Czech; the Moravian-born novelist Charles Sealsfield noted in 1828 that

There is no transition, no blending between the two nations; they are separated like Germans and French, and a union of three hundred years cannot stifle this antipathy, nor bring them to forget the nicknames with which they honour each other.[2]

After the Czech radicals had been ruthlessly suppressed by the Imperial Army in the summer of 1848, with the blessing of the German Liberals assembled at Frankfurt, the two nations drifted further and further apart. As the Czechs grew politically more articulate and culturally more distinct, the Bohemian Germans surrendered to chauvinism and racialism, culminating in the rabid Pan-Germanism of Schönerer and his followers and the Sudeten problem of more recent times. The development can clearly be traced in the provincial literature of the area. There were, of course, notable exceptions : Stifter's *Witiko*, for instance, or the stories of Marie von Ebner-Eschenbach. Yet both these writers were rooted in the past. The characters in *Witiko*, a monumental historical novel, are still the old type of 'Bohemian' whose ethnic origin is of little importance either to themselves or to the author. The stories by Ebner-Eschenbach which are set in the pre-1848 period do not shrink from criticising the despotic abuse of feudal privileges; those set later in the century record the dwindling of aristocratic wealth and power, together with the latent hostility of Czech villagers towards the German-speaking landowners. The Slavs who appear in these tales are peasants or servants, mostly loyal, or else members of a Germanicised professional class, depicted against the background of villages and estates in Moravia and Hungary. Ebner-Eschenbach's fiction scarcely ever reflects the rise of an urban Czech-speaking bourgeoisie. She regarded Czech nationalism as a painful aberration and feared that in the provinces of the Empire nationalist resentment might unleash a terrible ally in the form of social unrest—at the risk of being itself engulfed by the upheaval that would ensue. Though acquiescing with tolerance, humour and occasional regret in the inevitability of social change, she never transcended in her fiction the values of an enlightened paternalism. Stifter and Ebner-Eschenbach continued to convey or invoke precisely that 'Bohemian' consciousness which had already begun to break down in the middle of the century. Neither could envisage any other response to the new challenge. When a new response was forthcoming, it appeared not in the provinces but in *fin de siècle* Prague.

After 1880 the majority of middle-class Germans in Bohemia and Moravia came to consider themselves an embattled minority, fighting jealously to preserve their privileges and status. In Prague, where the *haute bourgeoisie* consisted predominantly of cultured Jewish liberals, German nationalist feeling did not run as high among the leading circles, although a form of cultural apartheid still prevailed. On the other hand, the non-Jewish German middle class (Prague had no German proletariat) and the German students fully shared the antipathies of their cousins in the Czech-speaking provinces. The German-Jewish bourgeoisie occupied an uneasy position between a rising Czech middle class and the anti-semitic 'Sudeten' Germans. They preserved a cautious neutrality on the nationalist issue but by acknowledging their allegiance to a German cultural heritage they effectively cut themselves off from the world of the rapidly expanding Czech population of Prague. Max Brod and Egon Erwin Kisch, who were among Werfel's Prague contemporaries, recalled in their memoirs the hostility between German and Czech schoolboys that was a daily circumstance of their education. Oskar Baum lost his sight in one such brawl and seemed to Kafka a symbol of the unhappy position of the German-Jewish population, suffering for their allegiance to a nation which never in fact accepted them as Germans. Kisch remembered vividly the language riots of December 1897 following the rescinding of ordinances which would have given Czech parity with German as the official language of the internal administration in Bohemia; his family barricaded themselves into their flat as mobs stormed and sacked German buildings and business premises. (Werfel was seven at the time.) In 1900 the Germans of Prague who by then constituted only 7.5 per cent of the population—half the percentage recorded in 1880—still maintained for their exclusive use two theatres, a concert hall, a university and a technical college, four secondary schools, two daily newspapers and several large clubs. Certain swimming baths, parks, playgrounds and many restaurants, shops and cafés were in practice reserved for Germans, while the Czechs for their part kept their own company just as rigorously. Contact between the two nations was often confined to the contractual relationship between German employer and Czech servant, or German customer and Czech tradesman.[3]

Shortly before the War, however, efforts were made by a group of young German-Jewish intellectuals to bridge this gap, attempts which were informed by a very different attitude from the pre-1848 ethos of Stifter or Ebner-Eschenbach. Brod became an advocate of Smetana and Janáček, translating several of the latter's texts; Otto Pick translated some of the work of Ottakar Březina and F. Šrámek; Pavel Eisner introduced his friends to the writing of the Czech classics Bozena Němcová, Jan Neruda and K. H. Mácha, and in 1917 published a *Tschechische Anthologie* in Hofmannsthal's series, the *Österreichische Bibliothek*; Rudolf Fuchs translated the poems of Petr Bezruč to which Werfel contributed an introduction when they appeared in 1917;* Friedrich Adler translated the poetry of Jaroslav Vrchlický while Hugo Salus was an admirer of Dvořák. In a slightly earlier generation Rilke had for a time been in contact with the leading figures of Czech decadent literature Arnošt Procházka and Jiří Karásek. Kafka's contacts with Czech culture were according to Eisner 'for a Prague German Jew quite extraordinary'. He knew the language, read books in Czech and attended Czech political assemblies and debates where he made the acquaintance of Jaroslav Hašek. All these attempts were aimed at mediating between the two cultures in the intellectual and artistic sphere. It is doubtful if the young writers involved had any clear idea of the wider political implications of their activity. Werfel was not alone in interpreting their attempts as being totally divorced from politics. For him they were a token of 'authentic' relationships as distinct from the strait-jacket of political ideology and a corrupt power struggle. He rejected the intolerance or indifference of the Prague German bourgeoisie, thereby demonstrating the role of youthful rebelliousness in this whole trend. But he betrayed how deeply even he was imbued with the idea of German cultural hegemony when he wrote in April 1914:

---

* Fuchs recalled twenty years later that when Werfel was first approached about this project, he had never heard of the Czech poet. '[Werfel] had as much knowledge of Czech as, say, your maid has of German, perhaps a bit more', he wrote to a friend in Prague. After the War Werfel collaborated with Emil Saudek on a translation of the poems of Ottakar Brezina which ran to two editions.

For it cannot be denied that Czech culture can only exist as a ward of the German culture in the midst of which it dwells. Prague is only seven hours away from Vienna and Berlin by express train. And if in a sudden fit of arrogance this nation, oblivious of historical necessity, begins to vaunt its independence, it will have lost its unique and remarkable cultural opportunity and, for all its fashionable European elegance, succumbed to barbarism.[4]

The sentiment brings to mind Bahr's cultural imperialism and the young Rilke's attachment to a 'naïve' rural, patriarchal culture which he desired the Czechs to retain. Werfel's reference to 'historical necessity', with its spurious appeal to a metaphysical tribunal, bears the imprint of his upbringing in a wealthy German-Jewish family. Though muted and conciliatory, the voice of the Frankfurt Parliament of 1848 can still be heard in Werfel's words.

The First World War was to set a penultimate seal on the division of the two cultures in Prague and the Czech provinces. Yet the Sudeten problem of the inter-war years should not be allowed to obscure the fact that individual German-Jewish intellectuals such as Brod and Fürnberg continued to live and work in the new Czechoslovak Republic until driven out by the threat of National Socialism. As late as 1937 F. C. Weiskopf published a translation of Czech and Slovak poetry. And Werfel himself was a citizen of the Republic and was awarded the Czechoslovak State Prize for literature in 1927.

The years he was later to term the 'weekend of world history' were abruptly terminated by the declaration of war. To judge by a sketch entitled *Cabrinowitsch* (1915) Werfel, like most Austrians, was unmoved by the assassination of Franz Ferdinand. He also appears to have resisted the fever of patriotism which swept the country a month later. Max Brod testifies that he and Werfel, together with another friend, approached T. G. Masaryk in the early days of the War with the request that the Czech leader should use his good offices with Italian public figures in order to bring about a peace initiative. Brod alleges that the deputation was rebuffed with the admonishment, 'You should see to it instead that your compatriots do not deliberately provoke us.'[5] (Shortly afterwards Masaryk went into exile to work for the cause of Czechoslovak independence.) What *is* certain is that

Werfel did not join the chorus of acclaim for the War. A poem entitled 'Der Krieg' dated 4 August 1914 indicated that he was not deceived by the slogans and misplaced romanticism of the first weeks; but it remained unpublished until 1920. At the end of the year he publicly denied having experienced any elation and suggested that modern civilisation had by no means been purged in the bloodbath. Shortly afterwards a piece called 'Ein Ulan' appeared in a volume which also contained Rilke's tribute to the greatness of the hour, 'Wir haben eine Erscheinung', and Hofmannsthal's patriotic hymn, 'Österreichs Antwort'. In such company Werfel's contribution sounded a note of cautious reservation : to him the War was something evil and infernal whose ultimate goal was power and from which no good could come. In the figure of an Austrian trooper driven insane by the knowledge that the enemy he had killed was a fellow Jew, Werfel paradoxically saw an omen of a better future.[6] And a poem published in the same year attacked the intellectual propagandists who had betrayed the ideal of the brotherhood of man. Werfel's criticism was limited and his protest faint : but he retained a sense of outrage and refused to acquiesce blindly in the excesses of his fellow Austrians.

On the outbreak of war Werfel had to report for military service. In 1915 he was transferred to a regiment of heavy artillery on the Eastern Front where, after a short spell as a gunner, he became a telegraph operator. He had little or no experience of combat. In August 1917 he was seconded to the so-called 'literary group' in the War Archives in Vienna at the instigation of Count Harry Kessler, thus becoming entangled in the very propaganda machine which he had earlier attacked. His estrangement from his former mentor Karl Kraus was made public in November 1916 and throughout the following year the quarrel, exacerbated by their incompatible temperaments, grew in intensity. One of several sins which Kraus found unforgivable was Werfel's activity in the War Archives, above all a propaganda poem commissioned from the young writer to celebrate the recapture of the Austrian base at Gorizia in October 1917. However, Werfel undoubtedly found his duties irksome. On a lecture tour of Switzerland from January to April 1918, sponsored by the Austrian authorities, he caused some consternation by revealing anti-war sentiments and criticising official policy towards the Imperial nationalities.

He produced only one full-length work during the war years. *Der Gerichtstag*, a volume of verse written between 1916 and 1917, is full of turgid expressions of loathing and guilt, punctuated by nightmare images of death and decay. But it is not anti-war poetry in the conventional sense. Its condemnatory title is not matched by any specific indictment of the War or of those responsible for it. In the absence of a contemporary record, we are obliged to look to a much later work, the novel *Barbara oder die Frömmigkeit* (1929), to see how the War impinged on Werfel's writing. (This, of course, tells us less of Werfel's reactions to the War than of the way in which he intended his readers to view it in retrospect.) In this book he echoed the social protest against the War which had been articulated a decade earlier or more by Karl Kraus, Andreas Latzko and Egon Erwin Kisch. Within a conventionally realistic framework Werfel attempted to depict the horror of war through the experiences of his hero on the Eastern Front. He chronicles the corrosive distrust which undermined the morale of the Imperial Army after the desertion of a whole Czech regiment. The Austro-German commanders, convinced of the effectiveness of harsh repressive measures, order the summary execution of suspected deserters, traitors and mutineers. There is no glorification, no justification of the War in the novel. The encounter between the hero, Ferdinand, and a bath attendant who delicately admits to having been a military hangman in the 'good old days' before the authorities took to shooting prisoners, conveys a powerful sense of evil and perversity. The man recalls with relish the harvest of civilian suspects reaped during the first months of the War in the Bukovina and in Serbia, voicing an obscene pride in his work. Not only are men executed without proper trial, they are also denied the respect paid in peacetime to the enormity of the penalty inflicted on them: for, as the number of executions rises, so too the stipulated size of the escort and the rank of the officer in charge are steadily reduced. Even the stilted convoluted prose of the Army Manual sets more store by human dignity than the casual indifference attending executions in the field. There is a fatal discrepancy between the treatment of Slav units by the Austrian military command, and the gestures of goodwill directed at the Slav nationalities by the Emperor and certain liberal-minded politicians in Vienna. Werfel implies that each individual participant must bear a measure of responsibility for the prosecution of the War. He shows how

Ferdinand, by rebelling against the military machine and freeing the soldiers he has been ordered to execute, prevents yet another crime from being added to the needless catalogue of shame and misery. Like the train driver at the end of Arnold Zweig's *Der Streit um den Sergeanten Grischa* (1928), Ferdinand's example proves that military discipline need not preempt the dictates of conscience. But whereas Zweig's novel closes on this note of optimism because it is *also* a committed political statement, Werfel recognises that his hero's action is an isolated decision which saves the lives of the condemned men at the cost of his own safety. The functioning of the military machine is not seriously disrupted by his insubordination. Werfel's vision of war is confined to the experience of the infantry. There is little attempt at historical analysis. The hero's mentor, Alfred Engländer, who in some respects represents the novelist's *alter ego*, is contemptuous of generals and politicians alike, and dreams of a Papal peace march to end hostilities. Weiss, another of Ferdinand's acquaintances, regards war as a self-contained activity, the absurd pastime of idle politicians and military experts. But Ferdinand himself does not reflect upon the wider issues of the War even on this rudimentary level, while the narrator-novelist is content to suggest that the War constitutes the fitting culmination of a long period of moral decay. The War is envisaged as a stage in the hero's development which reveals to him the evil of which man is capable. The novel endeavours to present an emotional argument against war, that is, it appeals to our moral imagination —but not without a certain degree of constraint. The account of frontline conditions is generalised and superficial, imparting little sense of a searing experience re-created, as with Jünger or Renn or Latzko, while the style is too sententious to suggest the successful transcending and assimilating of wartime impressions which characterises the work of Hans Carossa or Theodor Kramer.

At the end of the War Werfel was actively involved in the 'revolution' which erupted briefly in Vienna amid the confusion and terrible hardship ensuing from military defeat and political disintegration. His progression from the cultural criticism of the prewar years to political revolution by way of antagonism towards the War would be a series of logical steps, were it not for the fact that he had hitherto professed a deep scepticism with regard to political activism and denied its efficacy as a cure for human ills. In a dispute with Kurt Hiller between 1916 and 1917, Werfel referred to Christian values—particularly as refracted through the writing of Dostoyevsky—to refute Hiller's contentions. At this time Hiller was the moving spirit of 'Activism' among the German writers; with a traditional emphasis on spirituality, he and his friends were dedicated to the task of transforming human life through the power of the Word. In an open letter to Hiller entitled 'Die christliche Sendung', Werfel discussed the issue of social change.[7] He claimed that all political parties desired the same end, no matter what their ideology : they sought power in order to ensure human happiness according to their own lights. But power had a corrupting influence, and the revolution of today inevitably became the establishment of tomorrow. Whatever social changes were effected, there would always remain those who travail and are heavy-laden, for no political system could remove human misfortune. Politics, he wrote, proceeded on the basis of several false assumptions. First, it regarded social relationships as the be-all and end-all of existence, to the neglect of the human soul. Secondly, it tried to ensure human happiness, but by thinking in terms of pluralities it disregarded the uniqueness of the individual. Thirdly, it claimed to be realistic, but laboured under the delusion that abstract theories, statistics, and so-called economic laws contained the secret of life. Werfel maintained that the only true reality was the religious duality of God and the individual soul. Political idealists dealt simply with external circumstances, unaware that the fundamental ground of our being resisted change from without. Even an exemplary social environment could not relieve the burden weighing on men's souls. At the same time, Werfel indicated that the practical expression of charity was of prime importance in Christian ethics, provided that good works sprang from faith and spiritual regeneration. Society needed to be changed, but only from within, through the dedication of individuals seeking their own salvation. Because Werfel was indifferent to specific reforms, because he was concerned less with an equitable distribution of power than with the abolishing of authority altogether, and because he saw the need for Christian action on a purely personal level, he displayed a lack of that social consciousness and political sense which the Austrian reformer, Karl von Vogelsang, had successfully combined with his Catholicism. In rejecting the existing imperfect world out of hand, Werfel was moved by the spirit of anarchism : he preferred total chaos to the survival of the old order, and declared that 'anarchism', the struggle against all power principles, was the only appropriate political attitude for a Christian. Werfel's social ideal was the community (*Gemeinschaft*), a spontaneous associ-ation of like-minded individuals joined together in love, a frame-work within which harmony, not conflict, was the spring of human relationships. Against this he set what he saw in the modern world : *Gesellschaft*, an involuntary association of indi-viduals who were swallowed up in an amorphous mass and whose relationship one with the other was that of perpetual con-flict, barely contained by arbitrarily imposed legislation. (Here he adopted the conventional conservative distinction in the service of a Christian utopianism, instead of a hierarchical social structure.) The weakness of his argument lies precisely in his denigration of social conflict and political organisation, in his exclusive emphasis on individual regeneration : he fails to allow for the possibility of productive tensions, or for an acceptable adjustment of means to ends.

'Die christliche Sendung' was followed by a private letter to Hiller from the Eastern Front. Werfel there reaffirmed his views, but also wrote of the need to avenge the victims of authority and regimentation. He placed a new emphasis on the 'messianic poss-ibility of a community of mankind united in knowledge and love'.[8] On his visit to Switzerland early in 1918 he prefaced a reading of his work before an audience of workers at Davos with a tribute to physical labour and an attack on bourgeois intel-lectuals and modern art as parasitical products of a capitalist society. In November of that year he was inciting a Viennese crowd to storm the offices of the Wiener Bankverein. In 1919 he joined Franz Blei, Albert Ehrenstein, Albert Gütersloh, Bahr and others in protesting—albeit as an afterthought—against the impending execution of Ernst Toller. Werfel and his fellow signatories referred to the vengeance of a bloodthirsty bour-geoisie, but ignored the atrocities committed by some of the Munich revolutionaries. At about this time, Werfel took out Czech citizenship, proclaiming his solidarity 'as a class-conscious worker of the mind and heart' with the people of the 'socialist republic' of Czechoslovakia. In July 1919 he and Ehrenstein were among the signatories of an appeal for the found-

ing of a 'Socialist Council of Intellectual Workers' published
in *Červen*, the organ of the Czech Anarcho-communists.
(The council was to encourage the dedication of all intellectuals, regardless of nationality or race, to the cause of
the working class.)[9] Adolf Klarmann has rightly observed that
Werfel's revolutionary enthusiasm was a temporary aberration. It
was not so much a refutation of previously held convictions as an
emotional response to the pressures of the moment, born of a
naive overestimation of the aims and motives of his fellow revolutionaries. To police interrogators who questioned him about his
political affiliation (Bahr protested against this 'harassment' of
the young writer), he is alleged to have replied that he thought of
himself as a 'Tolstoyan'.[10]

In the gratuitous fiasco of the Viennese 'revolution' he and
his café companions, Franz Blei and Egon Erwin Kisch, played
a conspicuous, if superficial role. A Viennese evening paper went
so far as to accuse Werfel, Kisch, Blei and Gütersloh of being
responsible for the casualties that had occurred after the fracas
in front of Parliament on 12 November 1918, the day the
Republic was declared. Kisch, a well-known Prague journalist,
had seen active service in Serbia and Galicia earlier in the War
and had been wounded. (He related his experiences in *Schreib
das auf, Kisch!*) He had spent the rest of the War in the War
Press Department, as a member of the 'literary group'. From late
1917 onwards he was active in the socialist underground movement
and at the end of the War became the leader of the Red Guard in
Vienna.[11] On 12 November he was prominent among the soldiers
who occupied the offices of the *Neue Freie Presse* and, despite the
non-cooperation of the staff, produced one brief and comparatively
moderate broadsheet. Unlike his coffee-house companions, Kisch
remained a life-long Communist. Two other well-known fre-
quenters of the Café Central were Blei and Gütersloh, who together edited a short-lived periodical called *Die Rettung*. Its
confused, strident articles, echoing Werfel's 'Die christliche
Sendung', called for moral regeneration and proclaimed distrust
of mere political solutions; this did not prevent it from also supporting international conciliation, attacking the plan for union
with Germany, and proposing a new federation of Austria,
Hungary and Czechoslovakia (this in December 1918!). In
February 1919 the editors made a public appeal on behalf of the

Social Democrats, announcing that they were the only party capable of running the new state of *Deutschösterreich*; but a month later Blei condemned the Social Democrats for their politicking and *embourgeoisement*, and called for some form of dictatorship. The career of this periodical culminated in the cry 'Long live Communism and the Catholic Church!'—an affirmation of Blei's own Christian anarchism. His warnings of the danger implicit in the political immaturity of the Austro-German middle class were subsequently complemented by an attack on the conservatism of the new socialist-dominated government of the Republic.[12] Werfel too was rapidly disenchanted by the 'revolution'. He began to criticise the shortcomings of the intellectuals who had tried to unleash it, and in the first postwar decade his attitude towards social change was wholly negative.

The problem of revolution impinged upon the majority of Werfel's works during the 1920s. Both the extravagant Expressionist allegories *Spiegelmensch* (1920) and *Bocksgesang* (1921) illustrate this concern. But his most sustained critique of revolution was formulated in the novel *Barbara oder die Frömmigkeit*. Here for the first time Werfel dealt specifically with the events in Vienna, re-creating the atmosphere and personalities of the period when the city faced the threat of a Communist coup. After a series of harrowing experiences on the Eastern Front, Ferdinand, the hero, arrives in Vienna in the last weeks of the War to find the capital utterly demoralised and on the verge of starvation. Moved by compassion and anger he frequents the company of the bohemian intellectuals and would-be revolutionaries who gather in the Café Central. He becomes involved with the Red Guard and is eventually arrested when the authorities take retaliatory measures against agitators. By this time, however, Ferdinand is bitterly disillusioned with politics. Released after interrogation, he sets about completing his academic education.

This account of Ferdinand's experiences in revolutionary Vienna occupies the third of the four sections into which the novel is divided. Werfel depicts with a degree of asperity the activities of dilettante intellectuals who indulge in politicking to gratify their vanity. Their cliché-ridden, impulsive harangues lack any real ideological conviction. The professional revolutionary, Elkan, is portrayed very differently : he has no idealistic or even ideological pretensions, he is cynical, pragmatic, and committed to the ruthless pursuit of power.* The Communists, led by Elkan, and the Social Democrats vie with each other in appealing for the allegiance of the soldiers and workers. The Red Guard thirst for revenge and redress, but betray a crippling political naivety; confused and fickle, they have no clear purpose beyond removing the yoke of military discipline and putting an end to the War. The city crowds for their part are merely apathetic. Werfel elaborates his theme of hollowness and futility by highlighting the unreal, theatrical quality of the 'revolution'. One of Ferdinand's friends, Weiss (Kisch), addresses a meeting of disaffected soldiers and workers, and wins their support with a histrionic gesture and a coarse joke. 'Comrade Weiss' becomes a password forthwith and finds himself at the centre of events, eager to play out the part assigned to him but viewing with growing alarm the depth of his involvement. He is a creature of the masses; like some erratic compass needle, he reacts involuntarily to the emanations of the mob. Since he shows himself to be weak and amateurish, his position is subverted by Elkan. (Werfel's strictures are irrelevant to his model, Kisch. More significantly, his theory of leadership as the dance of a puppet, whether the role be that of a general or a rebel, is scarcely convincing; Thomas Mann's *Mario und der Zauberer* conveys a far more perceptive idea of the *reciprocal* relationship between a political leader and his followers.) Werfel exploits the inherent absurdity of the trouble on 12 November when the Red Guard, mistaking film cameras mounted on the roof of the Parliament building for machine guns, storms the entrance with rifles blazing, only to be placated by defenceless Social Democratic deputies. Thus the novelist articulates his disenchantment with the men who had sought to change the world, criticising them severally for their vanity or insincerity, inconsistency or ruthlessness. Only those dedicated to havoc and destruction, to the unprincipled manipulation of the masses, are even moderately effective. Those who are inspired by some form

* There were two possible models for this character: (a) Josef Frey, chairman of the National Executive of Soldiers' Councils, and a leader of the *Volkswehr*; (b) Ernst Bettelheim, the envoy of Béla Kun, who took over the Viennese Communists and planned the abortive June uprising of 1919. Elkan is certainly an oversimplified portrait of these two activists. Like other figures in the novel he is a psychological type, rather than a fully-realised character.

of idealism can offer only empty phrases, and fail to channel the
emotions released by the collapse of the old order.

Werfel's novel interprets History as the working out of a providential design. Ferdinand's political initiation issues in fatalism :

> Men have not the slightest influence on their destiny. The signa-
> ture of an idiot, a weakling, a poltroon or a fool ignites the
> gigantic fuse. Then science comes along, full of wisdom after the
> event, runs its fingers in vain along the tightly woven plait
> of incidents, and arbitrarily (according to the political loyalty of
> the would-be unraveller) posits certain causes and effects. Fer-
> dinand learnt to appreciate the ancient idea of Fate. No man,
> not even for a fraction of a second, could comprehend the
> spontaneous train of his thoughts, let alone direct it ... The
> secret of history lay not in the will, not in the mind of man,
> but in the cunning jigsaw of life itself, which like human con-
> sciousness was nothing but a breathless, febrile succession of
> images, whose inner logic God alone could decipher.[13]

Ferdinand realises that he was wrong to think that he could help
to make history through political activism. He was wrong too in
assuming that anarchic freedom was any less burdensome than
military discipline. But he blames himself above all for having
thought that the structure of society could ever be fundamentally
altered—and here his conclusions apply to evolutionary change
no less than to revolution. He learns that there will always be a
gulf between the privileged and the underprivileged, between
rich and poor : the only thing which changes is the definition of
these terms. The 'messianic possibility', the potential transformation of society which Werfel had postulated in 'Die christliche
Sendung' as a corollary of individual regeneration, appears to
have receded. The novelist is not apathetic, nor does he endorse
the status quo. On the other hand he refutes the possibility of ever
achieving a more equitable social structure, on the grounds that
man's baser instincts demand self-assertion and self-aggrandisement at the cost of his fellows, no matter how much his spirit
may yearn to lose its individuality in the Kingdom of God or the
classless society. Werfel can conceive of only two alternatives :
unrestrained social conflict which produces injustice, and the
temporary restriction of social conflict through political tyranny.
A third political possibility—enlightened legislative controls and
the channelling of conflict as the essential productive element in

a healthy society—this other possibility remains in abeyance. It is characteristic of the political inexperience of a generation brought up within the authoritarian social institutions of the Habsburg Monarchy that Werfel cannot at this point envisage a workable open, just and democratic system.

The inadequacy of his conclusions is underlined by the problematic way in which his hero eventually achieves the good life. After defining political activity at any level as the irrational pursuit of self-interest, totally divorced from man's only meaningful (that is, moral) existence, Werfel tries to show that his hero is capable of living his life on the margins of society, free from the pressures of social conflict. Ferdinand's pilgrimage through peace and war, guided by the example of his faithful Czech nurse, the Barbara of the title, culminates in his renunciation of the world of 'telegrams and anger'. Yet his withdrawal leads him into the career of a ship's doctor, pandering to the medical and social needs of the rich. He who would be absolutely free remains dependent upon the material support of a society he professes to renounce. He who would be truly humble retires into the citadel of inwardness and self-righteousness. Ferdinand's ending is defeat, not victory—escape, not fulfilment. The philosophy of fatalistic acquiescence induces in practice a considerable measure of apathy and impoverishment, an abstract *caritas* untarnished by contact with social realities. And by evading his social responsibilities Ferdinand effectively ignores the lesson implicit in the story of the worthy Barbara who ostensibly inspires and guides his moral development.

The problem of activism is treated in two other works of the first postwar decade. The dramas *Juarez und Maximilian* (1924) and *Das Reich Gottes in Böhmen* (1930) both portray idealistic social and political reformers who are corrupted by power. Both plays emphasise the evil which results from giving rein to political ambition. It is not until the publication of the novel *Die vierzig Tage des Musa Dagh* in 1933 that a turning point is reached in Werfel's attitude towards activism. In this novel, for the first time since the War, he suggests the possibility of reconciling political action with personal integrity. The book describes the persecution suffered by Armenian communities at the hands of the Turks during the First World War. It tells of one community in particular which succeeded in defending itself against the Turks until saved from impending extermination by the intervention of an

Allied naval force. The leader who inspires this successful resistance against a greatly superior enemy is Gabriel Bagradian, an expatriate who is marooned in Syria by the outbreak of the War. His leadership is supported by the village priest who, in addition to his spiritual duties, directs the political life of the village. The religious sanction of military and political acumen is also embodied in Gabriel himself, as the Mosaic parallels clearly indicate. The source of Gabriel's political commitment is racial : even after twenty years of 'assimilation' in France he is still bound by a sense of obligation towards the past, by the memory of the persecution suffered by his forefathers in their Syrian homeland. His wife, his culture, his whole way of thinking are French—yet in Paris he was never really able to overcome his feeling of alienation. In Syria, on the other hand, he is painfully aware of the cultural differences between himself and the Armenian community. He is a *déraciné*, the ambiguity of whose position is never completely resolved. Nevertheless he is driven to identify ever more closely with the Armenian community as the threat of persecution looms over it.

Werfel no longer equates activism with self-aggrandisement and the ruthless pursuit of power, but allows that political action may constitute a proper combination of spirit and matter. The base element is still subordinated to and informed by the spirit; nonetheless it is the marriage of the two which the novelist now shows to be essential. In the figure of Gabriel the 'Law of Love' and the 'Law of Violence' are reconciled. By contrast, the apothecary, Krikor, is a parody of the 'non-political' intellectual, who passes from mere contempt for the material mode of human experience to utter solipsism. With his gospel of inwardness and his indifference to the social nexus, Krikor embodies an attack on mere intellectualism; his terrible physical decline symbolises the inadequacy and sterility of his philosophy. Like Ferdinand in *Barbara*, he is paradoxically dependent upon the community and the social life he disdains. Here, however, Werfel is fully aware of the paradox, for he shows how Krikor's self-imposed isolation is violated by the external world and how his dream of spiritual independence is shattered. Krikor is one of the first to see the mutilated body of Gabriel's son, murdered by the Turks, and at this sight a wave of pain, compassion and anger engulfs him. Here the social world cannot be ignored : it demands to be acknowledged as the cruel, imperfect but ineluctable context of man's earthly life and his sentient being. Later in the novel, when Krikor is finally confined to his bed, he attempts to erect a wall of books between himself and the room where the representatives of the community meet to argue, discuss and plan. And again the tumult of society and politics encroaches on the realm of pure spirit. Werfel's attitude towards this character is unambiguously critical.

Werfel's reappraisal of activism sprang from his awareness of the threat of Hitlerism to the Jews of Central Europe. He read excerpts from the novel on a tour of Germany in November 1932, choosing the chapter which relates the confrontation between a liberal German observer, Pastor Lepsius, and the fanatical Turkish leader, Enver Pasha. This political gesture, together with the Mosaic parallels in the novel, testifies to Werfel's identification with the Jews in the face of threatened persecution. The son of an assimilated German-Jewish family, Werfel appears to have shared Gabriel's sense of rootlessness; the dilemma of an assimilated Jew forcibly reminded of his origin occurs in the prose fragment *Pogrom* (1926) and in the unfinished novel *Cella oder die Überwinder* (1938/9). The writer's attempt to come to terms with the problem took the form of an endeavour to reconcile Judaism and Catholicism as complementary elements of God's design. (This is the issue facing Alfred Engländer in *Barbara*; it is central to the story *Die wahre Geschichte vom wiederhergestellten Kreuz* which appeared in 1942.) In the thirties Joseph Roth allied himself with Catholic royalism in an attempt to overcome his feeling of alienation; Austrian legitimism went hand in hand with a new respect and compassion for his orthodox kinsfolk in his native Galicia. Stefan Zweig, on the other hand, was left bewildered by the sudden undermining of his apparently secure assimilation by arbitrary political legislation, and refused to lend public support to the Jewish cause.

In *Die vierzig Tage des Musa Dagh* the hero stresses the need to resist Turkish oppression at all costs. The majority of Armenian communities in Syria submit to the Turks and are destroyed. And even Gabriel's village is saved only by a *deus ex machina* in the shape of a French naval squadron. Here the historical and literary realism of the novel begins to break down, for the *manner* of the deliverance is intended to illustrate the mysterious operation of Providence. The French cruiser's attention is attracted by the glow of the very fire which finally threatens to pitch the

Armenians into the hands of their enemies, while the tactical reasons for the Turkish withdrawal that permits the unhampered evacuation of the survivors are not delineated with sufficient narrative care. The story verges on the miraculous, and salvation is bestowed with the knowing connivance of the novelist, rather than against the greatest odds his imagination can devise. The pattern is too neat, the rescue lacks conviction. It brings to mind the reservations of the poet Ottfried Krzyzanowsky (the original of Krasny in *Barbara*) who once reproached Werfel, 'You like to think of yourself as God's advocate—but God doesn't need an advocate!'[14] For most of the novel, however, the affirmation of activism is matched by a grasp of the political process far superior to anything which Werfel had previously attempted. The Armenian community is led by an élite who govern through and with a council of elected representatives. The latter champion conflicting interests and are frequently swayed by jealousy, greed or ambition. The majority of them lack political acumen and frequently ignore their social responsibility. Yet Gabriel and the other leaders are compelled to work through this council, even at the cost of having some of their best plans frustrated. Werfel now accepts that human shortcomings necessarily bedevil political life but do not of themselves render all activism absurd and futile. Instead of condemning social tensions, he shows that they can be harnessed, controlled and directed.

Gabriel's estrangement from his wife, though compounded with the strain of physical hardship and political responsibility, cannot break his spirit. What finally crushes his moral will is the death of his son. This is the ultimate penalty exacted for the salvation of his people, a supreme loss which Werfel conveys with vibrant compassion. (Here the narrative realism is not relaxed.) Now that his mission is accomplished, Gabriel realises that he has no desire to return to his former life, and as the ships depart he remains behind on the Mount of Moses. On that high plateau, alone and aching with grief, he comes to know God. His life, his destiny, the rescue of his people and the death of his son all merge into a pattern of providential design and he experiences a mystical elation. Now at peace, he wakes at his son's grave. And then the distant sirens of the French ships summon him to take up once more the burden of social involvement. As his spirit is suffused with a new affirmation of life, he is shot by Turkish scouts cautiously reconnoitring the summit which has defied them for so long. Gabriel too is at the last prevented from entering the Promised Land.

In one respect, the account of Gabriel's culminating experiences is analogous to the entry of the Child King in Hofmannsthal's *Der Turm* : both works transfer the action from the plane of political realism to that of religious experience. But there is a significant distinction between them. Whereas Sigismund's death (in the book version) is interpreted as an atonement for the self-compromise he has inevitably incurred in the struggle against evil, Gabriel's death is an ironic contingency brought about by his passing spiritual desolation. Sigismund's death is the logical culmination of his mission; the zenith of Gabriel's experience is the mystical revelation and the decision to re-enter social existence—in short, his death is irrelevant to his ethical pilgrimage. Equally important, however, is the fact that both Werfel and Hofmannsthal choose to justify the political commitment of their heroes by reference to a metaphysical authority. Where the problem of activism is more or less resolved on the human level of politics and ethics, a metaphysical sanction is invoked to offset the taint of corruption that politics, when all is said and done, is still felt to carry. The absolute standards dear to the non-political mind are not easily relinquished, even when a determined attempt is being made to reconcile activism and morality.

Werfel's residual reservation becomes readily comprehensible if one recalls that during the period he was writing *Musa Dagh* he was also developing his view of the moral and spiritual degeneration of the modern age. In the address 'Realismus und Innerlichkeit' (1931), echoing his wartime letter to Kurt Hiller, he condemned the 'radical realism' predominant especially in the United States and the Soviet Union, an attitude which reduced individuals to abstractions. In the course of his remarks a dubious anti-intellectualism becomes evident. In a second homily 'Können wir ohne Gottesglauben leben?' (1932) he inveighed against the surrogate religions of Communism and Nationalism, both of which issued from nihilism; against them he set the moral and spiritual values of Christianity. He delivered these two addresses in various German towns, trying to show that the real choice was not between right and left but between heaven and hell. He knew, however, that his audiences had already made the wrong choice. Subsequently the religious emphasis came increasingly to

the fore. In the mid-thirties he was the poet laureate of
Schuschnigg's Austria where his wife's *salon* was a meeting place
of prominent public figures and intellectuals. Werfel's hypostasisation of the political conflict complemented the Catholic
conservatism of the 'Austro-Fascists'. During the PEN-Club
congress in Paris in 1937 he championed 'pure art', an art which
dealt with eternal verities as against topical issues and political
tendentiousness. His attitude ran counter to the whole tenor of
the congress which was concerned with the need for political
commitment in the struggle against fascism. To left-wing writers
such as Feuchtwanger he inevitably appeared resigned and
escapist.[15]

Before the War Werfel showed no interest in the political problems of the Austro-Hungarian Empire beyond the local tensions
in Prague. After the War his attitude ranged from bitter criticism
to detached irony. In the twenties his respect was reserved not
for the Imperial 'idea' but for the human virtues of the Imperial
civil servant. Claudio Magris in his study of the Habsburg myth
mentioned earlier has suggested that Werfel displayed a tendency
to idealise the Habsburg world as early as 1924; he perceives in
Juarez und Maximilian, a play based on the fate of the ill-starred
Habsburg Emperor of Mexico, 'the opposition of an idea of
supranational religious power and an irrational, barbaric nationalist drive'.[16] Such an interpretation, evoking as it does the internal
problems of the Habsburg Monachy, is not convincing. In some
ways Werfel's drama adheres more closely to the historical facts
than Magris would have us believe. Maximilian's ideals are
social, not supranational; his concern for the Mexican Indians
springs from humanitarian feeling, rather than from any attempt
to persuade them of the follies of nationalism. Confining himself
to the contrast between the Emperor and Juarez, Magris overlooks the fact that there is a third faction in the play, the
Royalists, who are consistently portrayed in an unfavourable
light. By comparison with *them* the republican nationalists
emerge for the most part as courageous and honourable. Juarez,
it is true, may appear 'barbaric' when he implacably insists on
Maximilian's execution—but the basic conflict in the drama is
between political expediency and idealism. Maximilian's only
relationship to the Habsburg tradition lies in his nostalgia for a
direct link between Emperor and peasant, in his idealisation of a

paternalist, authoritarian political framework devoid of national or social conflict, in his stylisation of a feudal structure. This notion owes its prominence less to Werfel's alleged Imperial nostalgia than to his prejudice against politics and political institutions. It is no accident that Maximilian is highly critical of Franz Joseph, whom Habsburg apologists normally treat with great respect.

In a later story, *Der Tod des Kleinbürgers* (1927), we find further evidence of Werfel's attitude towards the Imperial past. Here he describes the valiant struggle of a retired civil servant to stave off death until his life insurance payments are completed. In defiance of medical opinion he succeeds in staying the course. He is driven as much by the bureaucratic tradition of duty as by the need to provide for his dependents. In a delirium he sees his struggle against death as equivalent to remaining at his former post in the *Finanzlandesprokuratur* until the arrival of his relief. His impending release is heralded by a vision of Franz Joseph driving into Vienna from the summer palace in the suburbs, Schönbrunn, and the 'good and faithful servant' is finally rewarded with a place in the Imperial procession. Werfel's characterisation is lively, the tale is told with a pleasing economy of means, and the danger of sentimentality is avoided through realistic observation and ironic detachment. To the extent that the admirable conscientiousness of the Habsburg bureaucrat is related to the wider context of the Imperial tradition, Werfel's tale partakes of a tendency to idealise characteristic features of the Empire (what Magris calls the 'Habsburg myth'). In a very modest way he anticipates Musil's lovingly ironic exhumation of the past. But far from echoing Hofmannsthal's or Bahr's invocation of supranationalism and the 'Austrian mission', Werfel here does not go beyond a genuine and affectionate respect for the individual merits of the old type of civil servant. The same respect colours his ironically sympathetic treatment of the schoolmaster Kio in *Der Abituriententag* (1928):

A hundred times he had given proof of his warm heart and of a certain kind of passionate fair-mindedness, this epitome of the old Austrian character and officialdom which seemed to have died out with him... Refusing to belong to, or even serve the interests of any one particular nation or class, Kio, this typical old Austrian, was imbued with the sublime dignity of a suprapersonal hierarchy that would not tolerate any racist arrogance.[17]

Now, perhaps, the individual portrait has a limited political relevance. Lest it be assumed that what we have here is an uncritical idealisation, it is pertinent to indicate that Werfel *also* describes Kio's absurdity, his narrow-mindedness, his paranoic fear of subversive elements in state and school, and his blind faith in bureaucracy as the human activity closest to perfection. But our final impression of Kio is of someone honest, unselfish, devoted to his vocation and, with all his faults, endearing.

The character of Kio and the system he represents plays only a subordinate part in *Der Abituriententag*. In an almost contemporary story, however, Werfel's interpretation of the Imperial past is central to its theme. *Das Trauerhaus* (1927) is a critical recreation of the atmosphere of the Monarchy in its closing years, as distilled in the aura of a Prague brothel. The only real event in the story is the death of the proprietor on the night of the assassination at Sarajevo. Werfel's irony is here of a kind which precludes nostalgia :

> We are here concerned with an establishment which can confidently repudiate the designation accorded it in vulgar parlance. At the very least one would have to precede the name with the title 'Imperial and royal', for plush furniture, convoluted gilt embellishments, mirrors, velvet curtains, the etchings on the walls which depicted not only gay respectable love scenes but also horse races, the renaissance opulence of a haughty, even at that time long since vanished decade, the Imperial portrait hanging in the kitchen—from the midst of all this dusty and already slightly tarnished splendour the sheepish gaze of the old Dual Monarchy looked out at the spectator.[18]

The overfurnished, ornate, antiquated décor reflects the superannuated values of an Empire stripped of its self-confidence and ashamed to look the world in the eye. Significantly, the official portrait of Franz Joseph hangs in the kitchen, a scurrilous little detail not unlike the disclosure in *The Good Soldier Schweik* where it is seen to hang in the lavatory.

One of the clients of the 'house of mourning' is a typical *Feschak*, the stupid, irresponsible and fatuous army officer obsessed with the smartness of his turn-out and with cutting a dash. (The type was clinically dissected in *Leutnant Gustl* and lampooned in Kraus's *Die letzten Tage der Menschheit*.)

Although Werfel was prepared to respect the virtues of the Imperial civil servant, he usually displayed a degree of hostility towards the representatives of the Army. It is in *Barbara oder die Frömmigkeit* that his criticism becomes most vehement—when he describes his hero's wartime experiences. There is one exception, however : Ferdinand's battalion commander is depicted as the traditional regular officer, a counterpart of the civilian Kio. In November 1918 Colonel Prechtl is shattered by the collapse of authority and discipline, and by the disintegration of an Empire which he has served for so long. Having fulfilled his duty to the bitter end, he learns from Ferdinand that the Monarchy has been dismembered and that the Emperor has laid down his powers. Prechtl cannot accept the situation which threatens to undermine his whole existence : he simply does not know where he belongs any more. When two unruly soldiers insult him, Prechtl commits suicide. His plight, like his solution, is akin to that of Colonel von Radosin in Franz Theodor Csokor's play *3. November 1918*, which appeared in the same year as Werfel's novel. There too the Imperial officer displays wholehearted dedication to his mission : at the end of the War others may discover their local ties, but he cannot put aside a lifetime's service to the supra-national dynastic ideal. (It is perhaps appropriate to recall that two of Ludwig Wittgenstein's brothers, both army officers, committed suicide in Italy in November 1918.) Prechtl cannot comprehend how the Emperor could break his oath of loyalty to his soldiers—a muted reproach which in Alexander Lernet-Holenia's war novel *Die Standarte* (1934) becomes a bitter indictment. Emperor Karl's withdrawal from affairs of state, his decision to release his soldiers from their oath of loyalty, is there construed as a shameful betrayal of their trust and an insult to their sacrifice.

Just as the threat of National Socialism drove Werfel to affirm political activism, so too it brought about a revaluation of the function and nature of the Habsburg Monarchy. In 1936 he wrote a prologue to an anthology of some of his stories in English translation, in which he tried to analyse the meaning of Imperial Austria. The essay is informed by an apprehension of chauvinism, *Blut und Boden* and power politics. Werfel's account wavers between idealisation and perceptiveness : the 'Habsburg myth' is sustained by a polemic against contemporary ideologies. He now

reiterates the quasi-religious concept of the Imperial mission
advanced by Bahr and Hofmannsthal during the War :

> Empires have been, and will be, founded only in the sign of a
> higher idea. Nations can only found states. By their very nature,
> national states are daemonic entities and (like everything
> daemonic) fetish-worshipping, irritably 'dynamic', menacing and
> menaced. But true empires arise only when a supranatural,
> divine element is mingled with the daemonic 'natural' entities,
> to lift them above themselves : a revelation or a sublime idea.
> For every true empire is an unrealised effort to establish the
> Kingdom of God upon earth. At least in the hour of its birth it
> is that.[19]

(By 1939 Werfel's publicistic writing was even warmer in its
approbation, extolling Austria as the legitimate heir of the Holy
Roman Empire and condemning the Prussian usurpers. He
stressed the necessity for a union of all small nations that might
become the organic heir of the old Monarchy.[20]) The Habsburg
Empire was, of course, constructed for the greater glory of the
House of Habsburg. Yet the notion of an Imperial mission is not
entirely without foundation. Compared with the ruthlessness of
German imperialism under Wilhelm II and again under Hitler,
the Habsburgs from the eighteenth century onwards displayed a
sense of paternal responsibility towards their peoples—provided
their authority was not challenged. To the rulers and their more
enlightened administrators, the Slavs were no *Untermenschen*
but children whose gradual material and cultural advancement
Vienna was obliged to foster. As colonial records go, Austria's
is by no means one of the worst. (Compare, for instance, Russian
or Prussian rule in Poland with that of Austria before 1914.)
The paternalism became an encumbrance, once the nationalities
felt they had come of age; the assumption of the superiority
of German culture, on which the whole 'Austrian mission' rested,
inevitably bred discontent and resentment among the subject
peoples. But one should not forget how long a supposedly back-
ward and creaking Empire held together even under the extreme
pressures of war; it was as much a token of the political realism
of its internal critics as a measure of the strange loyalty commanded by the remote bewhiskered father-figure in Vienna. From
one point of view, Habsburg imperialism may be seen as a
relatively felicitous blend of arrogance and generosity, idealism

and exploitation. Werfel (in 1936) acknowledged that decay had set in long before the final collapse. He probably had in mind the upsurge of Pan-Germanism towards the end of the nineteenth century, or the new-found Austrian ambitions in the Balkans. The point is that there was always another, grimly realistic side to Habsburg imperialism which the propagandists naturally choose to ignore—the absolutism of Metternich and Bach, the repression in Italy and Hungary following the separatist revolts of 1848–49, the war to keep Lombardy within the Empire. Habsburg paternalism did not represent a triumph over nationalism so much as the expression of a feudal relationship which *preceded* the awakening of national and class consciousness. The claim advanced for the merits of the supranational ideal was, as we have seen, originally a weapon against Napoleon, then a defensive action against emergent nationalism, an attempt to cloak the maintenance of power and privilege with an acceptable 'ideological superstructure'. The crucial distinction between the 'Austrian mission' and post-1918 plans for supranational unity— a distinction too often ignored—hinges upon the question of chronology: subsequent schemes imply the transcending of local loyalties and the renunciation of nationalism, whereas the Habsburg ideology was designed to *forestall* the growth of nationalism and to protect an existing power structure. Writing from the perspective of the 1930s, Werfel thought in terms of an era moulded by the doctrine of the self-determination of peoples —and he superimposed this modern conception of supranationalism upon the mundane reality of the Dual Monarchy.

His essay offered a perceptive illumination of the Austrian mood after Sarajevo:

> It is enough, they said, we must not wait any longer; before it is too late we must show the world that we are a great power. Generals who displayed their genius at manoeuvres saw that it was now or never. Feudal-minded ministers, weary of adroit *fortwursteln*, were pleased to assume the Prussian 'hard line'. They were abetted by all sorts of people dreaming rosy dreams of success. And in the background were the [Austro-]Germans and Hungarians, ardently hoping to thrust the other races to the wall after a victorious war.[21]

In fact the Hungarians were a good deal more cautious in July 1914 than Werfel's account states, but before the War they had pursued a notorious policy of Magyarisation among their subject peoples. In general the historical documents of the period leading up to the ultimatum to Serbia certainly reveal that the mood in Austrian government circles was not far removed from what Werfel described.[22] There was an obsessive concern with national prestige, a feeling that their patience was finally exhausted, a desire to resolve once and for all the South Slav problem which had eluded conventional political solutions. And in Berlin, without whose support the Austrians would never have plucked up the courage for a final reckoning with Serbia, there was a feeling that this was the last chance of preventing the Habsburg Monarchy from further decline and eventual disintegration.

Werfel's essay on the meaning of Imperial Austria veered back towards an amalgam of insight and wishful thinking when it put forward the argument of cultural synthesis. In advancing a similar thesis, Hofmannsthal and Bahr had been primarily concerned with an alleged symbiosis between the German, Magyar, Slav and Latin cultures of the nineteenth century empire; Werfel at least looked beyond the Imperial frontiers of that period to the historical influences which had earlier converged upon Austria— to the Celts and the Romans, the Germans and the Tartars, the Turks and the Spaniards.

This essay was accompanied by short introductory comments on individual stories. Werfel's remarks demonstrated how his attitude towards the old world had mellowed. He admitted that only recently had he come to place any value on the 'imperial idea'. He had little patience with the more prominent survivors of the Dual Monarchy who carefully cherished their resentment towards the postwar world, since he felt that such an attitude was determined by regret for lost privileges. At the same time he himself regretted the loss of the dignity and majesty with which the Monarchy had once been invested. As a young poet before the War he had been incensed by the corruption of the old world : now, looking back upon the War and its aftermath, and aware of the political extremism that was rending Europe asunder, it seemed to him as if in those far-off days distinctions between social classes and political parties were less pronounced, their conflict less virulent. Werfel even misinterpreted his own stories in order to stress the civilised ambience of the Habsburg Monarchy, attributing to the clients of *Das Trauerhaus* a tradition of philosophical and political discussion for which the text itself provides no justification. The following passage epitomises the interplay of detachment and muted nostalgia—even defiant sentimentality—which marks Werfel's commentaries in *Twilight of a World* :

> Idea, Empire, Decline and Fall—what sonorous words for an eternally repeated drama! No earthly collapse is so great that it does not at the same time merit laughter. One thing replaces another, that's all! Like the changing of the guard! That's right, one day at noon the palace guard led by the band march to their posts for the last time. The roll of drums echoes over the wide courtyard in the heart of the palace, once more the hoarse raven's croak of command rends the air, the goosestep of the sentries traces a final dotted line across the paving stones, the glorious, venerable, battle-torn standard of a much-travelled regiment dips its golden point to the ground. Tomorrow perhaps it will be rotting in a museum. What has happened? Nothing! Time has cleared its throat, History has batted an eyelid. But we, hurrah, we were there! And our splendid technologically-minded grandchildren will have no conception of what sentimental events were there enacted.[23]

Towards the end of the thirties, Werfel drew on the Austrian monarchist movement for what promised to be a major novel. He viewed the movement with a mixture of sympathy and political realism, unlike Roth who became committed to the cause of Otto von Habsburg. *Cella oder die Überwinder* was begun in September 1938 and appears to have been abandoned in March or April 1939. Like *Musa Dagh* it is marred by emotional complications more appropriate to a romantic best-seller. But the recreation of the atmosphere in Austria before and after the Anschluss is a considerable narrative achievement. When depicting the wild hopes of a small monarchist group, or the weakness of Schuschnigg's government, or the corrosive core of anti-semitism in Austrian society, or the appeal of National Socialism to the younger generation, Werfel displays his capacity to convey the essence of a political crisis through its impact upon individual characters involved in it. In his account of the Anschluss, in the poignant story of the 'restoration of the damaged Cross', and in his description of the hero's imprisonment and entrainment for Dachau, Werfel's narrative powers are admirably adjusted to the task he sets them. The hero, Bodenheim, is an ex-officer affiliated to the monarchist movement. His royalism is essentially a matter of personal prejudice rather than political conviction. He betrays the sentimental attachment to Franz Joseph characteristic of a whole generation of middle-class Austrians who outlived the Empire. (There are Polish families today in Cracow who still refer to the 'dear departed Franz Joseph'.) To Bodenheim the image of the old Emperor is synonymous with peace and security, the golden days of childhood. The small association of ex-servicemen to which he belongs is even less politically committed than he himself. They are merely bent on recalling nostalgically their own moments of glory as compensation for the taunts of their recalcitrant children, and on forgetting for a time their middle-aged paunches, their unsuccessful careers (or empty retirement), their worries and their shabby-genteel façades. Nonetheless the leader of the group is a fervent and convinced legitimist, a former colonel and now a confidant of the Austrian Pretender. Grollmüller's courage, his upright soldierly bearing, and Spartan dedication to the Habsburg cause make of him a worthy successor to the line of Imperial officers and civil servants in Werfel's fiction. Grollmüller believes that the Habsburgs, with their tradition of disinterested and non-partisan devotion to the State, have a new mission—to unite all the anti-fascist factions now warring among themselves, and to overthrow with their aid the Antichrist, the Dragon of Berchtesgaden, thereby sweeping away an age of brutal tyranny and rampaging self-interest. As he is aware that external political pressures make it impossible for the Schuschnigg regime to call for the Pretender's return, Grollmüller dreams of a direct appeal from the Austrian people.* When the Anschluss appears imminent, Grollmüller summons over two hundred former Imperial officers to report in uniform, so that he may lead them to the Austrian Chancellor and offer their services in defence of their homeland. Twelve respond. The situation is absurd, yet curiously moving. The pathetic deputation is utterly out of place amid the scurrying aides, the excited politicians and the bullnecked Nazi emissaries in the Chancellery;

* As a matter of historical fact Archduke Otto sent an urgent letter to Schuschnigg on 19 February 1938, suggesting that the Chancellor should resign in his favour; he advocated a direct approach to the Western powers, a strengthening of the Army, and a reconciliation between government and workers. For further details of the monarchist movement, see pp. 110–12.

and Bodenheim finally realises that the Monarchists in their uniforms, wearing decorations that no longer belong to the real world, constitute a superfluous, indeed a ridiculous obstacle, as the embarrassing remnants of a defunct era. Grollmüller is a sympathetic character, but Werfel is under no illusion about the impracticable nature of his romantic ideals. The former officers and civil servants who might have helped are intimidated by fear, or simply unconvinced, while the younger generation remains impervious to the appeal of such dated values. It is significant that the monarchist ideology, even in Grollmüller's case, is sub-servient to the desire to resist Hitler. He does not indulge in dreams of a restored Imperial glory, but is totally absorbed in the struggle against the Antichrist. It is this determination to resist evil that most of all elicits Werfel's respect. As for Bodenheim, he merely sees that his life was more pleasant under the *ancien régime* than it has been since : again the affirmation of the past is qualified by the needs or deprivations of the present. One of the reasons which Bodenheim adduces to help explain his attachment to the Monarchy involves his position as an assimi-lated Jew. In those days, he claims, the Austrian Jews were accepted unreservedly and without prejudice both by society and by the State. He is acutely conscious, on the other hand, of the spread of anti-semitism in the postwar years, and in the course of the novel attains a new conception of the historical role of the Jews, exemplified in the present crisis. Yet his memory of more tolerant conditions under the Empire seems to be belied to a certain extent by his recollection that as a child he was rarely invited to another boy's home, though he himself often enter-tained friends at his house. He remembers too that a friend once asked him whether it was true that there were still real magicians among the Jews—the words 'among your people' clearly giving the game away. Even this vague awareness of concealed suspicion represents a dilution of what Werfel once wrote, for in a rejected variant of the opening pages of the novel he specifically described the embarrassment and inhibition which dogged any social contact between the Jews and their neighbours.[24] In short, the whole issue is deliberately played down in the text intended for publication, because Werfel wished for polemical reasons to stress the tolerance of the prewar world.

Two related concerns inform the whole of Werfel's writing : the problem of political activism and the affirmation of religious faith. In the works which appeared from 1933 onwards, such as *Der veruntreute Himmel* (1939), *Der Weg der Verheissung* (1937), *Das Lied von Bernadette* (1941) or *Stern der Ungeborenen* (1946), religious themes predominate. Throughout the first postwar decade, however, Werfel was preoccupied with the nature and meaning of political action. His attitude towards social change was governed by his belief that human society contained an ineradicable flaw, springing from man's basic moral inadequacy. He felt that social reform could never provide more than a palliative for human ills. But within the limitations imposed by this belief his attitude towards activism evolved from intransigent condemnation to qualified approbation. The rise of National Socialism contributed materially towards this revaluation. Similarly the development of Werfel's attitude towards the Habsburg Monarchy was closely linked to the contemporary political situation. Initially far less shaken by the Collapse of 1918 than Hofmannsthal, he gradually came to see in the Imperial past an era of humaneness, tolerance and ethical integrity which was thrown into sharp relief by the barbarity of the thirties.

5

Joseph Roth: A Time out of Joint

It is time that Ahasver found peace somewhere.
Sigmund Freud (in 1938)

Joseph Roth is best remembered as the chronicler *par excellence* of the Habsburg Monarchy. He was its most outspoken postwar champion among the writers included in the present study. When he died in a Paris hospital in 1939 at the age of forty-five, a descendant of the House of Habsburg ordered a wreath to be placed on his grave. Yet Roth's first novel appeared in the *Arbeiterzeitung*, the organ of the Viennese Social Democrats, and his early journalistic pieces were explicitly anti-monarchist and anti-clerical. It is this change of attitude which supplies my theme—the nature and circumstances of his commitment to monarchism and its influence on his fiction.

Roth was a student at the University of Vienna when war was declared. In the first year of the War a friend considered him to be a pacifist with anarchist leanings but in the autumn of 1916, despite a weak constitution, Roth volunteered for active service and was soon posted to the Eastern Front. He seems to have deliberately sought after war experience because he thought it would provide valuable material for him as a writer. Although he found his initial military training uncongenial he adapted easily to life behind the lines in Galicia where he helped to edit an army newspaper in Lemberg. When the paper was closed down he reverted to being an ordinary soldier but he does not appear to have seen front-line duty. The only extant record of his attitude at this time conveyed a would-be sense of exhilaration and resilience:

The main thing is experience, the intensity of feeling, the strength with which we penetrate to the heart of events. I have witnessed terrible moments—and moments of hideous beauty.[1]

But the pseudo-Nietzschean cliché and the self-conscious paradox betrayed a mind eager to seize on experiences for their potential aesthetic value. Not surprisingly the letter concluded with a complaint that he had little opportunity to write poetry. (When he did the result was little more than sentimental kitsch.) In later life he claimed that he had been a brave, disciplined and ambitious soldier who might have made a career for himself in the Army but for the collapse of 1918. He cultivated the image of a former Imperial lieutenant or at least ensign, who had been decorated for valour, had spent some time as a prisoner of the Russians and had even fought in the Red Army before making his way back to Vienna. However, recent painstaking research by David Bronsen has revealed that these details, like most of the biographical information Roth volunteered to friends and correspondents, are false.[2] At the end of the War Roth took up journalism in Vienna and not long afterwards moved to Berlin on the first stage of his wanderings across Europe.

The major part of Roth's early writing was concerned with the difficulty of reorientation in the postwar world. He viewed the civilisation of the twenties from various perspectives and found it wanting. In several novels Roth described the plight of the 'lost generation', the *Heimkehrer* (returning soldier) without a home, the revolutionary without a faith. Again and again, in stories and essays, Roth attacked a world built upon the sand of the Paris peace settlements and the inflation. His heroes are haunted by a sense of rootlessness and disillusionment. His writing at this time explored certain themes common to his Austrian contemporaries Hans von Chlumberg, Theodor Kramer and Ödön von Horváth. In the novels of the first postwar decade Roth's protagonists are typically (though not exclusively) *hommes de bonne volonté* caught in an impossible historical situation.

His first novel *Das Spinnennetz* (1923) takes a topical problem as its theme : the difficulties experienced by an ex-officer in the German Army in adjusting to peacetime conditions. The protagonist longs for a return to the simplicity, contentment and sense of self-importance that he enjoyed during his wartime career. In civilian clothes Lohse is an obscure failure who is driven by his personal inadequacies, his frustration and resentment to join an organisation of right-wing extremists, pledged to destroy socialism, the Jews and the Republic. In other words he is 'representative' of hundreds of such restless, disinherited ex-servicemen who fought in the *Freikorps* campaigns against Communists and Slav nationalists in the first years of Weimar, or who joined the 'Black Reichswehr' and various other clandestine, anti-republican military formations. For all its modish 'telegraphese' and wooden characterisation, the book provides a perceptive analysis of the growth of a fascist mentality. As we follow Lohse's career from betrayal and intrigue, through the first acts of violence and suppression of a workers' demonstration, to murder, we glimpse in the background a wholly corrupt Germany and a Europe ravaged by economic exploitation and political terrorism. (Two days after the last instalment of the novel appeared in the *Arbeiterzeitung*, Hitler launched the Munich putsch.) The narrative is imbued with an impressive detachment: Roth conveys his compassion for the victims of violence and unbridled capitalism without becoming overtly tendentious.

However, Roth was concerned less with nationalists smarting under political indignities, or with militarists unable to adjust to civilian life, than with the hapless, drifting victims of the European upheaval. Whereas his attitude towards Lohse is fairly objective, his portrait of Gabriel Dan, the hero of *Hotel Savoy* (1924), is unmistakably sympathetic. Gabriel, returning from the War, rests for a time in a small Polish town. As his insight into the functioning of the grandiloquently named hotel and the capitalist society of the town grows, he becomes increasingly estranged from his environment. He is ever conscious of the tide of *Heimkehrer* streaming westwards, driven by a dull yearning for home. Gabriel is admittedly in a better material situation than these, since he still has money and friends. But he identifies with them. Hungry, ragged and lousy, they go back to wives who have been unfaithful and to children who will not recognise them. By the end of the novel Gabriel feels as alienated and as hopeless as the ex-servicemen dependent upon the soup kitchens and derelict barrack huts outside the town, for like them he is separated by a deep rift from the ordinary bourgeois world.

Franz Tunda in *Die Flucht ohne Ende* (1927) is another variation on the *Heimkehrer* motif. In the passage that follows the substitution of 'we' for the initial 'he' is surely significant; Tunda, gazing at the Tomb of the Unknown Warrior in Paris, feels as though he himself lay there, as though all of us lay there who had marched away from home, had been killed and buried, or had returned but never found our homes again—for it makes no difference whether we are alive or dead. We are strangers in this world, we come from the valley of the shadow.[3]

He speaks for a generation estranged not merely by the traumatic experience of war, but also by the awareness that they have been forgotten, exploited and betrayed by a society in which henceforth they have no place. Nor do Roth's heroes find consolation in defiant memories of a glorious struggle, of heroism unto death which gives meaning to the destruction of war. The 'storm of steel' no longer plays any part. Tunda interprets the memorial under the Arc de Triomphe as a sop to the conscience of the living; he is appalled at the sight of fathers paying their respect to the memory of those very sons for whose deaths they themselves are indirectly responsible. This problematic relationship between the generations is the basis of the story *Zipper und sein Vater* (1928). The son, Arnold, uprooted by the War, sees his career and his marriage wrecked. His father, a caricature of the *Spiessbürger*, authoritarian and chauvinistic, philistine and wildly ambitious (and himself a failure), hails the War which his sons then have to fight. The theme is trite, even sentimental : Arnold's sacrificial role causes him to remain a blurred and shadowy figure. Ironically it is his father who comes to life as a clearly defined, energetic literary creation.

In Roth's writing during the twenties the Habsburg Monarchy is never a point at issue. It is, of course, implicated in his arraignment of a malevolent authority which inflicts war on its citizens, or turns a law-abiding, respectful individual into a social rebel. *Die Rebellion* (1924) tells of one Andreas Pum, a disabled ex-serviceman who, as compensation for the loss of a limb, is granted a licence to ply a hurdy-gurdy in the streets of Vienna. Quite by accident, Pum comes into conflict with the Law, thereby losing his licence, his freedom and his self-respect. He is not by inclination a social rebel—on the contrary, before his brush with authority he had great faith in its majesty, justice and infallibility which not even the War could undermine. But the events related in the story show that the State is unjust, callous and all-too-human. Roth's identification with his character is such that towards the end he attributes to Pum a degree of conceptual

thought and articulateness which is inconsistent with his personality and background. But here Roth's criticism of the State is
relevant far beyond the frontiers of Austria. Again : in *Der
stumme Prophet*, a novel written by 1929 but not published
until 1965, Roth specifically attacks the conduct of Austrian
society during the War, but his strictures apply equally to the
European bourgeoisie in general. He records the egoism and self-
delusion of the patriots, intellectuals and racketeers. Echoing Karl
Kraus, he criticises the blunting of the human imagination by a
combination of technology, commercialism and propaganda. The
soulless nature of this milieu is well illustrated by the mechanical
and sterile relationship between the hero's erstwhile mistress and
the Director of the Central Potato Bureau where she is now
employed :

> And the hours of love were no different from the office hours
> from which they were so to speak subtracted, with a cool eroticism
> which felt the same to the touch as the brown leather of the
> office couch on which they were spent. The yellow pencil and
> the shorthand notebook lay meanwhile on the carpet, waiting
> to be brought into play, for the Director did not like wasting
> time and would start dictating even while he was still busy ful-
> filling the requirements of basic hygiene at the wash basin. It
> was, one might say, a love idyll *à la* Pitman, and it was per-
> fectly suited to the importance of the hour and to the perils
> facing the fatherland.[4]

The shorthand notebook has the same function as Eliot's gramo-
phone in *The Waste Land*, implying an incapacity for vital
experience, a vacuous female passivity, the crude gratification of
male vanity. In Roth's landscape of the postwar world the emptiness of sexual experience is not as important an element as in the
contemporary writing of Eliot and Lawrence, but the social and
political disenchantment of his heroes is frequently compounded
with an inability to achieve a stable erotic relationship.

The novelist's political sympathies in the first decade after the
War were more or less socialist. For all the objectivity and reticence of *Das Spinnennetz*, its publication in the *Arbeiterzeitung*
constituted a political gesture. Roth's compassion for the plight
of the working class emerges from this novel, from *Hotel Savoy*
and from *Die Rebellion*. But he seems to set little store by a
Marxist solution. As the influx of *Heimkehrer* (in his second

novel) swells and the strike drags on, Gabriel Dan senses the inexorable approach of the revolution from the East. Yet the workers' riot is an act of blind and futile destruction which inflicts no fundamental damage on capitalist society. Politically the demonstration means nothing to Gabriel; on a private level it brings him grief and a renewed feeling of isolation. Roth, unlike Hofmannsthal or Werfel, does not suggest that revolution is morally wrong. On the other hand he does emphasise its cost and the overwhelming odds pitted against it. Neither the hero nor the narrator hints that another revolt might succeed where this one failed. As in Gerhart Hauptmann's *Die Weber*, bourgeois society is shown to be corrupt and brutal, its economy to be unsound, but the old order is still strong enough to ride out the storm of rebellion.

In his publicistic writings up to 1924 Roth takes a similar attitude. There is no doubt of his hostility towards anti-republican forces such as militarists, nationalist writers and reactionary academics. His *feuilletons* and satirical pieces in *Vorwärts*, the Berlin organ of the German Social Democrats, and *Lachen Links* attack war-mongering patriots, social injustice and the life-style of a stock-exchange bourgeoisie. Yet Roth is concerned with only the surface phenomena of society. Rarely does he explore deeper causes or discuss issues in a broad historical perspective. Although he gave his socialism as a reason for resigning from a middle class newspaper in 1922, he added that a higher salary or a more appreciative recognition of his talents might have persuaded him to swallow his principles.[5] His contributions to non-socialist publications during this period were notably less 'committed' than his work for the socialist press. Moreover, his biographer notes that in the early twenties he never lost his respect for the upper bourgeoisie.[6] It appears then that Roth's socialism was largely emotional and to some extent opportunistic. Certainly it never included any study of economic and social theory. Small wonder if by 1925 his 'commitment' began to tail off.[7] He slowly resigned himself to the triumph of right-wing radicalism and despaired of the working class ever achieving true emancipation. He grew ever more sceptical of democratic systems, in particular of a Weimar Republic which elected a Junker and Field Marshal as its President, which tolerated the Reichswehr as a state within the state and allowed the proliferation of anti-republican para-military formations, and which was powerless to curb the wave of assassinations by right-wing terrorists or the overtly reactionary bias of the judiciary. A visit to the USSR in 1926 left him with grave reservations about the course the Revolution had taken there, with its closed society, its rigorous atheistic propaganda and the dominance of mediocrity and petit bourgeois values. He saw many notable attainments and was tremendously impressed by the alien, exotic world of Russia—but he also observed a society riddled with careerism and sycophancy where the old classes had merely been replaced by a new hierarchy based on the degree of affiliation to the Party.

These impressions colour two of Roth's later novels which are set in Russia at the time of the Revolution. Tunda, the hero of *Die Flucht ohne Ende*, is a former Austrian officer who has fought with the Red Army and received his political education from his Communist mistress. With the triumph of the Revolution, however, Tunda grows increasingly disenchanted with the new society, which he feels to be ominously similar to the society it has replaced. In the second novel, *Der stumme Prophet*, Friedrich Kargan likewise criticises the *embourgeoisement* of the Soviet leaders and the stultifying power of a pettifogging Soviet bureaucracy. He objects to the tendency dominant in, though not confined to the new Russia : the practice of regarding individuals as cyphers who exist merely by virtue of their social function. Both Tunda and Kargan attack certain aspects of the Revolution and its aftermath, but their disillusionment springs from something deeper than the inevitable disparity between ideological principle and political practice. In post-revolutionary Moscow, Tunda reflects that only in a deserted Red Square at midnight, with a solitary red flag fluttering in the beam of a floodlight on the Kremlin roof—only here can one still experience the authentic meaning of the Revolution. This is not the observation of a party supporter frustrated by the inadequate translation of the party programme into reality : what Tunda feels is something more personal and more fundamental—it is the dissociation of a romantic idealist whose real concern transcends the cares and compromises of a workaday political world.

> Tunda remembered the red war, the years when one knew only how to die and when life, the sun, the moon, the earth, the sky were only a frame or backcloth for death. Death, the red death,

marched day and night over the earth, with a splendid marching song, with great drums that sounded like hooves galloping over iron and shattered glass, it scattered handfuls of splinters, the shots sounded like the distant cries of marching masses.

Then the orderliness of everyday life overpowered this great red death, it became an ordinary death slinking from house to house like a beggar and carrying off his victims as if they were gifts of charity . . .

It is no consolation to reflect that a desk and a pen, plaster busts, and shop windows full of displays in honour of the revolution, monuments, and blotters with the head of Bebel for a handle, are probably necessary to the founding of a new world; it is no consolation, no help.[8]

(The hollow rhetoric, the repetitions striving for effect, the deliberate pathos and the general slackness of the style are not uncharacteristic of Roth's writing; they grow more pronounced in his later work.) Tunda's aspirations for adventure and glory are more important to him than the political achievements of the revolution, and the relationship of ends and means is seen in a highly personal light. Though his socialism is more positive and constructive than that of Gabriel Dan, it is similarly limited in that it springs from an unreflective emotional response. The novelist attributes to Tunda's mistress a pertinent criticism of his attitude from the point of view of a committed Marxist, when she remarks that it is more important to run a hospital than to revel in private passions. On the other hand, Roth indicts through this same figure the clinical, impersonal approach to political reform which is carried over into sexual relationships. He is perceptibly biased in Tunda's favour and appears to affirm his decision to lose the world in order to gain his soul. Tunda's tragedy lies in the fact that he cannot opt out of a world he repudiates. In the case of Kargan we are again confronted with a disillusioned romantic. Roth suggests no third possibility between the ruthlessly realistic politicians on the one hand, and the dreamer and individualist on the other who deprecates the sordid conditions of political activity. Both Tunda and Kargan are anarchists, after a fashion. Both desire to sweep away the old world and rebuild a new society on new foundations—something which the Revolution has not achieved. They are also both critical of the highly organised modern state. They are at only one remove from a character in *Das Spinnennetz* who exults in the death throes of a corrupt civilisation and bids his emigrating brother pursue his researches into a new explosive with which to blow up the whole of Europe. Roth is aware of the naivety of Tunda and Kargan, he knows that society will never in fact be changed by such men as these. Yet he appears repelled by the only alternative which presents itself to him.

From the mid twenties Roth was hostile towards party politics, even on the left. His cynical remarks (in a letter) on the Socialist Congress in Marseilles in 1925 showed that he considered the democratic socialists outmoded and ineffective against modern industry. He objected to the intellectual blindness that he associated with a political ideology and resented the pressure to make him take sides. The very title of his novel *Rechts und Links* (1929) conveys this. Roth thus joins with most Austrian writers of his day in seeking to preserve his integrity in the face of ideological blandishments. At the same time he seems to agree with Hofmannsthal and Werfel, for instance, that no social upheaval would alter the basic structure of society, with its polarity of wealth and poverty, privilege and exploitation. In *Die Rebellion* the narrator describes Pum's plight as the work of 'fate'; in spite of Pum's Promethean defiance of authority, secular and divine, the social (and religious) hierarchy remains intact, and there is no hope of it being overthrown. The narrator of another story reflects :

All roads everywhere look alike. All the bourgeois in every country look alike. The sons look like their fathers. And when one realises this, one could be driven to despair by the thought that things would always remain the same. However much fashions, constitutions, styles and tastes may change, the old eternal laws are just as evident beneath every form, the laws according to which the rich build houses and the poor build huts, the rich wear clothes and the poor wear rags, the laws which decree that rich and poor alike love, are born, fall sick and die, pray and hope, despair and wither.[9]

The political corollary of this fatalism is acquiescence, however critical or reluctant, in the status quo. It has therefore been argued that Roth was a conservative at heart even before his affiliation to the monarchist movement.[10] Certainly, a reluctant fatalism could of itself lead to the affirmation of an immutable social hierarchy.

There are, however, more detailed affinities between Roth's ideas in the twenties and his subsequent monarchism. His cultural and political criticism in the early postwar years represents in the first place an attack on the dehumanising tendencies of urban industrial society, on capitalism, on the decadence of modern culture and on the moral bankruptcy of the age. All this is consistent with left-wing sympathies, but equally these are commonplaces of the right-wing ideologies of the period. The corpus of Roth's social criticism would not therefore be rendered invalid by a change of political allegiance. Moreover, Roth advances even in his early writing notions which are by no means commonplaces of socialist thought but which could easily be integrated into a conservative ideology. The figure of Brandeis in *Rechts und Links*, who longs to return to an 'authentic' existence on the land, is probably inspired by anarchist leanings; nonetheless he has obvious parallels in the grass-roots idea of right-wing literature. Gabriel Dan's appraisal of a living tradition in which the quick and the dead are partners in a common enterprise recalls a *locus classicus* of conservatism, the binding tie of tradition. One could also adduce Roth's regret that the style and elegance of prewar aristocratic society had given way to the vulgarity, ostentation and greed of a self-assertive middle class (this despite his acknowledgment that the War was largely the responsibility of incompetent or ambitious aristocratic diplomats). These are mere scattered references but they suggest that Roth's espousal of monarchism did not involve any radical transformation of his social and cultural values. To be sure, Roth could on occasion express an unequivocal hostility towards certain right-wing traits. One has only to read his articles on the Hitler trial of 1924 (that 'illiterate house-painter'), on the conspiracies of the *Freikorps* nationalists or the stupidity and megalomania of Ludendorff, the former military leader who abetted Hitler's Munich putsch, to be assured of his opposition to nascent fascism. However, the way remained open for the endorsement of a conservative ideology which was neither chauvinistic nor racialist, neither militarist nor committed to violence. Although Roth's Habsburg legitimism did not manifest itself until the thirties, its foundations were laid a good deal earlier. He himself hinted at his ambiguous position in a letter of 1925, criticising the Austrian Socialists for urging Anschluss with Germany. Roth recalled that at the time of Franz Joseph's death he was one of the soldiers who lined the route of the cortege to the Capuchin crypt in Vienna, the traditional burial place of the Habsburgs. Although already a 'revolutionary', Roth had wept unashamedly. For with the old Kaiser, he felt, a whole epoch of history was finally laid to rest. Union with Germany would extinguish the last embers of the culture that remained. He averred, with an echo of the supranational ideal, that an independent Austria still contained the promise of a future united Europe. Two years later, conveying his condolence to Bernard von Brentano whose father had just died, he wrote of his affection for the aura of the old 'Roman Empire of the German nation' but added that most of those who breathed that atmosphere had political ideas very different from his own.[11] In other words, he was attracted to the values of a universalist Catholic Empire without being a political reactionary or obscurantist.

Roth's monarchism finally crystallised in the fight against National Socialism. He was an early critic of Hitler and of political anti-semitism but after the Nazis had won their first major electoral successes he began to write a series of polemical articles such as 'Vom Attentäter zum Schmock' (1930), 'Bekenntnis zu Deutschland' (1931), 'Ursachen der Schlaflosigkeit im Goethejahr' (1932) and 'Die Nationale Kurzwelle' (1932). When Hitler became Chancellor, Roth left Germany, never to return. He would have no truck with those intellectuals who achieved a *modus vivendi* with the new regime and his voice was prominent among those of the German emigrés who continued their protest against Hitler in exile. At the same time he strongly resented being associated with left-wing intellectuals who were similarly campaigning against fascism, particularly the novelists Lion Feuchtwanger and Arnold Zweig, and the group centred on the periodical *Die Weltbühne*. There were complex reasons behind his distaste for these unwelcome allies. On an ideological level he would argue that their rationalism and materialism were partly responsible for creating a climate of opinion in which fascism could thrive. On a deeper level his criticism of these intellectuals—who were by no means all Marxist—was governed by a form of Jewish anti-semitism, a contemptuous aversion for what he called *chuzpe* (chutzpa), aggressive, brazen insolence, a combination of presumption and arrogance.[12] Similar sentiments coloured his comments on the Social Democratic leadership in

Austria. They ensued from Roth's experience of the predicament of Jewish assimilation. The result of this combination of political scepticism and personal resentment was that faced with the rise of Hitler, Roth could not resort either to democratic liberalism or to socialism. Only one other anti-fascist choice remained open to him, the least realistic of all, Habsburg legitimism.

His earliest public comment on the Habsburg Empire occurs in *Juden auf Wanderschaft* (1927), a series of vignettes centred round the life and character of the Jews of Europe. In the course of this book Roth contended that the concept of the 'nation'—by which he meant the nation-state—was an invention of Western European scholars. Though erroneous the idea was apparently substantiated by the decline of Austria-Hungary. The Monarchy, being a potentially supranational structure, might have disproved the theory of the self-determination of peoples : instead it was so ineptly governed that it encouraged the growth of nationalism. Roth indicated that in a situation where questions of national allegiance, national unity and national territory predominated, it followed that the position of the Jews grew highly problematic. One way in which they reacted was to revive their own nationalism in the form of the longing for a return to Palestine, a retrograde step in terms of Jewish history. In other words, the Zionist movement founded in Vienna by Theodor Herzl was a direct result of internal conflicts within the Habsburg Empire. Roth's attitude towards the Empire here was still critical. In the essay 'Seine k. und k. apostolische Majestät' (1928) Roth took up the theme of an earlier letter. He admitted that although he had been hostile towards the Empire he had known as a student, he now felt a spontaneous and irrational nostalgia for it, because he associated memories of the Monarchy and of Franz Joseph with his childhood and youth. (This is precisely the feeling experienced by the hero in Werfel's *Cella*.) Roth reflected upon the death of the Emperor in a mood which anticipated certain passages of his novel *Radetzkymarsch*. His own convictions were silenced at the thought of the tragedy of Franz Joseph's political existence. At about this same period Roth articulated for the first time the idea that the collapse of the Empire was brought about by a loss of faith, purpose and direction among the ruling class; the novelist put this notion in the mouth of von Maerker, a character in *Der stumme Prophet*, who declares,

'And yet it seems to me that we knew beforehand exactly what would happen. I saw with my own eyes year in, year out, how the state slowly fell apart and people grew more indifferent. But more malicious too, yes, more malicious... We cracked jokes, we all laughed at them... Every nation joined in the mockery. And yet in my day, when the individual still counted for more than his nationality, there existed the possibility of turning the old monarchy into a homeland for all. It could have been the model in miniature for a great new world of the future and at the same time the last reminder of a great era of European history when North and South were united. Now it's all over...'[13]

A similar reference to the demoralising witticisms of the ruling class had occurred in a passage written by Karl Kraus in 1919, where he recalled that it was characteristic of prewar Austria to tell funny stories about the mental deficiencies of Franz Joseph and to proclaim the State ripe for collapse.[14] The indifference of Schnitzler, Zweig, Werfel or Musil to the problems of the Empire before 1914, and Hofmannsthal's belated acknowledgment that the Monarchy had lost its idealistic impetus, complement or confirm the attitude of which the satirist and Roth's fictional character speak. As yet Roth does not advance these arguments *in propria persona*, nor is von Maerker a figure with whom he closely identifies. But in the publicistic articles of his last years Roth himself endorses both the accusation and the idealisation inherent in the above passage.

A turning point in Roth's attitude towards the Empire is at the same time his finest literary achievement, the novel *Radetzky-marsch* (1932). Here he recounts the history of the Trotta family, beginning with the elevation of the family to the nobility. Lieutenant Trotta, a Slovene and the son of a former NCO, saves the life of the young Franz Joseph at the Battle of Solferino, and is duly rewarded. A tradition of Imperial service and Imperial favour is thus established. Yet even at the outset this is vitiated by untruth. The incident at Solferino is recorded in school textbooks, falsified, embellished and romanticised out of all recognition. Trotta's rectitude leads him to protest against the falsehood and his appeals culminate in an audience with the Emperor himself. But here too he is put off with an argument that he has heard countless times before: that it is perfectly justifiable to adapt historical truth to the needs of the State—in this case, the education of the young. Bitterly disenchanted, Trotta resigns his commission. That the civil service and the Emperor himself endorse a gratuitous lie implies that the society they represent is already undermined. Moreover, as has been pointed out, the battle which brought good fortune to the Trottas was in fact an inglorious defeat for the Monarchy which thereby lost the province of Lombardy. Thereafter, the Imperial motifs— the ubiquitous official portrait of Franz Joseph and the sound of the Radetzky March itself, written by Johann Strauss senior to commemorate the victorious campaign against the Italian rebels in 1848—are constantly associated with guilt or decadence or death. The music, the most popular of all Austrian marching tunes, evokes the boyhood holidays of the hero of the novel, the youngest Trotta, Carl Joseph, in a house rigidly administered and lacking in human warmth. It is played as a grotesque parody when a group of officers troops into a sordid brothel; and again when Carl Joseph converses with a Jewish medical officer, as the latter prepares to meet certain death in a pointless duel for which the hero is ultimately, if unwittingly, responsible. The cold blue eyes of the Imperial portrait are a reminder of the Emperor's remoteness, and of the inhibition of natural emotion which the tradition of Imperial service is seen to entail.

Roth's description of life in the Imperial Army is imbued with critical detachment. He exposes the outmoded training, the monotony and the sense of futility which springs from a want of purpose. The gloomy atmosphere of political decline is deepened by the prophecies of the Polish magnate, Count Chojnicki, who claims that the Empire is held together only by a residual quasi-superstitious loyalty to the person of Franz Joseph. This loyalty does not extend to other members of the dynasty, and with Franz Joseph's death the Monarchy will fall apart. Habsburg power, he maintains, was founded on a belief in the divine right of kings; it cannot survive in an age of science and scepticism. It is an archaism incompatible with emergent nationalism, socialism and parliamentary democracy. (Roth himself echoed this notion in a letter to Ernst Křenek in 1932 : 'Yes, we are indeed Austrians ! We do not belong any more in this world. We live, think and write as though still in the Middle Ages . . .') The loss of direction and cohesion within the ruling class is illustrated by the way in which news of the Sarajevo assassination is received. A regiment of dragoons is holding its summer ball and the proceedings are well under way by the time the message arrives. In the ballroom a military band breaks haltingly into a slow march; the drunken revellers dance to the mournful strains; and as the music quickens, they celebrate *their* own bizarre funeral rite :

> The guests marched in a ring around the empty, shining circle of the dance floor. Round and round they went, each one a mourner behind the corpse of the man in front and in their midst the invisible bodies of the heir to the throne and of the Monarchy itself ... Gradually the orchestras began to play more rapidly and the legs of those in the procession began to stride out in a marching step ... Count Benkyö gave a leap of joy. 'The swine's dead!' he yelled in Hungarian. But everyone understood, just as though he had spoken in German. Suddenly some started to hop. Quicker and quicker blared the slow march. In between the triangle tinkled with its clear, silvery, intoxicated smile ...[15]

What the officers and their guests betray is not just Franz Ferdinand's feud with the Magyars or his general unpopularity, but the moral decay of a whole culture. Perhaps Roth had in mind an ostentatious society wedding which took place in Budapest shortly after the assassination.[16] (It is also worth noting that 'Benkyö' is not a properly Hungarian name : it is the equivalent of calling a Welshman 'Griffots'. The error is characteristic of the 'cultural synthesis' of the Empire as it impinged upon Vienna.)

Carl Joseph is ground to destruction between the millstones of history. He is heir to a semi-feudal mission in a society crumbling beneath the pressures of a modern age. What opportunities are open to him? Whereas his grandfather saved the Emperor's life, Carl Joseph rescues the Imperial portrait from its ignominious position in a brothel parlour; whereas the grandfather was wounded on the field of honour, the grandson is injured by workers demonstrating against intolerable conditions; and when Carl Joseph is obliged to show his loyalty by protesting against the insults to the Imperial family on the night of Sarajevo, his protest is ineffective, and the whole incident merely reveals to him the moribund nature of the Empire, leading him to resign his commission. Roth's achievement is to show that this private débâcle springs less from Carl Joseph's own inadequacies than from the temper of his age.

The principle of the Imperial tradition is loyalty to a dynasty, and the ideal of supranationalism that goes with it. Carl Joseph's father, the *Bezirkshauptmann* (a position roughly equivalent to that of a Lord Lieutenant, but carrying administrative responsibility as head of the local civil service), is deeply imbued with this ideology. Yet after 1848, and especially after 1867, it had become increasingly difficult to administer the State on these lines. As emergent nationalism drove the peoples of the Empire to rediscover their national identities, the supranational dynastic ideal came to involve the danger of rootlessness and emotional frustration on the part of those who tried to uphold it. It was to this that Werfel alluded when he described in his essay on the Empire the *sacrificium nationis* which freed the true Austrians from local ties, and thus from narrow-minded prejudice, but at the same time 'clipped the wings of nature's vital urge'. Carl Joseph is a victim of this crisis. Unlike his father, he longs to return to the soil once tilled by his Slovene forebears. To Carl Joseph the Emperor appears a cold, remote figure. The concept of dynastic loyalty has no living reality for him. And this lack of commitment comes to the fore at a period when the Emperor's function is increasingly to represent the one apparently stable and disinterested authority *au-dessus de la mêlée*.[17] As Hermann Broch has pointed out, the price of disinterestedness is abstraction.[18] Through his characterisation of Franz Joseph, and through the relationship between the *Bezirkshauptmann* and his son, Roth illuminates further the personal consequences of the abstract Imperial ideal. The remarkable physical similarity between the Emperor and the civil servant is an outward manifestation of a shared ethos. Both are governed by their conception of duty, both are unselfish, inflexible and distant. In the Emperor's case, his sense of responsibility to the Habsburg mission encloses him in a prison of his own making. (Again Broch makes a similar point.) Franz Joseph's life as portrayed by Roth consists in acting out the Imperial role; it has become a petrified pose, lacking vitality and truth, and involving human isolation and emotional deprivation. We, the readers, know that the cloak of Imperial majesty hides a lonely old man whose memory is fading, who realises that death will soon summon him and his Empire alike, who is more perceptive than is commonly supposed, and whose feelings are always misinterpreted by his entourage. The historical accuracy of Roth's portrait is not at issue : as a novelist he is simply concerned with translating the political inadequacies of the official ideology into human terms. The *Bezirkshauptmann* too allows himself to be dominated by considerations of duty and obligation to such an extent that his relationship with his son is seriously impaired. Father and son are admittedly inhibited by their natural taciturnity and fear of showing emotion. But a closer, warmer relationship is eventually established, as Carl Joseph's career slowly traces a downward curve. The *Bezirkshauptmann* gradually awakens to his responsibilities as a father, as distinct from those of the civil servant, and is made aware of the emotional void which has hitherto characterised his existence. There is a bitter irony in the fact that he and his son achieve their closest understanding at the point when Carl Joseph's career lies in ruins and when it is clear to both men that the Monarchy is irrevocably doomed. There is a still greater irony in the fact that in its death throes the Empire demands yet another sacrifice from the Trotta family. For a short time before the outbreak of war, Carl Joseph returns to the simple rural existence for which his heart has always yearned. But when war is declared, he reports for duty once again. He is killed during a retreat, trying to fetch water for his thirsty men; his unsoldierly death as a 'drawer of water' is a fitting end to a misguided career.

There is no trite moralising in Roth's novel. He shows that the Habsburg mission as viewed by the Emperor and his civil service could not be reconciled with national aspirations. He suggests that the tradition of Imperial service was too narrowly interpreted. He implies that men need more than an abstract ideological concept, that they need to be rooted in a regional culture. Carl Joseph would be quite capable of combining his local loyalties with allegiance to the House of Habsburg and the Imperial commonwealth, just as in his own way he would have served Franz Joseph more constructively on a country estate than in the Army. Subsequently Roth was to argue that the most steadfast and loyal of the Imperial peoples were those non-industrial nationalities who were both rooted in their own soil *and* devoted to the Emperor as a father figure. We are reminded of Bahr's diagnosis of the Austrian disease, when in 1909 he wrote that the problem was to reconcile the desire for cultural autonomy on the part of the Germans, the Slavs and the Italians with allegiance to the Austrian State. The political corollary

5—TBE * *

of what Roth suggests in his novel—though this is never adduced —is some form of federalism. Perhaps the problem is not clearly enough defined, inasmuch as Carl Joseph's desire to return to a local culture stops a long way short of the self-assertive national-ism which challenged the existence of the Empire. But the novelist hints that if the initially modest regional demands had been met, the destructive clash of national interests might have been avoided. However, the strength of the novel lies in the fact that it does not toy with the great 'ifs' of history, but explores imaginatively and sympathetically individual reactions to a concrete historical dilemma.

After *Radetzkymarsch* Roth's attitude towards the Empire grew steadily more partisan. As the shadow of the Antichrist lengthened—*Der Antichrist* (1934) was the title of Roth's polemic against the evils of modern civilisation and politics—so the Habsburg star shone more and more brightly. On 28 April 1933 he announced to Stefan Zweig that he had become a monarchist in obedience to his instincts and his convictions. Thereafter Roth's tone became increasingly sentimental and didactic. *Die Kapu-zinergruft*, published in 1938 as a sequel to *Radetzkymarsch*, is ideologically strident and an inferior creative achievement. The transition from literary re-creation to propaganda is marked by a short story which appeared in French in 1934 under the title *Le Buste de l'Empereur*. It tells of the life of a Polish count under the *ancien régime* and then under the postwar Polish Republic; it describes his inability to adapt to the new world of national frontiers and parliamentary democracy, a world which to him seems bereft of ethical responsibility. The image of the Empire presented in this story is perceptibly different from that of *Radetzkymarsch*. The narrator now praises the supranational-ism of the Monarchy, its benevolent nepotism, its uniformity amid diversity; and he condemns the ruling class for their cynicism and irresponsibility. This criticism is no longer attributed to the character alone, as in the case of von Maercker, but is also en-dorsed by the narrator. There is no longer any attempt to explore the crisis of the Imperial ideology itself. It is not fortuitous that the loyal Morstin is a Pole, for in Roth's opinion those who hastened the Empire's decline were not the dissident nationalities but the Austro-Germans who had succumbed either to scepticism or to the delusion of racial superiority. Roth is particularly hostile towards those Austrians who were beguiled by the 'dynamism'

of the Wilhelminian Reich. Anger at the shabby treatment meted
out to the Imperial peoples combines with a deep mistrust of
Vienna and all it represents. In the words of the hero of *Die
Kapuzinergruft,*

[The younger generation of the prewar years] 'had grown up far
too spoilt in Vienna, a city nourished incessantly by the provinces
of the monarchy; they were naive, almost absurdly naive children of the pampered, far too often acclaimed capital which sat
like a shiny, seductive spider in the middle of the huge black
and yellow web of Austria-Hungary, constantly drawing strength
and vitality and splendour from the surrounding provinces ...
The colourful gaiety of the capital city of the Empire throve
quite clearly ... on the tragic love of the provinces for Austria :
I say tragic, because it remained ever unrequited. The gipsies
of the puszta, the Carpathian Huzuls, the Jewish cabbies of
Galicia, my own relatives, the Slovene chestnut roasters from
Sipolje, the Swabian tobacco planters from the Bacska, the
horse dealers of the Hana in Moravia, the weavers of the Erz
mountains, the millers and coral-traders of Podolia—they were
all generous providers of Austria, the poorer they were, the
more generous.'[19]

The economic factor in the migration from the provinces into
Vienna is characteristically ignored. Carl Joseph's ambition to
return to the soil has by now developed into a diatribe against
the sophisticated (that is, depraved), urban (that is, inauthentic)
civilisation of the capital. The strictures recall those of Bahr and
Hofmannsthal. Roth's catalogue of names illustrates his infatu-
ation with the colourful tapestry of the Monarchy; it also betrays
the anachronism of his thought. His enthusiasm is reserved for
a pre-industrial feudal society, uncontaminated by education,
democracy and nationalism, for a society untroubled by the
emergence of a powerful bourgeoisie or by any form of political
consciousness on the part of the non-privileged classes. Roth's
argument is in the paternalistic tradition of Grillparzer and
Stifter. His historical criticism has now become historical escapism : he idealises, oversimplifies, makes wild generalisations and
draws the wrong conclusions. (For example, his account of the
decline of the Monarchy ignores the role of the Hungarian
aristocracy and gentry.) From the worthiest motives Roth con-
structs a travesty of the past. The monarchist essays which began

to appear in 1937 present a wide array of villains, from the followers of Schönerer and the cult of blood-and-soil, to Liberalism and the Social Democrats. They attack the Reformation, the Enlightenment, the French Revolution, the War of Liberation and the Revolution of 1848, tracing a direct line from Erasmus and Luther to the modern European dictators via Voltaire, Frederick the Great, Joseph II, Napoleon, Bismarck and Wilhelm II. They lash out in passing at clericalism, power politics, chauvinism, parliamentary democracy and the Anschluss. Though Roth had some contact with the Schuschnigg regime, his opinion of it, particularly after 1938, was not high. Had not Schuschnigg declined Archduke Otto's offer of help in the Anschluss crisis? Roth was critical of what he felt to be the petty manoeuvring and parish-pump politics of the Christian Socialists and doubtless remembered that the party's origins were closely linked with lower middle class anti-semitism. He had already broken off contact with the *Heimwehr* in protest against their brutal repression of the workers in the uprising of 1934. The ideal against which Roth measured the world of the thirties was the now familiar Romantic conception of the Holy Roman Empire, an organic community of peoples living together in harmony and in a common allegiance, uncorrupted by industrialisation and capitalism, a society neatly divided into a hierarchical structure from which all tensions were banished. The unbridled, even fanatical note of some of Roth's last polemics may have been due to some extent to his parlous state of health. He had for years suffered from cirrhosis of the liver which was soon to bring about his early death. From 1934 onwards his correspondence shows signs of persecution mania. But though extreme, Roth's ideas are recognisably akin to those of the 'conservative revolution'. Even his demonological hypostasisation of Hitler has parallels in the Christian writers of the so-called 'inner emigration', those conservative but non-fascist writers who chose to remain in Nazi Germany and who expressed their opposition in allegorical fictions or clandestine poetry.

The Austrian legitimist movement with which Roth was associated had not been prominent in the first postwar decade.[20] It drew its support from among former Army officers, civil servants and the nobility. A group under Colonel Gustav Wolff, known after 1923 as the Kaisertreue Volkspartei, gained some publicity but little electoral support. There were also legitimist circles

among ex-servicemen's organisations. Another group, the Reichs-
bund der Österreicher headed by Friedrich Wiesner, was not a
political party in the accepted sense but its policies enjoyed tacit
approval in certain Christian Socialist circles around Karl
Vaugoin who was for many years Minister for the Army, then
Chancellor for a brief period in 1930. It was with Wiesner that
Roth was associated. After 1934, the year of the Civil War and
the abortive Nazi putsch resulting in the murder of Chancellor
Dollfuss, the question of a Habsburg Restoration was discussed
far more openly and frequently. Legitimist propaganda was
tolerated by the government of Dollfuss' successor for although
Schuschnigg declared that a restoration was not a practical or
immediate alternative to the continued survival of the First
Republic, he was himself a monarchist at heart and maintained
personal contact with the exiled Pretender. Accordingly Roth's
friends campaigned for support in the Army and the civil service.
One idea mooted in the struggle against Hitler was a regency
with Starhemberg, the *Heimwehr* leader as regent; on a visit to
London in February 1936 this son of an old Austrian aristocratic
family caused an international stir by proclaiming his legitimist
sympathies. By the end of that same year nearly one thousand
five hundred local councils had made Archduke Otto an honor-
ary citizen. The monarchist campaign reached its climax in the
winter of 1936–7 and in February 1937 Schuschnigg sounded
possible German reactions to some form of restoration. In view
of the fact that the only German contingency plan for the invasion of Austria was code-named 'Operation Otto', the prospects
of Hitler standing idly by were slim indeed. As it transpired
Germany like the successor states remained implacably opposed
to the reinstatement of Habsburg rule. The Austrian working
class too was generally opposed to the Habsburgs. Thus in February 1938 Schuschnigg refused Otto's offer of help on the grounds
that it would merely seal the fate of their country.

It is clear that Roth's royalism was determined by events in
Germany rather than Austria. Only after pledging himself to the
Habsburg cause did he turn his attention to events in Austria
itself. As the son of middle class Jewish parents and as a journalist with former socialist affiliations, Roth hardly displayed a
typically monarchist background. He made up for this with his
invented commission and the zeal of a proselyte. His Catholic
legitimism coincided with a fresh creative interest in his Jewish

heritage. In the monarchist ideology he attempted to find a spiritual refuge and the means of identifying with a stable, universalist idea. Monarchism supplied a sense of belonging which compensated for years of restless wandering in an exile that was more than just geographical. Yet Roth's polemical pieces in exile newspapers and journals were paradoxically informed by an awareness that the Danube Monarchy and the Habsburg heritage were irrevocably lost. His articles contained no constructive proposals for a Habsburg Restoration. They were filled with nostalgia, bitterness and anger but expressed no hope for the future. It is not fortuitous that during his legitimist period his imaginative writing included a 'legend', a 'fairy tale' and a religious allegory, tales of moral disintegration and purely personal relationships which in the circumstances represented a flight from historical reality. Roth failed to overcome the fatalism to which he had always been prone.

At his grave-side in Paris were representatives of both the Communists and the Habsburg loyalists; while a Catholic priest gave a short address, Jewish friends offered the Hebrew prayer for the dead. His predicament and his conflicting loyalties outlived him.

6

Stefan Zweig: Pacifist Extraordinary

The only thing we ask of politics is that it should leave us alone.
                                                                  Zweig

In 1914 Stefan Zweig was known as the author of one or two
stories, plays and slim volumes of verse, and as the translator and
biographer of the Belgian poet Emile Verhaeren. Shortly after
the assassination of Archduke Franz Ferdinand on 28 June,
Zweig left Austria to spend his vacation in Ostende. At about
the same time Freud allowed his daughter to leave for England.
In Germany and Austria leading statesmen and generals likewise
went on holiday—in order to lull Europe into a false sense of
security. There was a conspicuous lack of bellicosity in Vienna,
as Franz Ferdinand had not been a popular figure and many
were relieved that he would never ascend the throne. Moreover,
there was nothing to distinguish this particular crisis from half
a dozen others which had occurred in recent years and which
had all been resolved without serious repercussions for the man
in the street.[1] Gradually, however, the mood changed. By 23
July tension in Vienna was high. That evening the Austro-
Hungarian ambassador in Belgrade handed over an ultimatum
to the Serbian government, and the juggernaut of war lumbered
into motion. Even as Zweig perused patriotic articles in the
French press, he refused to believe that war was imminent and
was adamant that Germany would never violate Belgian
neutrality. It took a squad of Belgian soldiers deploying in
Ostende to bring home to him the true dimensions of the crisis.
He joined the exodus of German tourists and left Belgium on the
last peacetime express to cross the frontier into Germany.

Continuing his journey southwards Zweig was greeted by a
memorable display of patriotic fervour. The nation seemed to
him united in the common experience of what promised to be a

historic event. War was seen generally as a heroic legend of gallant cavalry charges and clean, painless death. Zweig recalled later that every individual citizen desired to contribute to the national effort. The enthusiasm was infectious. In later life Zweig still thought of the atmosphere of these first days of the War as a unique and valuable experience. For the first time in his life he acknowledged his national loyalties. For the first time he felt involved in historical change—and it was an intoxicating feeling for one to whom politics and nationhood had meant so little. On the other hand, Zweig is remembered as a prominent European pacifist with a history of anti-war protest to his credit. His autobiography asserts that he resisted the general upsurge of patriotism, a point echoed in his wife's memoirs and in a recent biographical essay. But an earlier biographer, Erwin Rieger, admitted that at the beginning of the War Zweig succumbed temporarily to the mood of his compatriots. The most recent and most comprehensive account of Zweig's life by D. A. Prater goes some way towards clarifying the position but is still incomplete. The records of the War Archives in Vienna, the files of the leading Viennese daily, the *Neue Freie Presse*, and the unpublished correspondence between Zweig and Schnitzler help to build up a clearer picture of Zweig's wartime career.[2]

He was passed fit for military duty on 12 November 1914 having voluntarily enlisted for the duration of hostilities. (He was then aged thirty-three.) He was allocated to clerical duties with a service corps unit on the outskirts of Vienna. In mid-November the so-called 'literary group' was set up in the War Archives to assist the propaganda effort, with the popular writers Rudolf Hans Bartsch and Franz Karl Ginzkey among its founding members. The first recruit to be transferred to this group from outside units was Zweig. Others who joined included Alfred Polgar, Franz Theodor Csokor and—for a brief and wretched period—Rilke.[3] The group's first task was to rewrite citations for the benefit of the press, lending life and colour to the official text. In 1915 Zweig helped to produce two anthologies of these tales of gallantry and was actively involved in various other publicity projects. In 1916, at the behest of the officer in charge of the 'literary group', he submitted a memorandum to the Director of the War Archives, outlining a scheme for a monthly bulletin to be called *Das Kriegsarchiv*. From this idea was born a patriotic journal aimed at a middle and upper class civilian readership.

Zweig contributed only one original article to this periodical *Donauland* which Kraus acidly called 'the war service of those unfit for literature'. In February 1917, on his first visit to Switzerland, Zweig was fêted by Habsburg diplomats in Berne. At the beginning of September 1917 he applied for permission to spend his leave in Switzerland, where he was due to attend the première of his play *Jeremias* and give readings from his work under the aegis of the Austro-Hungarian Foreign Ministry, much as Hofmannsthal had visited Poland and Scandinavia or as Werfel was to be sent to Switzerland in January 1918. In the circumstances French Intelligence was not far wrong in assuming that Zweig was in Switzerland on a pacifist propaganda mission for the Austrian government.[4] There he remained for the duration of hostilities, securing further dispensation from military service through the agency of Moriz Benedikt, the publisher of the *Neue Freie Presse*, on condition that Zweig contributed monthly articles to his paper.[5] Zweig's reasons for staying in Switzerland were not particularly humanitarian : he could not face the prospect of returning to a starving, war-weary Vienna and to an irksome office job. He purchased his liberty, and with it the opportunity to proclaim his pacifism, at the price of supporting a newspaper that had shown itself to be one of the most strident and inflammatory advocates of the War. (It was as though Bertrand Russell had agreed to write for Northcliffe's *Daily Mail*.) It is necessary to view Zweig's pacifism in this context of compromise and weakness. Karl Kraus paid three strictly private visits to Switzerland during the War and each time returned to Vienna to continue his campaign against the authorities. Of Zweig, Fritz von Unruh, Hermann Hesse, Romain Rolland and other members of the international intelligentsia who sought refuge in neutral Switzerland, Kraus wrote :

> The 'good Europeans' from Vienna, Berlin and Budapest who have gathered in Zurich are there acknowledged as such, even though they have not yet made any attempt to profess these views at home; on the contrary, in their own country they have

---

* *'Donauland'*. This was a popular synonym for Austria-Hungary and the title of the periodical published by the War Archives. Kraus here alludes to the erstwhile patriotism of certain Austrian intellectuals but also reminds us that the extent of their military service was the production of a propaganda sheet.

shown themselves ready to die for the 'Danubian Realm'*, and they have even found credit with the good Europeans from Paris who are more deserving of the title but who would likewise be better advised to try and earn it at home.[6]

In order to clarify Zweig's position before he left Vienna, let us first look at some of his public statements. A piece which appeared in mid-November 1914 echoed the contemporary cliché of 'diese grosse Zeit' (the greatness of the hour). In another article published on 1 December he hailed (like Bahr) the moral and political regeneration of Austria-Hungary which had given the lie to gloomy prewar prophecies that the Empire was moribund and on the verge of disintegration.[7] At the same time he emphasised the common culture of Germany and Austria. In this moment of crisis he made no attempt to plead Austria's uniqueness or independence. He maintained that common interest had cemented even more firmly the bond of race and language which united the two neighbours. He praised German organisation, discipline and sense of duty. The article 'Ein Wort von Deutschland' of August 1914 had advanced the conventional propaganda argument that Germany had been deliberately encircled by her foes and now had to fight her way free. There Zweig revealed a trait which Kraus cited as one of the horrors of wartime Germany and which Musil was to satirise in the figure of Arnheim in *Der Mann ohne Eigenschaften*—the spurious synthesis of idealism and *Realpolitik*:

> Just as Germany, by virtue of the intellectual application of its physical powers, has wrested from its soil a greater quantity of fruitful produce than any other country, so too it is now forging from its teeming masses the highest expression of moral vitality and ethical energy.[8]

The dubious nature of the sentiments expressed is matched by the mannered rythms, the deliberate alliterations and rhetorical flourishes of Zweig's language at this time.

The article 'An die Freunde in Fremdland' which appeared on 19 September 1914 is perceptibly ambivalent; here Zweig indicated that he was caught up in a historical process which he had neither the right nor the will to resist. He refused to speak out against the chauvinistic outbursts of his compatriots.

He who is not yet in uniform [Zweig had not yet enlisted] must at least refrain from hindering those already under arms; he must not cast an exhortation to humanity in the teeth of one whose wrath and courage unto death obey a different law no less compelling than that which is binding upon the spectator. At the moment of pressing the trigger, the soldier must not reflect that his enemy did not want war and that wife and children await his return; so too an entire nation must not hesitate to hate another with all its might, as long as that other nation threatens the purpose of its existence. And this hatred against you [my friends abroad]—though I myself do not share it—I will not temper it because it produces victories and heroic strength.[9]

It is possible to interpret this as a humanitarian protest disguised as moderate propaganda; it is more likely a token of Zweig's susceptibility to the mood of the time and a mark of his moral confusion. At all events Romain Rolland, the French writer who was determined to remain 'above the conflict' and to whom Zweig was deeply attached, read this open letter as a negative statement and rebuked Zweig for thus taking leave of his friends. Many years later, in his autobiography, Zweig presented this article as a deliberate departure from the then current nationalism and as a declaration of fidelity to his friends, quoting from Rolland's reply the words 'No, I will never abandon my friends' : what Rolland actually wrote was 'I am more faithful than you to our Europe and I am not taking leave of any of my friends.'[10] Zweig ignored the rebuke in his relief at being able to renew his contact with Rolland. Meanwhile he continued to work for the War Archives and to repeat German propaganda slogans. An article of 18 November 1914 reveals his unabating hostility towards England. Another piece in the *Neue Freie Presse* in April 1915 defended the German invasion of Belgium and attempted to divert the attention of the neutral states to the sufferings of Galicia at the hands of the Russians. That spring Zweig was sent to Galicia to collect Russian posters and proclamations from the recently liberated areas for the Vienna archives. Describing this journey in his autobiography he stated that it brought him for the first time face to face with the realities of war. He claimed that he was profoundly distressed by the misery of the civilian population, by the appalling conditions in which the Galician Jews lived, and by the suffering of the men in the hospital trains which lacked morphine, bandages, attendants and doctọrs. On his return from the stricken areas he was able to compare the true picture with the accounts printed in the Viennese press and in retrospect he attacked the journalists for their lies and distortions. However, Zweig's published impressions of his Galician journey at the time told a rather different story. The whole emphasis of his article (which appeared in the *Neue Freie Presse* on 31 August 1915) is optimistic. Its purpose is to stress the reconstruction and regeneration of Galicia under German and Austrian administration. His description of the wounded is deliberately symbolic of such triumph over adversity, of confidence in recovery, and is unmarred by any account of the deficiencies of the medical services. Zweig's facile optimism was little more than an attempt to boost the morale of the Viennese bourgeoisie. Although in the same article he looked forward to the end of the War, he envisaged peace ensuing from a German victory rather than from war-weariness or humanitarian protest. During this same year Zweig wrote a mawkish poem depicting the kindness meted out to a disabled soldier on his return home; he did not dwell on how the man came by his wounds or on the bleak future awaiting him.

If we turn briefly to Zweig's private correspondence the anomaly of his position becomes manifest. In the first weeks of the War his ambition was to join the army in France and help punish French presumption and frivolity. He accepted the right of Germany, and for that matter Russia, to fight for 'ein erweitertes Volkstum' (an enlarged nationhood).[11] In October 1914 he corresponded with Rolland about a planned conference of intellectuals to counteract the effects of propaganda on both sides. Yet towards the end of November he wrote to Schnitzler that he was 'looking forward tremendously' to joining the War Archives. On 29 November and on 3 December 1914 his correspondence with Schnitzler spoke again of the imperative need for maintaining one's personal integrity and combating the distortions of propaganda. An undated postcard to Schnitzler which certainly preceded the letter of 29 November referred to 'the tragic monotony of the continuing static battles' and to 'these senseless days of destruction'. A letter to another correspondent in April-June 1915 described the War as a catastrophe for those who believed in the European idea and spoke of his distress at having to hide his true feelings.[12] In April and September 1916 and again in August 1917 Zweig complained to Schnitzler that he found his military duties uncongenial and that he did not have enough time for his own work. There was thus a discrepancy between his true convictions and his public attitude, a contradiction which was eventually resolved when he decided to follow Rolland's example and declare himself a pacifist.

In the spring of 1916 he contributed an article called 'Der Turm zu Babel' to a Swiss periodical. Although it conveyed a certain revaluation of his position, the essay was not yet a firm commitment to pacifism. Zweig defined the pristine virtue of the human race as a Faustian striving which enabled men to progress as a harmonious community towards perfection. Such were their indefatigability and unity of purpose that they inspired fear in the heart of their Creator. Accordingly he sowed dissension among them through the medium of language, thus imposing severe limits upon human achievement. By the twentieth century, however (Zweig continued), a new spiritual tower was beginning to rise towards heaven, a structure built by the international fraternity of intellectuals. Again God intervened to sow disharmony and enmity in the shape of the War. The significance of this curious parable is to suggest that aggression and conflict, however cruel, are an inevitable divinely-ordained phase of human history. Responsibility for the War is transferred from man to God. Zweig depicts war as imposed from above because it seems to him impossible to explain it as the action of individuals or of merely human agencies. Zweig's article illustrates the bemusement of an apolitical writer peremptorily enmeshed in the toils of a continental war.

The memory of those anonymous forces that had controlled his fate during the War remained with Zweig long after he had reasserted his individual freedom of conscience, and inspired several stories. In *Episode vom Genfer See* (1918) the Russian soldier, Boris, cannot grasp the political factors which determine the conditions of his existence and prevent him from living his own life according to his simple desires. Now that the Czar whom he once served has been deposed, he sees no more reason to fight and wishes to return to his home and family. But on escaping from a French camp he discovers that the only road open to him leads to a Swiss internment camp. Unable to communicate with people around him because he cannot speak French or German, and unable to comprehend his situation, he commits

suicide. The hero of another story, *Buchmendel* (1929), is techni-
cally a Russian citizen but in spirit an Austrian. His birthplace
only becomes important when war breaks out and an accident of
geography leads him into an internment camp for enemy aliens.
Soon after the end of the War Mendel dies, a broken man. Again
a completely apolitical individual is caught up in the impersonal
machinery of war and destroyed by it. In *Der Zwang* (1920) one
of the central issues is the struggle of the protagonist to resist
the compulsive influence of wartime bureaucracy. He is on the
verge of succumbing to its pressures when he is saved by the sight
of sick and wounded French prisoners of war who restore his
feelings of common humanity. The moral of the story is vitiated
by the fact that the hero's dilemma is artificial; it is not the
authentic problem of the conscientious objector, but the fabri-
cated conflict of a man who is already safe in Switzerland and
who simply has to decide whether or not to return to Vienna for
a further medical examination. The lesson is still, however, clear :
Zweig feels that even if one cannot control one's material fate,
one can still resist the moral blandishments of political forces.

On 25 September 1916 he wrote to Schnitzler that he had
been working on his anti-war protest, the drama *Jeremias*, for
eight months. (When it eventually appeared, he claimed that he
had begun writing it at Easter 1915.) Throughout 1916 he hinted
publicly at his change of heart. A forthright statement of his
attitude appeared in July 1917 in a review of the French anti-war
novel, *Le Feu*. His account of the book left the reader in no
doubt that he was in full agreement with Barbusse. Two months
later his own protest was published. By this time the climate of
opinion in Austria had considerably changed : 1917 was a year
of reappraisal. The hope of a decisive military victory had
receded, food shortages were growing more acute, and there was
a new emperor on the throne who had begun his reign by
promising to bring about peace as soon as was consistent with the
security and prestige of the Monarchy. In January the declaration
of Allied war aims with regard to the Habsburg Empire was
interpreted as a policy of dismemberment, and in March Emperor
Karl initiated secret peace proposals with the French government.
On 30 May the Austrian parliament was recalled for the first
time since the spring of 1914, and in its debates that summer
the extent and consequences of military government and emergency jurisdiction were revealed to a hitherto largely unsuspecting

Austro-German public. Reports of the desertion of Slav troops at the front were matched by the speeches of Slav deputies in Parliament, who pressed for constitutional reforms. On 2 July the Emperor issued a general amnesty to civilians sentenced by courts martial. The censorship was relaxed and the activities of the *Kriegsüberwachungsamt* (the security authorities) curtailed. In the autumn Count Czernin, the Foreign Minister, publicly denied that Austria-Hungary harboured any territorial ambitions; he urged a return to the boundaries of 1914, freedom of the seas and a limitation on armaments. And Rolland, drawing on information supplied by Zweig, noted in November that anti-war sentiments had become fashionable in Austria, even semi-official (allegedly to Zweig's embarrassment, since he felt himself compromised by unwelcome allies). It was against this background that *Jeremias* was passed by the censor and published. Zweig later claimed that the play rapidly sold twenty thousand copies : in fact, up to 1919 only eight thousand had been printed, which suggests that its impact was less than sensational. Shortly after the play's publication Zweig left Vienna for Switzerland. Between February and November 1918 he wrote monthly articles for the *Neue Freie Presse*, few of which alluded to the War. Only one merits our attention, an appreciation of the life and work of the pioneer Austrian pacifist, Bertha von Suttner, author of the novel *Die Waffen nieder!* (1889). In this article, Zweig acknowledged the need for political organisation as the condition of political influence, asserting that those uncompromising individualists who, though sincere pacifists, had refused to join the organised pacifist movement, must bear a measure of responsibility for the failure of the movement in prewar days. Even here Zweig's conception of political action was rudimentary—and in the postwar period he disavowed all forms of political organisation on the grounds that they were conducive to fanaticism and dogmatism, and encroached upon the moral freedom of the individual. He was drawn to actions which, though ineffective, represented the moral triumph of a solitary individual protester.

Such is the situation in *Jeremias* : a lone voice crying in a wilderness of chauvinism and selfish passions. The plot and setting owe much to the Biblical account given in the Book of Jeremiah, but Zweig has modified the traditional story in two important respects. In the first place, the Biblical model prophesies doom because the Jews turned away from God; their guilt lies in their

sinfulness, and the prophet summons them to renounce their evil
ways and to do penance for their sins by surrendering to the
Chaldeans who are besieging the city of Jerusalem. In Zweig's
play the guilt of the Jews is that they sue for war in a vain desire
for conquest, booty and glory; it is their war-mongering which
leads to their being punished at the hands of Nebuchadnezzar. In
the second place the Bible narrative ends with a laconic statement of fact—that the Jews were driven into exile. Zweig,
elaborating on this, shows them leaving as though in triumph,
resolved to rebuild the razed city in their hearts. The story of
Jeremiah and of the Jewish king Zedekiah is transformed into a
vehicle of protest against the First World War. The *leitmotiv*,
'Jerusalem shall endure for ever!' changes its significance as the
play proceeds. At first a sign of security and self-confidence, of
defiance and self-assertion, it becomes by the end of the play an
expression of trust in God and of faith in the integrity of man.
Zweig commented on the peculiar aptness of an episode from
Jewish history to illustrate the theme of 'victory in defeat': the
whole history of the Jews, he felt, the centuries of suffering and
tribulation, persecution and dispersion, revealed how spiritual
values could be cherished and preserved amid the most terrible
adversity.

Jeremias is not a subtle drama. Its highly coloured rhetoric
does not allow of intellectual argument, and the main issue is
reduced to the simplest terms: should the Jews wage war upon
Assyria for material gain, or not? There is no provocation, no
urgent pressure in favour of war. Aggression is suggested by the
Egyptians as a profitable course of action; all that remains for
the Jews to do is to decide whether they should accept the offer.
Politically the situation is unreal because it is oversimplified. This
is partly due to Zweig's polemical purpose, the desire to present
the crux of the problem in the clearest possible terms. But it is
also symptomatic of his lack of sympathy with, or appreciation
of the complexities of political life. His intention is not to casti-
gate one nation in particular but to condemn the phenomenon of
war and to show the suffering and destruction which it brings in
its train, irrespective of the specific political circumstances. He
argues that if only ordinary men and women would communicate
across the international frontiers, they would discover their
common humanity and forthwith put an end to war and aggression. Zweig's attitude is one of humanitarian individualism: his

model is an archetypal individual free from social ties and political pressures, humanity in limbo.

The construction of *Jeremias* is untidy, its prose turgid, its passages of verse uninspired. The argument is emotional and unrealistic. As the play avoids identification with specific details of the contemporary situation, the polemic loses a good deal of force. Zweig is a victim of the time lag between the situation in which he began writing and the less repressive conditions in which *Jeremias* eventually appeared. An example of what form an effective protest could by then take is provided by the contemporary collection of short stories *Menschen im Kriege*, written in Switzerland in 1917 by a fellow Austrian, Andreas Latzko. This book which Kraus called 'a scream which silences aesthetic reservations', presents a sequence of graphic images of the destruction, horror and filth of war, illustrating conditions at the front, behind the lines, in hospital and in the hinterland. The social protest against the War and those who live by it is more direct, more urgent and more compelling than Zweig's stylised Old Testament epic.

During the last year of the War Zweig openly avowed his pacifist views and contributed to pacifist periodicals. On one occasion he occupied a prominent space in the *Neue Zürcher Zeitung* with an appeal for the 'devaluation' of all ideals or ideologies that brought suffering in their train. He held that peace should be achieved at any price. He came to see Austria as the hapless tool of Berlin, and although he approved of Karl's attempt to negotiate a separate peace, he criticised the Emperor's weakness in bowing to German protests when news of his indiscretion became public. (Karl Kraus too attacked the Emperor's lack of integrity in denying his own initiative—but with considerably more justification than Zweig.) When the Empire finally collapsed, Zweig was unmoved for he had never felt any emotional attachment to it as a political structure. The Armistice seemed to him to mark the ultimate defeat of militarism, and he looked forward to a new era in international relations. He placed great faith in President Wilson, and was optimistic about events in Russia. He believed that a united Europe had at last become a realisable ideal. This was the intoxicating 'dreamland of the Armistice period'—prior to the Peace Conference—into which Musil also strayed. Zweig's hopes were soon dashed. Wilsonian self-determination endorsed the emergent nationalism of Central and Eastern Europe and militated against European unity. Zweig objected to the way in which the Entente exploited their victory to the detriment, as he saw it, of a more noble and far-sighted vision. He felt that Wilson's ideals had been tainted and degraded by diplomats, politicians, generals and industrialists. Twenty years later Zweig still looked back on Versailles with bitterness.

The key to Zweig's attitude towards the political situation of the postwar years is his renewed emphasis on the need for European cooperation and unity. He was aware that in some circles 'internationalism' had become a convenient slogan : he pointed out that in fact it was a radical commitment demanding the renunciation of patriotism. Only through the success of the European movement, Zweig maintained, would it be possible to keep the militarists and their supporters in check. A visit to Paris in 1922 brought home to him the depth of anti-German feeling in France, and he resolved afresh to work for Franco-German friendship. Apart from articles such as 'Internationalismus und Kosmopolitismus' (1926) and 'Die moralische Entgiftung Europas' (1932), several of Zweig's books in the postwar years were imbued with the spirit of internationalism, notably his tribute to Romain Rolland (1921) and his autobiography *Die Welt von Gestern* (1941) which was subtitled 'Memoirs of a European'. He was under no illusion about the difficulties facing the movement, but to him the important thing was to keep its spirit alive.

Rolland was a shining example to Zweig of those who were magnificent in defeat—in this case, the defeat of the cause for which Rolland had worked before the War, friendship and cooperation between France and Germany. For another such example during a later European political crisis, Zweig looked to a historical figure, Erasmus of Rotterdam. In Zweig's biography of the great humanist, published in 1934, Erasmus shares several of Zweig's characteristics—his reluctance to brave the storm of fanaticism while this was at its height, his cavilling and his weakness. Zweig was aware of his hero's shortcomings as he was aware of his own.[13] He offset them, however, by indicating that Erasmus survived to argue the case for reason and humanity when the clamour had died down. By being prudent, he preserved intact his spiritual resources and his faith in mankind. There was here consolation for the setback and failure which Zweig himself had experienced. (In an analogous position Brecht's Galileo cannot acquit himself so easily.) Zweig knew that the aggressive instinct was deep-rooted in man; he held out the tenuous hope that this aggression might eventually be curbed through a lengthy process of education. But he distinguished between primitive instinct on the one hand, and its exploitation for political ends on the other. The targets of Zweig's criticism were the chauvinist, the warmonger, the irresponsible or incompetent diplomat and the unscrupulous propagandist, for without their manipulation, he argued, human aggression would be more limited in its extent and less pernicious in its effects. By transforming the climate of opinion, Zweig hoped that one could minimise the consequences of violence.

Before 1914 Zweig had been indifferent to politics, but with the coming of war he was compelled to acknowledge that politics was indeed relevant to the life of the individual. At the same time his contact with the machinery of state and his glimpse of wartime politics confirmed his profound distrust of political activity. His moral condemnation of politics was overwhelming. He equated it with both stupidity and cunning, incompetence and cleverness, cynicism and fanatical idealism, the manipulation of will-less masses by power-hungry leaders and the tyrannical control of their leaders by power-hungry masses. Zweig's biography *Joseph Fouché* (1929), subtitled 'Portrait of a Political Man', attempts to present the French statesman as an object lesson in political behaviour. This man who served in turn the French Revolution, the Directorate, the Consulate, the Empire and the restored Monarchy, is depicted as opportunistic, ruthless and unprincipled. Loyalty to persons or causes is alien to his nature. Occasional references in the text underline the relevance of his dubious career to the present age. Zweig wrote to Emil Ludwig in 1928 that Fouché was to serve as a warning of the dangers of the professional politician for the peoples of Europe. To Rolland he remarked that his biography was directed against the contemporary politics of Stresemann and his like who lacked all faith and ideas.[14] Gustav Stresemann, who was first Chancellor and then Foreign Minister of the Weimar Republic, was responsible for restoring Germany's prestige in the West, a process which culminated in the Locarno non-aggression treaties. He was awarded the Nobel Peace Prize in 1926. On the face of it, one might have expected Zweig to endorse his efforts. Presumably what the writer objected to was the manoeuvring and horse-trading, the guile and ambiguities that accompanied Stresemann's achievements. It must have irked Zweig to see a former member of the Pan-German League fêted as an internationalist and a negotiator dedicated to Germany's interests hailed as a peace-maker. But then Stresemann was a realist who practised the art of the possible, whereas in politics Zweig demanded idealism and personal integrity above all else. His purpose in writing the bio-graphy of Fouché was too didactic to permit any noteworthy in-sight into the political history of the period with which he deals. His narrative assumes that history is entirely the work of individ-uals and their private motives. He avoids analysing social and economic forces, all the wider pressures to which individuals are subject in society. History for Zweig was largely applied psychology.[15]

There are many other instances in Zweig's postwar writing of his distaste for politics. He alluded scathingly to the 'hired labourers of politics' and asserted that morality and political power were usually irreconcilable. He condemned the League of Nations as the last refuge of secret diplomacy and intrigue, wholly invidious to the European movement proper. In his biography of Erasmus the repeated warnings against fanaticism apply no less to contemporary politics than to the ostensible subject, religion. Apart from such admonitions Zweig shied away from any gesture or statement which might have carried party-political implica-tions. He avoided associations of a political character because he felt that his moral independence would thereby be compromised. His English biographer D. A. Prater records many examples of this reluctance. As early as October 1918 Zweig refused to sign a 'republican-democratic declaration' drawn up by another Aus-trian pacifist Alfred Fried. However, it is in the face of the rise of fascism that his aversion to direct political statements becomes most marked and at the same time most questionable. In March 1932 Ernst Fischer begged him to write an anti-fascist article but Zweig felt that his biography of Marie Antoinette was a more appropriate contribution as a text that would bring inward hope and inspiration to his readers. In 1933 he dissociated himself (initially in a private letter to his publisher) from Klaus Mann's emigré periodical *Die Sammlung* on the grounds that it was an overwhelmingly political journal, not the literary periodical he had been led to expect. When his views were made public with-

out his consent, they caused consternation among other writers
in exile. His friend Joseph Roth questioned the propriety of his
non-involvement, arguing that there came a point where nobility
of soul was synonymous with dereliction of duty.[16] In 1934 Zweig
was asked by the Austrian government to collaborate like Werfel
in their propaganda for Austrian independence but he refused—
not because he did not believe in the need for Austria to remain
independent, but because during these years he did his utmost
never to commit himself publicly to any cause or party. Later
that year he was extremely distressed over false reports in the
French press that attributed to him remarks critical of Dollfuss.
(For a while the reports made him *persona non grata* in Vienna.)
Though keenly aware of the tragedy which had overtaken the
Jews of Germany he declined to align himself with any Jewish
political organisation for fear that public protest of this sort
would invite even more unwelcome attention. He refused to
attend the PEN congress at Dubrovnik in May 1933 on the
grounds that German Jews should abstain from provocative
demonstrations against Hitler. He felt that the exiled intellectuals
who constantly attacked the Third Reich diminished their own
effectiveness by dint of repetition and by stressing the Jewish
problem 'which in his view defeated its own end by tending to
create something that in many countries did not exist'.[17] He
averred that nothing had stimulated anti-semitism so much as
the prominence of Jews in politics. On a visit to New York in
January 1935 he evaded all attempts to elicit from him a condemnation of Hitler's treatment of the Jews lest words from him
might affect the fate of those still inside Germany. One cannot
but feel that behind all this lies the predicament of the assimilated
Jew who clings to the straw of unobtrusiveness amid the rising
tide of racialism. Only once did Zweig protest publicly against a
specific example of persecution—and then unhappily chose to
defend Ernst Lissauer, author of the notorious 'Hymn of Hate'
against England in 1914. Nevertheless in private Zweig helped
and supported several exiles including Joseph Roth and played
an active part in charitable organisations.

While one respects his concern for absolute moral standards
and impartiality of judgement, one cannot ignore the naivety of
his response to political problems. Reviewing the career of his
friend Walther Rathenau, the economist and statesman, after his
assassination by right-wing terrorists in 1922, Zweig carefully

overlooked Rathenau's political views and achievements and instead saw his life in terms of a heroic struggle against the impossible odds of Fate or History. Zweig accepted an invitation to attend the Tolstoy celebrations in Moscow in 1928 because his journey was occasioned by a cultural event and would not (or so he believed) be interpreted as a political gesture towards the regime. He contrived to write an account of his impressions which involved only a passing reference to the Soviet system. It was completely in character that he should try to interpret the Nazi victories in the elections of September 1930 as a perhaps unwise but basically natural and welcome 'revolt of youth' against the dilatoriness and indecisiveness of conventional politics and diplomacy. On this occasion Klaus Mann repudiated his excessive tolerance and objectivity which in the eagerness to comprehend overlooked the concrete implications of events and did nothing to change them. 'One can understand everything with the aid of psychology, even rubber truncheons.'[18] As the pressure on him to take a stand mounted, Zweig expressed his dilemma in a piece written in 1934.[19] The writer's dedication to his art demanded impartiality, neutrality, detachment, clear-sightedness, qualities which could only be acquired at the price of isolation. Yet the effect of his writing was to bring him back into contact with the social world. To write was to address an audience and in turn to give them a claim on the author. His public demanded leadership, guidance and solidarity. Zweig saw the problem to lie in the choice which the writer then had to make between his work and his public responsibility. Zweig uneasily chose to neglect the latter. He would have done well to recall a remark made by the Zionist leader Theodor Herzl who, as editor of the cultural columns of the *Neue Freie Presse* in Vienna, had been a patron of the young Zweig:

> There are ideas which one cannot escape. One commits oneself by saying yes, by saying no, and by saying nothing at all.[20]

Characteristically Zweig could not envisage for himself a role which would preserve his integrity as a writer while allowing him to heed the demands of the political situation.

To show that intelligent and critical political thought *sans parti pris* was indeed possible, one might cite the argument of Max Weber, one of the founders of modern sociology. In a short essay entitled 'Politik als Beruf' (1918/19) Weber expressed his conviction that one could not avoid the obligation to come to terms with politics. He defined politics as the bid for, or the exercise of power, but he distinguished between the desire for power as a means to an end, and the desire for power as an end in itself. The latter desire Weber rejected as reprehensible. The focus of his attention was the role of the idealist in politics. He made the general point that politics by definition involved compromise, that no ideal was ever realised in its entirety or in its original purity. So far Zweig would have been in full agreement. But Weber went on to assert that such practical limitations must be accepted, that they did not make a mockery of the ethical responsibility which should underlie all legitimate political activity. He described two categories of idealistic behaviour, what he termed *gesinnungsethisch* and *verantwortungsethisch*. The former insisted on absolute, uncompromising idealism; the latter was more expedient, it weighed up the practical implications of its idealism and modified its demands and expectations accordingly. In theory the first type of activist had his chances of achieving even a part of his goal greatly reduced, since he would have to reject every course of action which appeared to demand morally dubious means. Yet history showed that the uncompromising idealist, no matter how admirable his objective, could easily prove more dangerous than the politician who was prepared to compromise his personal integrity and his ideals within certain acceptable limits in order to ensure that something at least of the original vision was realised. All too often, Weber stated, one observed that the man driven solely by idealism suddenly changed into a chiliastic prophet and courted disaster. Weber here pointed to the reverse of the medal of German idealism, to that side of the idealist tradition of which Heine had prophetically warned in 1833 and which Thomas Mann perceived in the catastrophe of twentieth-century German history. Weber implied that it was impossible to judge whether or not certain ends really justified certain means : it *was* possible, on the other hand, to weigh up the given situation to the best of one's ability and to shoulder the responsibility for one's actions. If a politician were to accept this responsibility as his own, instead of transferring the blame to the imperfections, immorality or stupidity of the actual world, then he would rarely transgress the limits of acceptable compromise. Thus Weber acquiesced in the necessity for politics, warts and all; Zweig stubbornly rejected it. Weber advised that the man who could not accept the limitations inherent in political activity should confine himself to improving personal relationships between individuals. Was this not precisely what Zweig and Hofmannsthal and Werfel (before 1932) attempted to do? Certainly : but in response to problems which went beyond the bounds of this narrow private sphere—social unrest, economic disruption, political violence, the need for European unity, disarmament and peace. In its very intransigence, in its contempt for political adjustments, Zweig's idealism was doomed to founder.

Unlike many contemporary writers, Zweig remained indifferent to the Habsburg Empire and the Austrian heritage. His memories of his upbringing in an upper middle class family in Vienna, as recalled in his autobiography, were somewhat ambivalent. He criticised the hypocrisy, shallowness, monotony and misguided pedagogic ideas of *fin de siècle* Vienna, while at the same time admiring its faith in human reason, its respect for the liberty and privacy of the individual, and its belief in progress. Its notions, even if excessively optimistic, frequently served a humane and constructive purpose. Above all he remembered fondly the illusion of security and solidity in which he had spent his youth. Where Zweig nostalgically evoked the world before 1914, he had in mind a whole era of European civilisation rather than any qualities unique to the Habsburg Monarchy. As in Schnitzler's work, there was little indication in Zweig's memoirs that beyond Vienna lay the hinterland of a great empire. One of Zweig's last books, *Ungeduld des Herzens* (1938), ventures into the Imperial provinces for its setting : the backcloth of the novel is a garrison town on the Hungarian-Slovak border. But despite the introduction of a Magyar country house, Ruthenian conscripts, a peasant wedding, the background remains rudimentary and conventional, lending a touch of local colour but of no intrinsic interest. Zweig too was a Viennese, not an Austrian, in his indifference to the ways of thinking, feeling and behaving of the Imperial peoples. In his memoirs he claimed that the theatre, not the problems of the Monarchy, provided the focus of attention among the Viennese bourgeoisie in the last years of the Empire. In retrospect he saw that theirs had been an inward-looking world where imagination and creativeness were expended in 'aesthetic' pursuits. Zweig's own character was moulded in the image of the society he described. His indifference to politics before 1914, his one-sided individualism, his dilettante probing of the psyche, his inability to comprehend or accept the necessary limitations of political activity—all this is strongly reminiscent of the Viennese intelligentsia at the turn of the century. That early environment shaped his work to the end : although *Ungeduld des Herzens* suggests that for certain men the First World War provided an escape from intolerable problems, the idea is stated in purely private terms. There is no attempt to attach any wider historical significance to this rather mawkish story of a young cavalry officer who—out of pity—becomes deeply embroiled with a crippled girl and her wealthy Jewish father. Zweig's choice of theme and his treatment of the hero contrast markedly with Joseph Roth's historical novel *Radetzkymarsch* on the one hand, and with Musil's or Kraus's analysis of cultural decay on the other. It is characteristic of Zweig's writing that while the rest of the Empire is agog with the news of Sarajevo, his fictional hero is entirely absorbed in his personal dilemma.

Zweig tried to flee from the conflagration that consumed the last vestiges of the 'world of yesterday'. Shortly after his final autobiographical tribute to the culture and society of Edwardian Europe appeared under that title in 1941, he committed suicide in his Brazilian exile.

7

Heimito von Doderer:
The End of Ideology

And when [the devils] were come out, they went into the herd
of swine : and, behold, the whole herd of swine ran violently
down a steep place into the sea, and perished in the waters.

St Matthew, VIII, 32

At the outbreak of the First World War, Heimito von Doderer
was eighteen years old. He left school in 1914 and spent six
months as a law student at the University of Vienna before being
conscripted in 1915. He saw active service on the Eastern Front
later that year. At the battle of Olesza in Galicia on 12 July
1916 he was taken prisoner and spent the next three years in
Russian camps in various parts of Siberia. After returning to
Vienna in 1920, he took a doctorate in history and began to
write for various Viennese newspapers. His first literary work
appeared in 1923. In 1933 he joined the then illicit Austrian
National Socialist organisation, but appears to have been disillusioned some time before his formal resignation from the Party in
1938. During the Second World War he served as an officer in
the Luftwaffe, returning to Vienna in 1946 to resume his career
as a writer. He died in 1966, after having established himself as
one of a small group of writers responsible for the remarkable
efflorescence of the Austrian novel in this century. Most of the
work to which I shall have cause to refer was written in the last
twenty years of his life and is therefore much further removed in
time from the events which it describes than the work of the
other writers covered in the present study. But what his work
lacks in immediacy it gains in hindsight and perspective. In any
case there is, I believe, a continuity between the pre-1914 writing

of Schnitzler and the post-1945 writing of Doderer, a continuity
that is central to my theme of the 'defective vision'.

The literary precipitate of Doderer's experiences during the
First World War is the novel *Das Geheimnis des Reichs* (1930),
which describes the life of a group of Austrian officers in Siberia
from 1916 to 1920. The main character is René Stangeler, who
subsequently appears in the two major novels, *Die Strudlhofstiege* (1951) and *Die Dämonen* (1956). The personal history of
the prisoners centres on the relationship between two of René's
friends, Alwersik and Dorian, and a Polish woman called Katjä;
the hero is also an interested party, but remains on the sidelines.
Their private story is punctuated by passages of straight historical
narrative, tracing the course of the Russian civil war, the setting
up of a White Republic in Siberia, and its eventual collapse before the advance of the Bolshevik armies. Towards the end of the
novel, the private and the political spheres merge more closely
when the Red Army occupies the camp and the nearby town, and
Katjä's husband returns as a prisoner of the Bolsheviks. As
Alwersik pits his wits against a political commissar in an attempt
to save the lives of Katjä and her husband, the characters are
caught up far more directly in political events than has been the
case hitherto. The picture which emerges of life in the camps is
not excessively bleak. As officers René and his friends receive
better treatment than the other ranks, and while many camps
are ravaged by disease and starvation, René himself is not exposed to these dangers until after the Communist victory in 1919.
Atrocities are described indirectly—the Austrians survive
relatively unscathed.

For much of the novel, Siberia is in the hands of Admiral
Koltchak, whose regime depends to a great extent upon the
military prowess of the Czech Legion. (The Legion had been
recruited in 1917 from among Czech and Slovak prisoners of war
in Russia; it was intended to fight against Austria-Hungary in
the national liberation struggle. Although Thomas Masaryk was
determined that it should not become involved in Russian domestic
politics, it clashed with the Bolsheviks in May 1918.) The narrator's attitude towards the Legion is unambiguously critical. To
him they are not Czech patriots but 'bloodthirsty parasites', feeding relentlessly on the body of the Russian nation. He chronicles
bitterly their reign of brutality, oppression and terror, which
culminated in an act of cynical treachery against their Polish

comrades. In the chaos of the final collapse of the Koltchak regime, the Czechs succeeded in obtaining a safe conduct from the Bolsheviks and were allowed to leave the country unmolested and still in possession of their arms. But the Czechs omitted to include in the terms of the agreement any safeguard for the Polish Legion which had fought alongside them; they also failed to inform the Poles of their plans for evacuation. Consequently the Poles were delivered into the hands of the vengeful Bolsheviks and left at their mercy. The narrator is even more outspoken in his terse condemnation of the cruelty of the South Slav Legion.

The Koltchak regime and the Czech Legion are supported by the Entente with men and equipment. Again the narrator's bitter resentment is perceptible, partly because he objects to the political presence of the western powers, partly for what seem to be more personal reasons :

> In the town French officers bought up the women and the increasingly scarce butter, while for next to nothing English subalterns adroitly obtained from half-starved and frozen Austrians of their own class those decorations for courage in the face of the enemy which were made of pure gold—as a souvenir, so they said.[1]

(Can one not detect here the national stereotypes of German wartime propaganda?) The narrator scornfully dismisses the compromises of the bourgeois Kerensky government of 1917 which, he claims, invoked the support of the Russian people but ignored their legitimate demands; which promised peace to the Russians and a continuation of the War to an anxious Entente; which advocated land reform while assuring the landowner that their rights were inviolable. Yet the Bolsheviks are also attacked—for their vicious terror which is just as bad as the reactionary cruelty it has replaced. The novel is thus critical of White and Red alike. The narrator reserves his compassion and respect for the Russian people—for their spiritual resources, not their political organisation. He asks how one can explain the fact that in two years the Bolsheviks were able to train, organise and equip mass armies, and drive out an enemy which was backed by the resources of the Entente. He answers that although many external political factors may be adduced, the ultimate reason lies in the character of the Russian peasant. He suggests that the November Revolution represented the awakening of the Russian masses to historical and political consciousness. The contribution of the Bolsheviks was incidental. The misleading receptiveness of the Red Armies to Bolshevik propaganda should not blind one to the truth : the Russians obeyed their leaders not because they believed in an economic theory, but because they were using the Bolsheviks to assert their emerging nationalism. Despite the atheistic prating of the Red Armies, the masses were driven by the dimly sensed feeling that the godless foreigners, the enemies of Christ, should be expelled from the holy soil of Russia. The narrator thus replaces Marxist with national loyalty (as Stalin did). He emphasises that the emancipation of the Russian masses was due in the first instance to a personal religious feeling, to a new consciousness of self. It would be boring to show that such an interpretation is scarcely tenable as a historical explanation. It is redolent of Rilke's mystique of Holy Mother Russia, or of Dostoyevsky's salvation from the East, rather than of the political realities of 1917 to 1920. The narrator's distortion cannot be justified as fictional licence since it is offered as an objective statement in the context of the novel's interpolations of historical narrative.

Neither *Das Geheimnis des Reichs* nor Doderer's last and unfinished novel *Der Grenzwald* (1967), which reverts to the prison camp setting, contains any reflection of political events in Austria. René Stangeler is less interested in the implications of the Revolution or of the collapse of the Habsburg Empire than in the emotional dilemmas of his friends and in his own hobbies. (In captivity he tries his hand at writing—like Doderer himself.) It was not until after the Second World War that Doderer published his thoughts on the disintegration of the Monarchy; by then he had come to believe that the impact of 1918 upon Austrian culture had been considerably overemphasised, and the extent of the breach with the past exaggerated.[2] The First Republic, he argued, wasted time and energy trying to remove every vestige of the Imperial past, but succeeded only in changing superficial features such as street names, and in giving itself a bad conscience as a result. He alluded to the lack of any fundamental social transformation under the new republican system, a point also made by Werfel, Blei, Musil and Kraus. The Second Republic, in Doderer's view, was far more successful in coming to terms with Austria's past. Instead of trying to repudiate it, Austrian culture after 1945 drew sustenance from the wealth of tradition, without indulging in nostalgia for past glories. In *Die Strudlhofstiege* the continuity of the characters' lives before and after the First World War is clearly demonstrated, and the tangible political changes in Austria are deliberately ignored. This attitude contrasts strongly with, say, Stefan Zweig's impressions of Vienna in 1922 when, writing of Schnitzler's characters, he observed :

> The sweet young things have become whores, the Anatols play the stock market, the aristocrats have fled, the officers are clerks and commercial travellers—the effortless refinement of conversation has coarsened, eroticism has been vulgarised, the city itself proletarianised. But several of the problems which Schnitzler treated with such verve and acumen have grown far more urgent, above all, the Jewish and the social problem.[3]

It is not until *Die Dämonen* that we begin to glimpse the extent of these changes, and even here the characters are affected remarkably little by war, revolution and inflation. In later years Doderer viewed the disintegration of the Empire in a positive light, maintaining that within the supranational framework of the Habsburg Monarchy the Germans had already absorbed the optimum amount of alien cultural influences, and that by 1918 there existed a real threat of the process of assimilation being converted into one of cultural annexation. An already saturated Austro-German culture could not have preserved its unique identity much longer and would have lost its character over the coming years. The collapse of 1918 interrupted this process at a point when a delicate cultural equilibrium was still being maintained. Consequently the Austrians were able to continue their independent cultural development, enriched but not overwhelmed by the cultures of their neighbours.[4] This perverse twist to the familiar notion of cultural symbiosis has a dubious genealogy. It is rooted in Pan-German fears of *Überfremdung*, such as were expressed fairly moderately by Ferdinand Kürnberger or the politician Joseph Maria Baernreither, who accused Franz Joseph of furthering Slav expansionism for fear of too close an involvement with the Wilhelminian Reich. In the writing of H. S. Chamberlain or Adolf Hitler, however, these political fears were buttressed by a doctrine of racial superiority. Hitler too felt that the Germans had been saved from Slavonicisation only by the collapse of the Dual Monarchy.

The Imperial theme impinges only indirectly upon Doderer's most ambitious and important novel, *Die Dämonen*. Here the political background is the First Republic, or to be more precise, the year 1926 to 1927. The novel is set in the streets and squares of Vienna and on the wooded hills overlooking the city; this local flavour is heightened by the stylised evocation of the rhythm and idiom of the Viennese vernacular. The deliberate disruption of the conventional narrative sequence, and the attention paid to the minutiae of recollection mark the novel as a product of post-Proustian literature. It relates the adventures of a group of friends on the fringe of the Viennese *jeunesse dorée*. The involved plot hinges upon an attempt to embezzle an inheritance, but what really sustains the novel and imposes unity on it is the theme of a 'second reality'. The story culminates in an account of the rioting in Vienna on 15 July 1927, in the course of which the Palace of Justice was gutted by fire.* But this climax is seen as an overture to coming horrors. At the beginning of the novel the narrator, Sektionsrat Geyrenhoff, indicates the wider relevance of his tale :

Terrible things took place in my native land and in this, my native city, at a time long after the grave and lighthearted stories I wish to relate here had come to an end. And one thing that lay curled amorphous and germinal within the events that I must recount, emerged dripping blood, took on a name, became visible to the eye which had been almost blinded by the vortex of events, shot forth, and was, even in its beginnings, recognisable—gruesomely inconspicuous and yet distinctly recognisable for what it was.[5]

Die Dämonen then is ultimately a political novel, but of a curious kind. For the most part its political relevance is indirect; moreover, it embodies a radical critique of politics, or at least of certain kinds of political activity. It urges that the tyranny of

* In the Burgenland village of Schattendorf a clash between Socialists and members of an ex-servicemen's organisation in January 1927 resulted in the death of an old man and a boy. When the *Frontkämpfer* were acquitted by a Viennese court in July, the workers of the capital took to the streets. There was a heavy toll of casualties and destruction. The riot estranged even liberal sections of the bourgeoisie from the Social Democrats, strengthened the position of the fascist *Heimwehr*, and brought home to the Socialists that they could not rely on any support from the working class members of the police and the army in a crisis.

'ideology' or a 'second reality' be replaced by a brave realism and a determined individualism.

'Ideology' in Doderer's sense implies preconceived ideas, rigid thought patterns, any selective and distorted view of reality, political or otherwise. It is a denial of critical thinking and of each man's capacity to work out his own salvation. It is the habit of subsuming men under general headings which ignore the essentially private—and alone significant—aspects of personality and experience. All dogmas, programmes and theories intervene between an individual and the reality with which he comes into contact, they refract his perceptions, rearrange them in an arbitrary pattern and construct a 'second reality' at one or more removes from the actual world. To live in a 'second reality' means for Doderer to seek refuge from the difficulties, complexities and inevitable imperfections of human life in a utopian ideal of order, simplicity and clear-cut solutions. Armed with slogan and cliché, the 'ideologist' violates reality in order to gratify his own psychological needs. Most of the characters in Doderer's novel are the victims of some such 'ideological' delusion, ranging from Kajetan von Schlaggenberg's obsession with statuesque female forms to Eulenfeld's incipient fascism, from Quapp's dream of becoming a violin virtuoso to the riot of 15 July. (The title of the work refers to these demonic obsessions.) The political demonstration is interpreted as a purely ideological reaction in the conventional sense : the Viennese workers are shown to be motivated by a misguided feeling of solidarity with the victims of the Schattendorf fracas, and to be demanding the very class justice against which they are ostensibly protesting. The riot is crucial because in the light of subsequent developments it represents the 'Cannae of Austrian freedom'. Thereby political liberty is given a mortal blow from which it never recovers. With a significant change of tense the narrator—at this point not Geyrenhoff, but the novelist *in propria persona*—relates the workers' fateful error to the whole principle of political association :

> The so-called masses have always been fond of settling in a compact group upon the branches of the tree of liberty which tower into infinity. But they must saw off these branches; they cannot help themselves; and then the whole crown of the tree collapses. Sit where he will, the man who listens to the 'masses' has already lost his freedom.[6]

This criticism of political organisation and social regimentation is echoed by several of the more prominent characters and endorsed by Doderer himself elsewhere.[7] The implications of his rejection of ideology, made abundantly clear in *Die Dämonen*, are 'A plague o' both your houses./They have made worms' meat of me.' Looking back upon the events of the 1920s from the standpoint of the postwar period, Doderer insists that political reform and collective solutions must be subordinated to the moral renewal of the individual, for without *that*, he feels, grand political designs are just so many houses built on sand. The refrain is familiar from the work of Austrian writers of an older generation.

Since the middle of the nineteenth century Vienna had witnessed a plethora of ideologies. Between 1830 and 1914 the city was a proving ground for various substitute doctrines which attempted to fill the vacuum left by the decline of a unifying Catholic, feudal, imperial ethos. The 'confusion of values' in *fin de siècle* Vienna was reflected in the competing theories of Liberalism, Marxism, Christian Socialism, Zionism, racial anti-semitism, Pan-Germanism, Slav nationalism and the 'conservative revolution'; the schools of idealism, positivism, psychoanalysis; a ferment of aesthetic activity which produced its own conflicting factions and manifestos. (Musil brilliantly satirised this confusion in *Der Mann ohne Eigenschaften*.) Effective political direction could only come from Parliament, but this was virtually paralysed by bitter strife. After 1918 the Republic was again reft by ideological struggle, now between Christian Socialists and Social Democrats, neither of whom could win an absolute majority. A third ideological element entered the scene with the growth of the fascist movement. In the face of daunting problems, periodic attempts to forge a coalition of Right and Left (after 1920) were wrecked as much by irreconcilable differences of principle as by short-sighted politicking. The Anschluss merely intensified the process of ideologisation which was already a feature of Austrian public life.

It is against this background of many diverse ideological conflicts that Doderer's impatient abjuring of ideology and political association must be seen. What Doderer has in mind when he speaks of a political ideology is not a reasoned political programme : it is rather—as we have seen—the failure to come to terms with political realities, the tendency to evade the true issues

by cloaking them with metaphysical values or philosophical concepts. Yet Doderer's remedy is too facile. He does not confine
himself to the defence of his own independence and integrity as
an intellectual—in which case his strictures might up to a point
be justified. *Die Dämonen* offers a would-be panacea for the ills
of European civilisation in general and European politics in
particular. In fact Doderer solves nothing by advocating a consistent individualism, since for better or for worse the principle of
association is germane to the political process in a highly organised
modern society. The real problem is how to combine effective
political action with the maximum individual liberty—and of
that problem he has little to tell us. His analysis is inadequate in
that he makes no attempt to evaluate different ideologies : there
is, after all, a fundamental difference with regard to ends and
means between National Socialism and Social Democracy, a
distinction which in practice matters far more than the tenuous
formal link between them as ideologies. In short, Doderer swings
from one extreme to another, in a pattern similar to that noted by
Thomas Mann in Germany after 1918. Mann, seeing a connection between the non-political attitude of the bourgeoisie under
the Wilhelminian Empire and the susceptibility of the middle
class to the *völkisch* ideology after the War, asked in 1937 :

> Must the German always move from one extreme to another?
> Must he, in a grotesque over-correction, to show a 'thorough-
> ness' which denotes a terrifying exaggeration and a lack of
> human equilibrium, now take it into his head to make a totali-
> tarian cult of politics and the State—which is even worse than
> his erstwhile neglect of politics?[8]

Doderer moves back in the opposite direction, from a 'totalitarian'
position to the repudiation of politics as we know it. In spite of
his criticism of ideology, concrete political realities continue to be
veiled in sweeping abstractions.

Die Dämonen illustrates the havoc wrought by a 'second
reality' on both the political and the personal level. The weight
of the narrative is borne by the personal relationships between the
characters and by the idiosyncratic obsessions of Schlaggenberg,
Quapp, Guyrkicz, Herzka and others. One doubts, however,
whether the equation of the private and the public 'ideologies'

is entirely valid. The origin, nature and significance of Schlaggenberg's fantasies about stout women, or of Quapp's obsession with
her musical career, are of a different order from the factors involved in commitment to a political ideology. It is not simply a
question of degree : the private quirks—and the way in which
they are resolved—are so remote from our political experience as
to be irrelevant to it. Even the purported fifteenth-century manuscript describing Achaz von Neudegg's torture of two respectable
women whom he accuses of being witches—a document that
might have proved commensurate with the events of 15 July and
their aftermath—lapses into anticlimax. Here is no heinous crime,
no exercise in evil, but the mildly perverse, even farcical titillation
of a medieval *voyeur*. The disparity between the private and the
public 'ideologies' elucidates the situation at the end of the novel,
where a rash of happy marriages contrasts strangely with the
catastrophic political outlook.[9]

For a novelist whose concern is to exorcise the demons of
'ideology' and to advocate pragmatism and objectivity in all areas
of experience, Doderer remains paradoxically partisan in certain
respects. Though the overt political attitude of the novel's enlightened characters is one of critical detachment, the book contains the seeds of a political polemic. The view of the proletariat,
for instance, is highly selective. Apart from Leonhard Kakabsa,
the young worker who becomes a librarian and a PhD candidate
with the aid of a Latin grammar, and his friend Niki who protests, 'But I'm not the "masses" ', the lower orders are chiefly
represented by a handful of whores and criminals, by the rowdies
and gamblers of the Café Kaunitz, and by the rampaging demonstrators of 15 July. When a retired civil servant makes out a case
against revolutionary ideologies, or when a former NCO dissociates himself from the idea of working class solidarity and outlines his belief in a corporate society, it would be egregious to
attribute these opinions without further ado to the author : yet it
is surely significant that the opposite point of view is never argued
in the novel. And in the relationship between Leonhard Kakabsa
and Prince Croix, Doderer presents us with nothing more original
than a latter-day adaptation of the traditional relationship between the Austrian nobility and the *Volk*.

It is Doderer's account of the events of 15 July which raises
the gravest doubts as to his impartiality. To be sure, the novel

rightly pays warm tribute to the Socialist militia, the *Republikanischer Schutzbund*, for the part it played in supplying much-
needed first-aid teams. The fact that many of the excesses
committed in the course of the rioting are attributed to the
Viennese underworld seems to exonerate the workers to a considerable extent. However, the government which ordered the
police to use firearms against the mob later justified its decision
with precisely this argument; the Vice-Chancellor reported to
Parliament that many of the civilian dead and wounded had
police records. The debate about the tragic events of 15 July has
always revolved round the nature of the police reaction to the
demonstration. Both the Social Democratic Party machine and
the Vienna police showed a lack of foresight in failing to anticipate the protest and to take adequate precautionary measures for
that day. But the point at issue is whether the form which police
intervention took was commensurate with the extent of the
danger. At the beginning of his essay attacking the conduct of the
police, Karl Kraus published a harrowing collection of reports,
testimonies and speeches which together made up a powerful
indictment. The detailed and circumspect account of the same
events by an American historian states that 'even if full consideration is given to the psychological position of the police what
followed [in the afternoon] can be described only as a series of
acts of unspeakable horror and criminal cruelty.'[10] When
Doderer's novel pays tribute to the Vienna police prior to describing the events of 15 July, it implicitly anticipates this kind
of criticism of their conduct. The narrator claims that at that
time the police force was still a body of conciliatory, responsible
individuals; it took the rioting to transform them into a para-
military unit. The officers featured in the narrative, even on the
terrible day itself, are 'honest and civilised men' who are killed or
beaten as they seek to uphold law and order. There is no mention
of those members of the force who went berserk and fired upon
innocent bystanders, attacked dressing stations, used dum-dum
type ammunition and cut down women with drawn sabres. (The
casualty figures speak for themselves: of eighty-nine fatalities,
only four were policemen, and of these not one was killed on the
afternoon in question.) The selective nature of Doderer's account
exceeds the limits of fictional licence—it amounts to a covert
apologia for the police and the Seipel government which endorsed
their actions. It cannot be objected that Doderer, as a creative

writer, has no obligation to observe historical accuracy. In this case the novelist has chosen to illustrate a certain thesis about modern culture by reference to a specific incident. He has interpreted that incident as vital to our understanding of a concrete historical development, the spread of totalitarianism in Austria. If his thesis is to convince, he owes it to himself to offer a plausible account of the incident he is using as an illustration. What he offers instead is a travesty of events. Doderer is ostensibly concerned with achieving a breakthrough to an 'objective' reality : yet faced with a situation where most of the 'facts' are readily ascertainable, he bends the truth to serve his own purpose.

Geyrenhoff, one of the novel's two narrators, is a former member of the Imperial civil service who has resigned his post because in the Republic it carries with it none of that sense of higher purpose, none of that sense of mission which attached to it under the Empire. In any case he feels that the new system limits his opportunities. In other respects the events of 1918 have had relatively little impact on his life and outlook. But at one point he indulges in a fleeting mood of nostalgia; on a bright spring day in 1927, his mind reverts to Vienna in the 1900s :

When frontiers were open, Europe had poured through here, happily falling in with the polished local life-style, which maintained a pretty and inimitable mean between the great Empire outside and the here and now of hills, vineyards, old courtyards, and ancestral customs in the suburbs, as well as the modest gracefulness of the small townhouses of noblemen in a still and cool street in the heart of the Old City. Thus lay the here and now on the one side, which we might call the heart's side, the side of familial and social life, the little world of rounded forms; for outside lay the most variegated landscapes, climates and costumes, lay the ice of glaciers and lowland plains, blue sea and southern vineyards, all the multilingual richness of a vast empire, full of pomp and rituals to which the individual owed certain duties inherited from fathers and forefathers [not just incumbent upon him because of the office he happened to be holding at a given time]. In balance between these two poles moved the nonchalance of the round-dance, the smiles of charming, worldly-wise women, the handsome men who succeeded, with an often astonishingly small application of intelligence, in being fully qualified representatives of one of the most charming cultures that ever was among the many that have vanished from our hasty continent . . .[11]

Unlike Musil's subtle blend of criticism and affection, this confused and rambling sentence—despite the touch of irony towards
the end—is unleavened nostalgia. Geyrenhoff evokes a social fairy
tale, the world of *Der Schwierige* purged even of its muted dis-
cords. The Vienna he describes is not the busy expanding industrial and commercial centre of 1900, but an aristocratic spa. The
stylisation is heightened by the strong emotive overtones of the
language—'ancestral', 'gracefulness', 'Old City', 'pomp', 'vanished' (*urväterisch, Anmut, Altstadt, Prunk, versunken*); by the
significant contrast between the traditional 'fathers and forefathers' (*Vater, Ahn*) and the contractual 'office' (*Amt*)—the
familiar conservative distinction between *Gemeinschaft* and
Gesellschaft; by the picture postcard landscapes and the operetta
world of the carefree 'round-dance' (*Reigen*—compare Schnitzler's
play of the same name). To what extent does the author share
Geyrenhoff's feelings towards the Empire? Circumstantial evidence suggests that Doderer's views do not diverge materially
from those of his character. There is no express dissociation from
Geyrenhoff's views at this point, and several other political
opinions voiced by Geyrenhoff are anticipated in Doderer's published diary. There are other allusions in the novel which suggest
a tendency to stylise the past : for example, Gach's fond memories
of his military service before 1914 and of his genial paternalistic
officers; and the claim that Austrian statesmanship had always
protected the culture of the Croats—a claim immediately belied
by the narrator's reference to ruthless Magyarisation in Croatia
which the Austrians had been powerless to prevent. Doderer endorses the cultural aspect of the 'Habsburg myth' in an essay on
Austria :

> the essential Austrian patriotism has a supranational struc-
> ture ... A politically aware Austrian must today be heartily glad
> of every single Croat or Magyar farmer in the Burgenland, of
> every Slovene in Southern Carinthia : not because one sees in
> such valuable sections of the community a kind of springboard
> for certain [nationalist] aspirations, but because these compatriots
> of his offer his supranational nationalism a symbolic, concrete
> basis.[12]

Die Strudlhofstiege contains occasional observations on the more
civilised, more comfortable or more leisurely existence of Austria

before 1914. When Doderer named as the two great Austrian political novels Stifter's *Der Nachsommer* and Musil's *Der Mann ohne Eigenschaften*, or described Acts III and IV of Grillparzer's *Ein Bruderzwist in Habsburg* as being among 'the finest works of literature that I know', he again indicated where his sympathies lay.[13]

The majority of the characters in *Die Dämonen* belong to the upper middle class or the lower nobility. In spite of the loss of privilege and opportunity incurred through the collapse of the Habsburg Empire, they have emerged relatively unscathed from the War and its aftermath. It is therefore curious that Geyrenhoff should voice opinions more appropriate to the generation of dispossessed *Heimkehrer* than to the world of *Die Dämonen*. He reflects that the generation which is too young to have known war has been leap-frogged by history. This deprivation, he feels, is reflected in their freedom from any sense of loyalty or responsibility.

> Whereas we who had first awakened to personal consciousness on the battlefield acquired a tragic disposition from the start. We felt that we were not born for happiness, or that if happiness came our way it would quickly be lost again [but that we were conceivably destined to meet our end on the battlefield again]. And it seemed to me that we had a mandate not to lay down the burdens and the duties of youth ... until a new generation had grown up, one which unlike the faceless, overleaped generation would be caught in the gears [wheel] of history and thus would release us, their wearied predecessors, from our unduly protracted youth. The terminus of the journey for us would be the same sword that had once awakened us to consciousness. Our destiny could not be 'maturity'. The sword would return us, still young, on the unchanged battlefields to the unchanging earth. For no pitcher goes to that well twice ... Such was my general view of the situation around 1927.[14]

The lame disclaimer in the last sentence follows incongruously upon the pathos and rhetoric of the rest of the passage, which is vibrant with feeling and lapses (in the German) from an indirect mode into direct statement. It is a strange sense of values which disparages a generation mercifully spared the obligation of dying in war. The clichés: 'acquired tragic disposition' (*tragisch verfasst*), 'wheel of history' (*Rad der Geschichte*) and 'sword'

(*Schwert*), are designed to ennoble and justify an uncritical involvement in war and politics. And in the appeal to 'fate', the speaker betrays a compulsive surrender to whatever appears to have been decreed by History, irrespective of the merits of the political agencies through which 'history' in this sense operates.*

The passage is a temporary lapse on Geyrenhoff's part, but it anticipates a far more important event in the novel, the rehabilitation of Imre von Gyurkicz. Here too we find an emphasis on 'authentic' experience, on fulfilling one's destiny regardless of the socio-political implications. Imre is an imposter. He claims to have been a Hungarian officer during the War and to have helped put down the Béla Kun regime in 1919. In his room stands a skull surmounted by a steel helmet, while a Sam Browne with a bayonet and pistol attached to it hangs on the wall. These emblems, however, are but the spurious ornaments of a private mythology. Imre is not of noble Hungarian stock but an Austrian commoner; he is not old enough to have fought in the War; and though he has indeed been involved in political feuding, it was in a less glamorous role than he attributes to himself. In the course of the rioting in Vienna on 15 July, Imre is observed haranguing a crowd of workers. He braves the shots which suddenly ring out behind him and fires the hitherto purely 'emblematic' revolver in the direction of the attacking police. In this gesture the empty symbol assumes a concrete function and is endowed with true significance : his 'second reality' is finally shattered. Imre is killed—but his gesture has redeemed his honour and integrity. His action is not inspired by ideological conviction and his words to the crowd lack intellectual substance. Yet the important thing is that he responds sincerely and unreservedly to the pressures of the moment. This existential commitment represents his moral salvation in the eyes of Geyrenhoff who witnesses his death—and there is no suggestion that the novelist dissociates himself from the narrator's interpretation. Here then Doderer shows the attainment of 'authenticity' in the most unexpected and unpromising situation he can muster, a political situation. Compared with the kind advice, rational decision or mere disillusionment which brings other deluded characters down to earth, Imre's

---

* This 'heroic fatalism', the willing affirmation of one's own destruction for the sake of an ill-defined cause, is in fact characteristic of the right-wing war novels of the Weimar Republic and passed thence into the literature of the Third Reich.

return to a 'first reality' is a good deal more realistic. But neither Geyrenhoff nor the novelist reflects upon the context in which this salvation is won. The target of Imre's shots, the implications of his demagogy, the political validity of his role are never considered : and by failing to examine these political factors Doderer impairs his wider purpose, which was to present the rioting of 15 July as the consequence of the 'second reality' of socialist ideology. Imre transcends his second reality even though he fights on the side of the workers against the police. Authenticity is achieved in a situation which elsewhere we are to understand as the eruption of angry prejudice and criminal violence. The paradox springs from an exclusive concern with individual regeneration, untempered by regard for social and political consequences.

Doderer endeavoured to draw a distinction between 'political' history and the 'true' history of an age, which for him meant the history of private human experience. 'Political' history he dismissed as unimportant to the creative novelist. By nevertheless electing to write a politically relevant novel he undertook a task beyond his creative compass. The allusion to Dostoievsky's *The Possessed* implicit in his title merely serves to underline his failure. That Doderer felt compelled to write *Die Dämonen* at all, belies his artificial distinction between political and personal history. That the novel ultimately fails to illuminate our political experience in those areas where it raises that expectation, is an inevitable consequence of the non-political attitude which Doderer—belatedly—adopted. The paradoxes in the narrative suggest that the demons have departed from the possessed, only to enter the Gadarene swine.

8

Robert Musil: Vanity Fair

The fellows are insufferable and delightful at the same time.
Fontane (on the Prussian Junker)

The editorial of the *Soldatenzeitung* for 15 April 1917 bore the
title 'Vermächtnis' (Testament).[1] This was to be the last number
of a periodical which had circulated for over a year among the
Austrian troops on the Italian Front, and the editor took the
opportunity to sum up his past policy and to underline the tasks
facing the nation. He pointed out that the nationalities conflict
had merely been suppressed, not resolved by the War. He called
for less political wrangling and compromise, and pressed for the
clear, thorough and disinterested exploration of alternative
solutions to the nation's problems. He also urged that whichever
policy was chosen should be firmly and consistently pursued. He
demanded a 'critical patriotism' and a reform of Austrian public
life which would enable independent, solicitous individuals to
replace dilettante aristocrats and career politicians. His own
editorial policy, he admitted, had advocated increased centralisation as a remedy for some of the Empire's pressing problems;
but this was designed to stimulate discussion rather than to lay
down a basic principle.

The writer of this leading article was Robert Musil. After two
years' service with the infantry in South Tyrol, during which he
had demonstrated his physical courage, his cool head and his
administrative ability, he was declared unfit for frontline duty
and placed in charge of the local army newspaper. When this
closed down, Musil was transferred to staff duties and thence, in
the spring of 1918, to the *Kriegspressequartier* in Vienna where
he had charge of a propaganda sheet called *Heimat*, published
in German, Czech and Slovene.[2] Of his loyalty as an officer
there could be no doubt. Yet, in his own words, his patriotism

was 'critical', critical above all of political life in Austria. His editorial concern with the problem of the nationalities did not betoken any personal commitment to the dynastic or Imperial idea; he later maintained that a career in the Austro-Hungarian Army was not calculated to inspire an officer with enthusiasm for the official Habsburg ideology. Recalling his upbringing in military institutes from 1892 to 1897, Musil wrote that he and his comrades were neither dynastically nor patriotically minded but that certain moments had the capacity to thrill them to the core.[3]

The *Soldatenzeitung* was not the only platform from which Musil expressed his opinions on the issues of the day. As a detached but perceptive observer, he contributed essays to various journals on the state of politics under the Empire, on the implications of the War, on the meaning of peace and the challenge of the postwar world. I believe that these essays are directly related to Musil's culminating literary achievement, his monumental novel, *Der Mann ohne Eigenschaften*. The War plainly reinforced many of those insights into the state of European culture which were eventually woven into the warp of his novel.

Like the majority of his contemporaries, Musil experienced an intense elation at the outbreak of the War.[4] Like many others, he accepted the propaganda argument that Germany had been deliberately encircled and threatened with political extinction. He saw the War in terms of an act of self-defence on the part of the Central Powers. Where Musil differs from Hofmannsthal, Bahr, Schnitzler or Zweig, is in the value he attached to this initial experience of patriotic feeling. The corruption, incompetence and cowardice which appeared to him to have subsequently dominated public life failed to influence Musil's assessment of that original mood. On the contrary, the unique experience of the first few days was heightened in retrospect by a knowledge of what followed. Musil's reaction was intensified by a sense of dissatisfaction with his work and career, which in 1914 appeared to him to be in danger of stagnation. In August 1914 Musil was struck above all by the feeling of community which infused the whole nation, by the way in which the individual merged into the totality of his people. As artists regained a resonance which they had long since lost, so too the ordinary citizen found the isolation and anonymity imposed upon him by modern civilisation suddenly endowed with a new meaning and purpose. Society and its values had changed overnight : the individual was no less anonymous than before, but he had now achieved integration within his community. The release from individuation, Musil felt, had brought with it selflessness and a new attitude towards death, inasmuch as men would now gladly lose their lives that they might find them. The intensity of the patriotic experience was such that in describing it Musil used the words 'religious' or 'mystic', and never allowed its value to be diminished by an awareness of its dubious political causes and exploitation.[5]

For Musil the 'effective causes' of the European catastrophe soon appeared irrelevant. His concern lay rather with the 'final causes' of the War, with the collapse of European culture. In the article 'Europäertum, Krieg, Deutschtum' of September 1914 he wrote of a conspiracy to exterminate the German people, and of the elemental call to protect the *Stamm*. But even here Musil pointed to the wider relevance of the outbreak of war :

> Nevertheless it is uncanny how the sudden possibility of a war impinges upon our moral lives from all sides and seeks to transform them. Although today is not the time to reflect upon this question, we, perhaps for a long time the last Europeans, should not build in such a critical hour upon truths which are no longer valid for us; before we march away, we must bring our moral testament up to date.

By about 1917 [?][6] he saw the War as an explosive liberation from a stagnant culture. The idea was developed in the essays 'Die Nation als Ideal und Wirklichkeit' (1921) and 'Das hilflose Europa oder Reise vom Hundertsten ins Tausendste' (1922). Musil observed in the reactions of his contemporaries to the pressures of war, whether on the battlefield or in civilian life, a wide range of human behaviour which pointed to the flexibility and fluidity of the human personality.[7] The banal assertion that a man could be a hero one day and a coward the next, was for Musil of far-reaching consequence. It confirmed that individual behaviour was determined not by an immutable ethical code possessed of an absolute validity, but by psychic idiosyncracies and environmental pressures. Musil postulated the need for a revaluation of the traditional Judaeo-Christian morality. (So too Freud indicated in 'Zeitgemässes über Krieg und Tod' (1915), that the world crisis had borne out his belief in the disastrously repressive effects of bourgeois morality; and Musil's contemporary, the novelist Hermann Broch, saw in the War the final proof of the 'decline of values', of the fragmented nature of the modern world with its ruthless single-minded devotion to totally discrete, self-contained areas of activity.) Musil's imaginative probing of the 'dark gods' in his novel *Die Verwirrungen des jungen Törless* (1906) clearly anticipated this theme. The young cadet's *nostalgie de la boue* shown by his relationship with the prostitute Bozena, and his escape from the oppressive, constricting values of bourgeois society into her arms; his vision of the proximity of the world of reason, morality, progress and success—and the underground world of perversion, debauch, blood and filth; his awareness of the effortless transition from the one to the other; the whole contrast between the amoral depravity of the adolescents and the unsuspecting respectability of the adults—all this foreshadows the 'liberation' of July and August 1914. However, the insight is not fully rationalised until after the War. Musil thus proceeds from the analysis of the individual psyche to the critique of culture.

An heir to Nietzsche's criticism of contemporary values, Musil tried to show that the War was the concluding stage of a prolonged cultural decline,[8] caused by the inability of the civilisation of the nineteenth and early twentieth centuries to keep pace with its own evolving knowledge of the natural world. Scientific advance and a scientific way of thinking had undermined the traditional ground of our being. Yet out of lethargy, or fear, we had not accepted the consequences of this development. In religion, morality, jurisprudence, psychology, politics and even in science, we clung to outmoded conceptions of the world and of human nature. We deliberately closed our eyes to the fact that our actual conduct bore little relation to our cherished values, that our habitual ways of thinking about the world bore little relation to our scientific progress. From this discrepancy between our capacity for knowledge, or the true conditions of our existence —and our reluctance to meet the cultural challenge they posed, sprang the malaise which characterised European life before 1914. Systematically our lines of thought had been invalidated : first rationalism, then idealism, then positivism; yet we persisted in outworn traditions. Consequently, beneath the surface appearance of order and progress lay confusion, doubt and insecurity. The revolt against intellectualism was a symptom of the malady. But Musil defended the intellect on the grounds that it destroyed only that which was already rotten at the core,* and that far from being corrosively analytic, it offered the hope of ultimate synthesis.

The cultural scene up to 1914, then, was marked by a fatal hollowness, and a loss of direction and purpose, which contemporary politics mirrored in its confusion and cynicism. From this point of view, the War seemed to represent an escape from a peace that had become intolerable. Musil wrote of a 'flight from peace' and of a 'revolution of the soul'. He noted that 'in 1914 people were literally bored to death' and again, 'the age simply perforated like an ulcer'.[9] Despite the strong echo of Ernst Jünger's peacetime frustrations, Musil did not share Jünger's militarism. He did not believe that war of itself furnished any kind of solution. Musil was closer to the position of Karl Kraus, who maintained that in the War European culture, far from being renewed, had escaped the executioner by committing suicide.

In different ways many of Musil's contemporaries concerned themselves with the problem of the existential insecurity of the individual and his society. The theme may be heard in Rilke's lines—

> and the knowing animals see clearly
> that we are not very reliably at home
> in the interpreted world.

—or in Hofmannsthal's essays 'Ein Brief' and 'Die Briefe des Zurückgekehrten'. Musil, however, attempts to explain where Kafka or Trakl articulate their private nightmares; he relates his ideas to a social and political context where Freud probes the individual psyche; he adduces science and philosophy where Schnitzler is content to depict individual relationships; he rejects the sentimental simplifications of Werfel and the traditionalist solutions of Hofmannsthal. Perhaps Musil's suggestion (it is of course Nietzsche's)—that the world be treated as an 'aesthetic phenomenon'—approaches Rilke's solution, although he does not share Rilke's doctrine of feeling and *Innerlichkeit*.

In an essay entitled 'Politik in Österreich', written in 1913, Musil had highlighted the peculiar unreality of Austrian politics

---

* cp. 'That which is already falling should be propelled on its way.' (*Also sprach Zarathustra*)

before the War. Despite the frantic activity in and around Parliament and the power wielded by politicians, even the professionals declined in the last resort to take themselves seriously. So too Karl Kraus as early as the first issue of *Die Fackel* in 1899 pointed to the apathy underlying the clichés of political life; and Schnitzler made a similar point in *Der Weg ins Freie*. Musil also claimed that the Empire lacked any idealistic inspiration. Six years later, in 1919, he added that because of the uncertainty attending the decadal renewal of the Compromise with Hungary, Austria's economic and technological progress had been seriously impeded. Dynamic forward movement had been rendered impossible, and the internal conflicts, which might otherwise have balanced each other out, caused the Monarchy to topple over like a cyclist whose machine rolls to a halt.[10] Viktor Adler, the Austrian Socialist leader, had said of Austria-Hungary in 1889 :

The Austrian government is as incapable of being consistent where an act of justice is concerned as it is over an act of oppression; it veers constantly hither and thither—we have despotism tempered by slovenly incompetence.

Musil in effect echoed this view when (after the War) he described the Austrian administration oscillating uncontrollably between repression and leniency in its treatment of opposition groups.[11] From tragedy to farce, from farce to tragedy, the Habsburg pageant had gone its weary way. Musil dismissed the problem of emergent nationalism as a symptom of a more fundamental difficulty. From a political point of view, he argued, Austria-Hungary after 1867 was a 'biologically impossible structure', as Hungary pursued an independent course and no one nation proved strong enough to take the lead in the rest of the Empire. From another point of view, however, the political problem seemed to have been overemphasised. Musil felt that politics had become a convenient outlet of confusion and frustration, a means of evading the real dilemma of the age, which was moral and philosophical, not political. The passion which politics aroused was a mere camouflage for a lack of personal involvement and true concern. Politics had become a game, a method of whiling away the time, pending more important developments. Musil denied that the ideology of supranationalism formed an ethical

or cultural ideal : he saw it for what it was, a political response
to the challenge of emergent nationalism.

This semi-official doctrine, particularly as we have seen it adopted
by such apologists as Hofmannsthal or Joseph Roth, claimed
that Austrian culture was a unique synthesis of German, Magyar,
Slav and Latin cultures within the framework of the Habsburg
Empire. To Musil, on the other hand, in 1919 no less than in
1913, the Empire revealed only the co-existence of diverse
cultures, not a cultural symbiosis. In an area too long befogged
by idealisation and nostalgia, Musil brought his lucid and sceptical gaze to bear :

> First, neither the Slavs nor the Romance peoples nor the Magyars
> of the Monarchy acknowledged any Austrian culture, they
> recognised only their own culture and a German one which they
> disliked; 'Austrian' culture was a speciality of the Austro-
> Germans, who similarly would not have anything to do with
> a German culture as such. Secondly, even within the Austro-
> German area one had to distinguish between three regions which
> were totally different in character and manners—Vienna, the
> Alpine regions and the Sudeten lands. What kind of culture was
> common to all these? There was a great deal of provincialism
> in Austria, but where it became more enlightened, there like
> anywhere else people tried to make contact with the sphere
> of the mind and the way this was achieved was not through
> Wilhelminian or Austrian but quite simply through German
> culture. Admittedly Tyrol, which, though the least enlightened
> region, nevertheless had about it a tinge of Italian culture,
> possessed its own unique character—but what had this to do
> with the Bukovina or Dalmatia, and vice versa? 'Austrian'
> culture was an error of perspective on the part of the Viennese;
> it was an abundant collection of local cultures, to be familiar with
> them was an enriching experience, but that should not have
> deceived anyone into thinking that they constituted a synthesis.[12]

Those who talked of Austria's cultural mission were thinking of
the Empire before 1867 : since then the wheel of history had
rolled on and outstripped the ideals of *Altösterreich*. Musil's
point is that there was no essential difference between Austrian
and German culture. No distinctive feature or value had accrued
to Austrian culture by virtue of Austria's separate political
development. Therefore the argument that Austria would lose her

uniqueness if she were to merge with Germany was not a valid reason for opposing the Anschluss now, at the end of the War. Kraus, who likewise had little patience with this aspect of the 'Habsburg myth', castigated in 1919 an Empire

> where the ethnic kaleidoscope produced the unity of an indefinable culture which was forced upon the European palate as a so-called speciality—a muddy brown* coffee topped with a double helping of whipped cream—and displayed in the closet of the civilised world as a tourist attraction.[13]

The character of 'Austrian' culture cannot be analysed in any detail here. All that one can do is to suggest a possible line of enquiry. In the first instance, it should be acknowledged that the argument of cultural synthesis is *also* a political argument. By justifying the 'cultural' benefits derived from the close relationship of the Habsburg peoples one with another, critics were implying a judgement on the political structure of the Habsburg Empire which made the alleged cultural synthesis possible. If one examines the origin of the argument among the Romantic propagandists, and traces its subsequent development down to the First World War (see pp. 7, 17–18, 85), it becomes clear that cultural synthesis is invoked at a time when the Empire is threatened by disruptive pressures from without or from within, either by emerging nationalisms or by a foreign enemy. The argument becomes in effect an appeal for cohesion at a time when Imperial unity is no longer taken for granted.

One important point in this debate is made by Musil himself —namely, that there is no such thing as a homogeneous 'Austrian' culture, or even an Austro-German culture. When a claim is advanced on behalf of 'Austrian' culture, this really refers to the culture of Vienna. Vienna undoubtedly left her mark upon the Imperial provinces, just as the British Raj influenced the development of modern India. The educated classes in the Habsburg provinces regularly learned German as the precondition of a successful career in the Civil Service, in the Army, in commerce and in industry, in education, politics, the professions and

---

* The pun *gräuliche Melange* is untranslatable: *Melange* is Viennese for white coffee, *gräulich* means lit. 'greyish' but also suggests *greulich* = 'revolting'. Kraus uses the characteristic Viennese obsession with culinary 'specialities', coffee and cream, and the tourist industry, as a stick with which to beat his victims.

the arts. They attended Austrian universities (at least until the foundation of a Czech national university in 1882). Social institutions were moulded by Vienna, just as a familiarity with German music and literature formed part of the upbringing of middle and upper class families. The provinces may have revolted against this influence as nationalism asserted itself in the course of the nineteenth century but the impact of Vienna had already been assimilated and had become an ineradicable element in their cultural heritage, if only because of the social and economic benefits bound up with that influence. This was only to be expected within a fundamentally colonial framework. The crucial test of cultural synthesis is whether Vienna in return absorbed elements of the local cultures over which she held political sway. There is moreover a chronological factor involved. A true synthesis implies the meeting of equal partners, encompassing recognisable and relatively advanced national cultures on both sides. In the case of Austria-Hungary we are therefore limited to the period which began with the revival of the Slav cultures in the late eighteenth century. What we should seek is an awareness of the way of life and thinking, of the values and aspirations of neighbouring peoples at a conscious and reasonably sophisticated level—particularly then among the educated Viennese. Thus evidence of Croats, Poles, Italians and Hungarians who were bilingual and also wrote in German, or of Czech and Rumanian writers who appear to have been influenced by Austro-German literature, does not substantiate the claim of a reciprocal relationship between Vienna and the Habsburg territories. Nor does the impact of Spanish or Italian culture on Vienna before 1800 demonstrate the existence of a unique Habsburg synthesis in the sense in which it is usually meant. As for the debt of the Austrian classics to Czech and Hungarian material : this argument is, as I shall try to show, ambiguous and misleading.

What of the alleged synthesis ? Certainly the Viennese vernacular shows traces of Slavonic, Magyar and Yiddish vocabulary. The Viennese cuisine and certain traditional arts and crafts also reveal the influence of the imperial hinterland. Hungary sent to the Austrian capital wines and strange fish, paprika, fine horses, syncopated rhythms and eastern musical instruments. Bohemia and Moravia sent songs in a minor key, a taste for beer and floury dishes, the inflections of Czech speech and Czech names.[14]

Yet if one turns to the classical musical tradition of nineteenth-century Austria, it seems to have been affected little by the music of the other Habsburg cultures. There are two movements bearing Hungarian titles from the pens of Haydn and Schubert—indeed, a Hungarian rhythmic influence is manifest in the Haydn piece—but both are minor works. Brahms used foreign themes only for a handful of relatively lightweight works such as the Hungarian Dances and for the last movement of his violin concerto. Liszt, Hungarian by birth and upbringing but European in outlook, drew on certain Hungarian melodies, for example, in his Hungarian Fantasies, but smoothed out their irregularities of mode and rhythm. They are in fact a purely characterising device, similar to Haydn's use of Turkish music. On another level, Lehár, also Hungarian-born, shows a certain debt to Magyar and Slovakian folk idioms; in his *Merry Widow* the rhythms and highly-coloured musical language suggest the legacy of his native land, without however altering the basic Viennese quality of his work. Other composers from Beethoven to Mahler rarely display any creative interest in the musical culture of the Habsburg nationalities. One can only conclude that Slav or Magyar folk melodies are used simply as exotic and superficial interpolations (for instance, the *csárdás* in Act II of *Die Fledermaus*). The sophisticated national music of Dvořák, Smetana or Erkel makes relatively little impact. Dvořák gained a firm foothold abroad through the agency of a *German* publisher and critic, though Brahms and Hanslick both helped from Vienna; indeed, Hanslick advised him to abandon his nationalism if he sought success in Germany or Austria. Dvořák seems to have won the respect of the Viennese in spite rather than because of his Czech patriotism and his debt to Slavonic folk themes. As for Smetana, the success of *The Bartered Bride* was limited to Slavonic stages for twenty-five years, until it was performed in Czech at the Vienna Exhibition of 1892. Only then was the libretto translated into German.

The main line of development in Viennese music owes little to the traditional imperial provinces: it springs from a fusion of the German and Italian heritage. Conversely it can be shown that even the national music of Dvořák or Smetana is recognisably Viennese in structure. The greater the composer, the more he is assimilated to the 'western' musical tradition.

In literature we find a similar situation. The Habsburg provinces exerted little influence on Vienna since the Austro-Germans
saw no reason to learn any of the other Imperial languages.
To have acknowledged the existence of a literary culture among
the peoples of the Monarchy would have helped to raise them to
the full status of nationhood and reinforced the demands of the
nationalists. Grillparzer had a knowledge of French, English,
Italian and Spanish, but his command of Czech was limited to
the names of food, terms of abuse and a few hunting terms which
he had acquired during a spell as a tutor in Bohemia in his
youth. When in 1825 Czech students in Vienna and Prague
misguidedly greeted the drama *König Ottokars Glück und Ende*
with a storm of protest against what they deemed to be an insult
to their national honour, the scandal merely increased Grillparzer's deep-rooted prejudice against Czech arrogance. The
dramatist welcomed an honest patriotism which combined loyalty
to the Habsburgs with subservience to German culture, but drew
a careful distinction between 'nationality', 'race' (*Volksstamm*),
'idiom' or 'dialect' on the one hand, and 'nation' and 'language'
on the other. The physical beauty of Prague and the romantic
history of the Czechs impressed Grillparzer profoundly and
inspired some of his greatest work—but never to the point of
reconciling him to the demands of modern Czech nationalism
for cultural and political recognition. Other Austrian writers of
the *Vormärz* years expressed their sympathy with down-trodden
peoples without abandoning their faith in the supremacy of
German *Kultur*. For Austrian liberalism was synonymous with
centralism and harked back to the Germanicisation policy of
Joseph II. The playwright Eduard von Bauernfeld, a contemporary of Grillparzer, pungently characterised the general attitude
when demonstrating that the Viennese local colour in his own
comedies was perfectly compatible with a German orientation :

> 'I feel myself to be far more the compatriot of Lessing or Goethe
> than of some Wenzel or Janos or some other character whose
> name ends in "inski", "icki" and "vich", to whom I am tied
> by political destiny but who at heart want as little to do with
> me as I with them.'[15]

In general the Austrian liberals showed little understanding for
the national aspirations of the Habsburg Slavs which were still

the prerogative of small groups of Slav intellectuals; paradoxically they were more sympathetic towards Hungarian claims. Meissner and Hartmann displayed a sentimental attachment to the sweetly melancholy songs of their Bohemian homeland (Rilke's 'böhmischen Volkes Weise', airs of the Bohemian people) and to the hearth fires of Slovakian peasants. They glorified the Hussite rebellion and opposed Habsburg absolutism. Yet both were severely disillusioned when the Czechs invoked Slav solidarity in 1848. The Galician writer Karl Emil Franzos depicted in his fiction the cultural and political problems of the peoples in the eastern provinces of the Empire, oppressed by an alliance of Austrian administrators and Polish nobles. Again, however, he expected liberation to come only with the extension of German culture to these areas. His essays on Rumanian, Bulgarian and Ukrainian literature aroused as little enthusiasm among educated Austrians as Anastasius Grün's sympathetic translations of Slovene folk-songs published as *Volkslieder aus Krain* in 1850. In the Viennese literature of the nineteenth and early twentieth century the Habsburg provinces occasionally provide exotic settings, conventional local colour or an aura of mystery, as in Hofmannsthal's *Der Turm* and *Arabella*, Zweig's *Ungeduld des Herzens* or Musil's 'Tonka'. Far from demonstrating the existence of a cultural symbiosis, such works show rather the peripheral nature of the Habsburg influences. The Habsburg ideal of supranationalism must be seen against the kind of background which Friedrich Funder, a prominent Christian Social politician and journalist, recalled in his memoirs :

> The Austrian school boy was far more familiar with the causes of the Punic Wars and the mentality of the Carthaginians than with the history, political institutions and way of thought of the neighbouring nation that shared the same constitutional roof with us ... One learnt Sanskrit sooner than Hungarian. Thus all intellectual contact was lacking, the separation of the Austro-Germans from their racially isolated imperial co-rulers was insulting and nothing had been done over the decades to change this unhealthy state of affairs. Austrians and Hungarians met only to quarrel passionately over their respective contributions to the common budget and to listen to gipsy music.[16]

However, it was in Bohemia, not Vienna, that the greatest opportunity existed for cultural contact between the Austro-Germans and another Habsburg people. Here a long-established

German population lived side by side with the most advanced of
the 'nationalities'. And as we have already seen, it is the history of
the Czech provinces which most eloquently belies the myth of
cultural synthesis.

In Bohemia as elsewhere the relationship between Vienna and
the Habsburg peoples was essentially a colonial one. Such was
the insularity of the capital and the Austrian administrators in
the provinces that they absorbed even less from the 'nationalities'
than did other colonial powers such as the British or the French
from their subject peoples. Austria has no counterparts to Kipling
and E. M. Forster, no imaginative exploration of a colonial
situation as searching as Conrad's *Nostromo*. Conversely those
Polish, Croatian, Slovene, Rumanian, Italian and Hungarian
peasants and artisans who moved to the industrial suburbs of
Vienna in the latter decades of the nineteenth century usually
became assimilated within a generation under overwhelming
social and economic pressures. While adding a touch of colour
to the vernacular, they tended to merge comfortably into their
new environment without modifying it to any great extent.[17]
Where they retained a distinct sub-culture of their own, as in the
case of the Czech community in the working class suburbs, it was
in defiance of and quite apart from the Viennese milieu. As late
as 1934 there were still 50,000 Czechs in Vienna (with their own
primary schools), 30,000 Croats in the Burgenland and 30,000
Slovenes in Southern Carinthia, but there is little evidence of the
kind of cultural synthesis suggested by Habsburg apologists. If
one looks beyond Vienna to the urban, German-speaking
minorities in Slavonic- or Magyar-speaking areas, one finds that
resistance to the local culture formed part of a general endeavour
to preserve social, political and economic privileges against the
encroachment of a rival nationalism and a rival middle class.
Shortly before the War, the attempts by young German-Jewish
intellectuals in Prague to mediate between the German and Czech
cultures arose precisely from an awareness of the gulf that divided
them. In Austria-Hungary as a whole the nineteenth century was
less an era of cultural symbiosis than of hardening nationalist
prejudices on all sides. It should also be remembered that one
can scarcely speak of a modern Czech or Hungarian literature
before 1850. In the first half of the century Prague, and even
more so Budapest, was predominantly German in speech and
culture, and the smaller towns of the Empire (except in Galicia

and Italy) remained German in character even longer. In other words, just at the point where a fruitful contact might have occurred between the different cultures, political differences drove the Habsburg peoples further and further apart.

The Italian provinces ruled by Vienna until the mid-century were a special case. The Habsburg administration there found itself cast in the role of an occupying power rather than in that of a 'civilising' influence. Since the Austrians were now confronted with a mature culture to which they themselves already owed a considerable debt, their attitude was far more receptive. The music of such characteristically Italian composers as Rossini, Donizetti, Verdi (a figurehead of Italian nationalism) and Puccini was readily accepted in Vienna in spite of political difficulties with Italy. At their première the operas were often sung in Italian. After all, the influence of Italian opera was central to the development of the Austrian musical tradition. The Austrians for their part found it difficult to leave their mark on Lombardy and Venetia. The columnist Ferdinand Kürnberger declared at the time of the final ignominious Austrian withdrawal from Northern Italy in 1866 that the Austrians had nothing to give the Italian people and that their rule had been entirely superfluous. All they had earned was incomprehension, hatred and determined resistance.

Except for the Italian provinces then, the cultural relationship between Vienna and the Imperial territories was very much a one-way current. Yet when all is said and done Austro-German (or Viennese) culture reveals evidence of an openness to European influences unparalleled in Germany. The main outlines of the modern Habsburg Empire were established in the last two decades of the seventeenth century and the first two decades of the eighteenth. These years saw the expansion and modernisation of the Imperial Army and Civil Service whereby Italians, Germans, Frenchmen, Spaniards, Scots, Irishmen, Walloons, Austrians and Bohemians worked and fought side by side in the Habsburg cause. More than anything else, it was this period of glory following the defeat of the Turks that determined the supranational character of Vienna.[18] Spain, the Netherlands and Italy all helped to mould Viennese architecture, art, music, literature and manners, as Vienna developed from a frontier fortress into a European capital. Then, as later, the alien cultural influences flowed from Western and Southern Europe rather than from the

Slav and Magyar lands of the Empire. (Although one can point to subsequent Russian intellectual influences in the form of Turgenev and Dostoyevsky, these were common to Germany, if not to Western Europe, as well; they did not spring from a peculiarly Habsburg situation.) The alleged Habsburg mission to create (among other things) a unique synthetic Austrian culture out of the local cultures of the Empire was an ideological response to centrifugal pressures. Viennese cosmopolitanism is a different phenomenon altogether. One has only to glance at the moulding influences on those two supremely 'Austrian' figures Grillparzer and Hofmannsthal to perceive the reality behind the myth.

A lack of purpose and direction, a paradoxical lack of true involvement, confusion and insecurity—these are the features of Musil's description of the Habsburg Monarchy in its closing years. Alienation, paradox, self-delusion, the hollowness of accepted values and ways of thought—such are the features of Musil's critique of European culture as a whole. In the initial flood of elation in 1914 Musil believed that a new, more authentic mode of life had emerged from the ruins of prewar culture. At the end of the War he again experienced an intense joy of expectation, a fervid faith in a new world. It was a mood which permeated almost all shades of political opinion in the months between the Armistice and the Peace Conference; Ernst Troeltsch called this interval the 'dreamland of the armistice period'. For a time Musil advocated a reform of the basis of political life, above all a revised conception of the State.[19] Before the War the State had appeared as a soulless administrative machine, predatory and threatening. The individual citizen felt anonymous and impotent and lapsed into helpless passivity, while the bureaucrats evaded through indirectness and impersonality the human consequences of their decisions. Moreover, the morality of the State in its foreign affairs was painfully at odds with the personal morality ostensibly demanded of its citizens; international relations had been fraught with conflict and tension. (From a similar observation Freud concluded that the aggressive conduct of one State towards another helped to emancipate its citizens from the grip of conventional morality.) No improvement would be effected through palliatives such as partial disarmament or international arbitration. Musil believed that a complete transformation of the function of the State was needed; it should assume the nature of an ethical inspiration. He extolled the idea of a federation of states, each an autonomous partner in the whole, each a true national community based upon the bond of language and culture. In fact, Musil's ideal seems to owe much to the Habsburg ideology he rejected. Under the Empire, the State had not, of course, been the idealist community which, according to Musil, it should now become. Yet this was a question of the discrepancy between an ideal and its realisation. Romantic apologists of the Danube Monarchy, from Josef von Hormayr to Joseph Roth, habitually conferred on the Habsburg State an ethical value which was intended to be inseparable from its political function.

Musil's hopes for the reform of the State soon gave way to the search for a non-political remedy. He came to repudiate the mystique of the State, claiming that both 'nation' and 'state' were provisional concepts or structures, designed merely to fulfil immediate practical purposes. Without denying the reality of the feeling of national unity which most European countries had experienced in 1914, he now tried to explain it—rightly—as a momentary response to extraordinary external pressures. Normally, such a unity did not exist : neither race nor language could provide a valid basis for it, and each nation was divided within itself by social, moral and intellectual differences. Musil was now prepared to accept only a utilitarian and temporary justification of the concepts of 'nation' and 'state'. To elevate these two abstractions above the individual was, he felt, an obstacle to the natural organisation of society. His indication of a possible alternative remained vague. One thing was certain : no contemporary ideology had the answer. Conservatives and revolutionaries, nationalists and internationalists, militarists and pacifists, capitalists and socialists alike were in his view guilty of anachronism and oversimplification. He felt that political parties could at the most prepare the ground for reconstruction and that the task of actually building a new world lay outside their competence. When in 1919 he advocated the merging of *Deutschöster-reich* with the Weimar Republic, he was motivated less by economic or political than by exclusively 'cultural' considerations. (Yet in the climate of the time his 'cultural' argument must have had the force of a political statement.) The nearest he came to partisan involvement in politics at the end of the War was when he signed the programme of the 'Political Council of Intellectual Workers' set up by the self-styled Activist Kurt Hiller in

November 1918. Fellow signatories included many prominent
names of the Expressionist generation, among them Kurt Wolff,
Kasimir Edschmid, Fritz von Unruh, René Schickele and Kurt
Pinthus. The novelist Heinrich Mann was also a leading member.
The programme was a quixotic blend of social reform and
spiritual conversion, ranging from the abolition of war and a
more equal distribution of wealth to free love and a constitu-
tionally defined role for the intellectual elite of the nation. Not
surprisingly, the Activists' approach to the Berlin workers'
councils was rudely rebuffed.[20] This attempt to forge a path
outside the routine of conventional parliamentary politics,
together with the Messianic note of Hiller's manifesto, is consistent with Musil's state of mind for a brief period at the end of
the War, even if he did not endorse every item on the Activist
agenda.

Thereafter Musil's attitude towards politics remained free
of that sentimental distaste for the 'immorality' of political
activity which Stefan Zweig professed. Nor did Musil's scepticism
with regard to political remedies turn into political apathy.
His diaries and notebooks for the years 1918 to 1920 contain
several perceptive observations on the issues of the day. Foremost
among them was the question of socialism. Musil criticised
Marxism on the grounds that its division of society into exploiters
and exploited took no account of the large intermediate social
group of whitecollar workers. But he was even more critical of
the actual conduct of the Austrian Social Democrats in 1919–20.
He noted that they had been fatefully compromised through their
cooperation with German nationalists and Christian Socialists.
From the devious tactics of the Social Democrats in the
immediate postwar period, from their parliamentary manoeuvring and their failure to achieve any fundamental social or
economic reforms, Musil concluded that they lacked a strong
positive ideology. He felt that their programme was based on
little more than a romantic rebelliousness and the positive features
of nineteenth-century liberalism (that is, the spirit of 1848 rather
than the subsequent decline into 'national liberalism' and the
doctrine of ruthless private enterprise as propounded, for instance,
by the *Neue Freie Presse*). In short, Musil criticised the *embourgeoisement* of the Social Democrats. One can understand
his feelings. Although the Austrian Socialists did not have to call
upon the Army to suppress the workers as their counterparts in

Germany were obliged to do in 1918 and 1919, they were equally afraid of Communist extremism. In November 1918 the professed aim of Karl Renner, one of the party leaders, was to accomplish a smooth transition from monarchy to republic without creating any social upheaval. Not all the Social Democrats were as cautious as Renner but the majority were reluctant to imperil their political gains by totally alienating large sections of the population through excessive revolutionary zeal. There was also strong moderating pressure from the Allies. Despite substantial constitutional and administrative changes, there was no fundamental reform of the established social order. Attempts to nationalise key industries and to change property relationships were defeated. The party's only period in government (1919–20) was shared with the Christian Socialists. Thereafter the Social Democrats remained in opposition. They were split between the left-wing and the moderate faction around Renner which frequently advocated rejoining a coalition. Otto Bauer fell between the two stools: his speeches proclaimed a fiery revolutionary socialism, while his tactics were more flexible and opportunistic. Musil recorded his criticism only in the early years of the Republic (and in private notebooks). Karl Kraus, on the other hand, devoted a considerable part of *Die Fackel* throughout the twenties and the early thirties to what he called the 'corruption' of the revolutionary idea.

In the Viennese situation at the end of the War Musil observed a general confusion and the lack of any driving force; with a degree of acumen he related this to the traditional role of the Austro-Germans as the Imperial *Staatsvolk*. After accepting authoritarianism for so long as a means of maintaining their privileged position within the Empire (he wrote), the Austro-Germans were left politically inexperienced and ill-prepared for operating a democratic system.

At the end of the War Musil echoed the nationalist condemnation of the 'fraud' allegedly perpetrated by President Wilson when, having proposed his Fourteen Points as a basis for a peace settlement, he then 'revoked' the spirit of that programme in the actual negotiations. Musil considered that the Central Powers agreed to an armistice less out of political and military necessity than in eager anticipation of a new world. As in 1914, he employed a vaguely religious vocabulary, writing of an Eastertide atmosphere or of an advance towards the new Kingdom.[21] But his optimistic gloss on events was rapidly dispelled. Musil could not suppress a feeling of bitterness at the treatment meted out to the German-speaking populations of the South Tyrol and the Sudetenland in the immediate postwar period. In 'Der Anschluss an Deutschland' (1919) he defended the Empire against the charge of having oppressed the nationalities, and mocked the 'doll's house imperialism', megalomania, atavism and obstinacy of the Czechs. He felt that at Versailles the Entente had failed to seize a unique opportunity of reshaping European politics. As late as April 1921 he wrote in a letter of the unjust, intolerable nature of the Peace Treaties which were even less forgivable than the declaration of war itself, for they had prevented the birth of a new world, a chance to break out of the vicious circle of power politics and *revanche*. He opposed the fulfilment of the conditions imposed by the Allies not only on material grounds but also because it was contrary to his moral conviction. Again he blamed the Czechs for neglecting their mission no less than the old Monarchy.[22] But he acknowledged that Germany too had failed to purge herself of old errors. Musil's disenchantment in the early postwar years sprang from this awareness that, in T. E. Lawrence's words, 'the old men came out again' to remake the world 'in the likeness of the former world they knew'. Like Kraus, he condemned his society's incapacity to assimilate the true meaning of what it had experienced.

Musil's reaction to the rise of National Socialism was somewhat ambivalent. On the one hand, he seemed to protest against totalitarianism; on the other, he despised the clichés of democratic politics. While he criticised racialism and *Heimatdichtung*, he accepted Hitler as a historical necessity, the inevitable product of the collapse of prewar civilisation and of the trend towards collectivism. After the failure of democracy to replace 'the numerous sects of capitalist liberalism'[23] with a more positive system, National Socialism had achieved its aims simply by shattering the old scheme of things altogether; and its success went a long way towards justifying its method. Musil believed that the predatory states (*Raubstaaten*) of the present would eventually be succeeded by a higher order; in the meantime, however, they remained the dominant political system. They helped to clear the ground and sow the seeds of the future order. (In other words, possession was nine-tenths of the law.) Musil was clearly attracted by what he felt to be the modern, up-to-date

qualities of Fascism. He was also susceptible to the 'energy' and
'courage' of the 'movement' (*Bewegung*)—precisely the qualities
Hitler was eager to project in contrast to the effete *System* of
Weimar.

Musil appears to have admired determination and fanaticism
in politics, irrespective of means or ends. There are occasional
indications of this during and at the end of the War. Years later
he expressed his respect for Hitler's handling of Chamberlain and
Daladier at Munich, not because of the political merits of the
Nazi campaign, but because of the courage and determination
Hitler displayed.[24] Musil queried whether cowardice was inherent
in what he called *Pluto-Demokratie*, whether the spirit of the
system was not indeed morally corrosive, as its opponents claimed:
he asked whether they were witnessing the birth of a new, powerful attitude of mind. In its relations with Hitler the West boasted
that it was being practical and realistic : Musil riposted that its
compromises indicated a remoteness from the realities of the age.
The fact that democratic statesmen lacked the courage of their
convictions implied that those principles were hollow. (It is
the very fallacy in this argument that is significant.) At one
point Musil suggested that democracy was a more humane
method of resolving political differences, and that it supplied
perhaps a wiser form of government than recourse to the knife
and the pistol. Yet other diary entries indicate a predilection for
power, ruthlessness and authority, characteristic of the heirs of a
vulgarised Nietzsche.

Had Musil's reflections been systematically developed, he
might have realised that the fascist ideologies were as atavistic
as anything they replaced. It is a measure of his contempt for the
old Europe that he should thus have compromised himself
intellectually with those who endeavoured to destroy it. Conversely, it is indicative of his intellectual and political roots in the
last decades of the old era that he could distinguish between the
moral value (as he saw it) of a political movement, and its practical implications; that he could affirm its ethos and ignore its
political repercussions. Unlike Franz Werfel or Joseph Roth,
whose response to the rise of National Socialism took the form
of a reappraisal of the Habsburg Monarchy and of the values it
seemed to represent, Musil eschewed any such contrast between
the present age and 'the good old days'. His own literary
memorial to the Danube Monarchy owed little to the political

climate of the interwar period—and was in any case far more
sophisticated and subtle than the accounts of Roth or Werfel.

During the thirties Musil was drawn into a discussion of the
relationship between the creative artist and the State. He now
admitted the connection between political and cultural developments, and acknowledged that the artist was exposed to influences
at work within his society. Yet he insisted that the artist be
allowed to remain autonomous and free from political commitment. He protested—on two occasions in public[25]—against
attempts to harness art to a political programme. The function
of politics and *Geist*, though related, were entirely different. The
former dealt in terms of what was practicable, of what the age
demanded; the latter in terms of ideas or possibilities. Whereas
politicians and committed intellectuals worked for the present,
the creative individual worked for the future. And the artist's
preoccupation was with form, not with content. His aesthetic
commitment to his work, Musil felt, did not necessarily involve
any moral commitment to the ideas expressed therein. Somewhat
late in the day Musil echoed Mann's *Betrachtungen eines
Unpolitischen*. There, in the preface, Mann had warned that the
reader should not attribute to the author all the views expressed,
that irony was the capacity to see all points of view; as a novelist
he was accustomed not to state his own convictions but to create
characters who stated *theirs*. He could not divest himself of this
tendency to play the devil's advocate and to embrace simultaneously opposite points of view. Mann felt that Art was socially
irresponsible, even when it left the study or the studio for the
public forum. Musil for his part added that the preconditions of
artistic activity were precisely those concepts which had been
abused and debased in the political arena—freedom, courage, the
right to criticise, and a love of truth.

The position of the artist in relation to politics, as defined
by Musil in the thirties, was a necessary corrective to the demands
for a committed art prevalent in the rest of Europe at that time.
It appears that the most useful political function an intellectual
can perform is not to endorse a party programme but to act as a
control. By virtue of his gifts and training he is in a unique
position to evaluate critically the policies and tactics of parties
and politicians. Yet precisely because of his critical attitude,
he may appear fickle and irresponsible to those who are concerned
to achieve or to exercise power. Intellectuals make uneasy political

bed-fellows, as Brecht and Karl Kraus showed. On the other hand, the appeal for intellectual liberty can easily conceal a desire to remain uninvolved, to retreat into the sanctuary of Art or *Innerlichkeit*. It is this which lies behind Musil's argument. He overlooks the fact that in a highly-charged political atmosphere silence may be construed as acquiescence in the status quo, and that to remain detached from politics is itself a political decision. He also ignores the fact that the defence of certain moral and aesthetic values may sometimes call for a tactical alignment behind a political organisation or system, for as long as those values are imperilled. Musil condemned Thomas Mann's public support for the Weimar Republic because he neither shared Mann's values nor appreciated the distinction Mann drew (after 1918) between his political and his aesthetic statements. The problem, as Musil saw it, was merely to preserve the autonomy of the artist from the political claims made upon it. Thus he attempted to strip the concepts 'liberty' and 'the right of free expression' of their wider political implications. He appealed for artistic freedom while denying that this implied, in the contemporary situation, support for a democratic political system. Even though he claimed that he was not indifferent to all forms of government, he avoided committing himself to any one actual system; his ultimate criterion in political decisions was an excessively narrow definition of the prospects for cultural advancement.

At the end of the First World War Musil had concluded that a new way of life and a new mode of thought were called for. No single ideology would supply these, neither would the conflict of ideologies produce any valid alternative. The time was past, he felt, when one particular philosophical system could encompass the whole of reality as we perceived it. Our knowledge of reality had become so complex that our ideas could articulate only part of the truth. We had to accept the limitations of these ideas, acknowledge that there was something useful in them all, and attempt to devise fruitful confrontations between them. Musil appealed for the abolition of dogmatism and of an illusory certainty, demanding in their place an open mind and a receptiveness to new ideas. Instead of clinging to rigid standards and concepts which violated a reality that was fluid and mutable, we needed to revise our whole conception of knowledge. (Compare Doderer's hostility towards 'ideologies'.) And this was to be achieved through a synthesis of intellect and intuition, science and imagination, reason and the aesthetic sensibility.

> We possess not too much intellect and too little soul, but too little intellectual understanding in matters of the spirit.[26]

> This order of art, ethics and mysticism, that is of the world of feeling and ideas, admittedly draws comparisons and analyses and provides a synthesis; to that extent it is rational and intimately related to the strongest instincts of our time, but it does not contradict the soul; the latter has its own goal, and that is not the clarity whereby (let us say) ethos condenses into morality or feeling into causal psychology, but an overall picture of the causes, connections, limitations, the fluid meaning of human motives and actions—in short, an interpretation of life.[27]

Thus Musil endeavours to establish guide-lines for a new epistemology, which would combine the advantages of mathematical precision and objectivity with those of intuitive perception and imaginative truth.

As the figure of the millionaire, Arnheim, in *Der Mann ohne Eigenschaften* shows, Musil was aware that others had attempted —and failed—to achieve a synthesis of *Seele* and *Ratio*. At the beginning of the century Hofmannsthal described in *Ein Brief* his overwhelming realisation of the fluidity and complexity of reality, and the inability of the intellect to comprehend and express in language the nature of the world. Lord Chandos, the writer of the letter, believes that since our moral and intellectual concepts abstract from and transfix reality, they cannot convey any existential truth. It is a conviction which isolates Chandos from the natural and social worlds. On occasion, however, the barrier of individuation falls, to permit a moment of sublime empathy with ordinary, familiar things. Chandos then regains that community of being which he had once taken for granted :

> I then feel as though my body consisted of nothing but cyphers which hold the key to everything. Or as though we could enter into a new intuitive relationship to the whole of existence, once we began *thinking with our hearts*.[28] [my emphasis]

(There are similar experiences in Rilke's *Malte Laurids Brigge*.) Such moments remain inexpressible, for Chandos's soul in effect outstrips his intellect, his ability to formulate his experience. In a very different context Törless likewise attempts to fuse his perception of unconscious experience with rational analysis, by trying to formulate his own intuitive knowledge in conceptual terms and exploring the reactions of the hapless Basini to his degradation. Basini, however, proves inarticulate, and Törless eventually abandons his attempted synthesis in the conviction that language and reason draw a veil over the true nature of experience.

> I know that things are what they are and will presumably always remain so; and I suppose that I will always look at them now in one way, now in another. Now through the eyes of the intellect, now through the others... And I will never again try to compare them with each other.[29]

Subsequently Musil's ambition was to achieve a true synthesis, to extend the boundaries of thought and language, rather than to acquiesce in their limitations. Thus he pursued in his own fashion, without reference to a transcendental reality, the principle underlying Goethe's 'idea of scientific truth'.

In an essay entitled 'Politik in Österreich' Musil wrote (in 1913):

> Somewhere or other in this state there must be a secret, underlying idea. But one cannot discover it. It is not the idea of the State, nor the dynastic idea, nor the idea of a cultural symbiosis of different peoples (Austria could be a world experiment)— probably the whole thing is merely motion resulting from the lack of a driving idea.*[30]

And again, shortly after the end of the War:

> This Austria [prior to the division into two separate halves in 1867] was a remnant of the valiant old authoritarian state which in some respects was quite congenial. Since then, however, the wheel of history has taken one or two further turns...[31]

* The image of a *Weltexperiment* anticipates Kraus's 'laboratory of world destruction' ('Franz Ferdinand und die Talente', July 1914), though Musil's use of it is positive.

In these two quotations we are presented with a key to major sections of Musil's most ambitious work, *Der Mann ohne Eigenschaften*. For the setting of the novel, and the theme of its most successful chapters, are the closing years of the Austro-Hungarian Empire. The novel shows that the Empire outlived itself by fifty years or more. Yet Musil's treatment of it conveys a blend of ironic criticism and sincere affection. In the author's own words :

> In the *Man Without Qualities*, dissatisfaction with my country formed a gently ironic precipitate.[32]

Early drafts indicate that the novel was to be a critique of European culture, culminating in the outbreak of the War. It was to evoke uncritically the elation of August 1914, and to depict the subsequent corruption behind the lines and in Vienna. The mobilisation would have emerged as the inevitable resolution of an intolerable mode of existence, without, however, offering any real solution. In fact, the novel never progressed as far as the declaration of hostilities.

It is set in Kakanien,* in the year 1913–14, and the early chapters re-create the aura of a lost empire. Musil both reiterates and modifies the picture of the Monarchy that emerged from his essays. Here in the novel too[33] we read of the Empire's lack of dynamism (tempo, but not too much tempo); its paradoxes (a liberal constitution, a clerical government, a free-thinking way of life); the inconsequentiality of its authorities (when Parliament exploited its independence, absolutism reasserted itself, but just as the public became accustomed to absolutism, the Crown would decree the reestablishment of parliamentary rule); and the disruptiveness and peculiar unreality of the conflict between the various national groups (a rivalry which had developed into a 'sublime ceremonial'). In the discrepancy between the official title of the Empire (Austro-Hungarian Monarchy) and the intuitive allegiance of the Austro-Germans who simply called it Austria, thereby employing a name which had been formally renounced in the interests of Dualism, lies an intimation of that 'biological impossibility' which lay at the root of the collapse of

---

* The name is based on the initial letters of the ubiquitous Austro-Hungarian royal prefix *kaiserlich (und) königlich*, 'imperial (and) royal'; usually abbreviated to *k.(u.)k.* There was a subtle constitutional issue involved in the inclusion or omission of the 'and'.

1918. Musil several times exploits with ironic dexterity the constitutional absurdity of the Empire, as conveyed by names and titles. What has become more pronounced in the novel, as distinct from the essays, is the mood of ironic detachment and tolerance. This note was not entirely absent even in the 1913 essay 'Politik in Österreich' or in 'Der Anschluss an Deutschland' (1919); yet both these essays were more or less polemical in intent. Subsequently the whole emphasis changes, and it is this fusion of frustration and affection which endows the first book of *Der Mann ohne Eigenschaften* with its peculiar and exquisite charm.

The Empire's fatal lack of dynamism now appears as a principle of moderation, not as stagnation. Its aims, achievements and style of living are refreshingly modest (not too much, not too intensively, not too often, not so sophisticated, not so foolish)— so that it appears as a haven of calm and rationality amid neighbours who are driven to all manner of excess by overreaching ambition, wild imperialist dreams and surplus energy. Where previously, in 'Der Anschluss an Deutschland' and 'Buridans Österreich', Musil underlined the discreteness of the national cultures within the Empire, he now invokes the variety of the different landscapes and their wonderful totality, passing over in silence the question of cultural symbiosis :

> There was glacier and ocean, arid scrubland and Bohemian cornfields, nights on the Adriatic, filled with the chirping of restless crickets, and Slovakian villages where the smoke rose from the chimneys as though from skyward-facing nostrils and the village huddled between two small hills, as though the earth had opened its lips slightly to warm its child between them. (pp. 32–33)

He recalls the splendid road system of the Monarchy :

> Whenever one remembered this land abroad, one saw in the mind's eye the wide white prosperous roads dating from the age of foot marches and post-chaises, which traversed the country in all directions like rivers of law and order, like ribbons of light-coloured twill, entwining the provinces in the paper-white arms of the administration. (p. 32)

—suggesting without undue emphasis that this dates back to the pre-railway era, and that what the roads represent—a rigidly

centralised system maintained by a loyal army and bureaucracy
—no longer corresponds to modern demands. What was openly
stressed in 'Der Anschluss an Deutschland' is here gently in-
sinuated. The Civil Service, for all its conservatism and suspicion
of new ideas, is now described as 'enlightened', and its philistinism
considered to have the merit of common sense; earlier Musil had
emphasised its antiquated values and impersonality.

In the novel the note of nostalgia is clearly not uncritical.
Musil gives his assent to Kakanien only insofar as those of his
characters who are in some sense its representatives appear to be
aware of its defects. The Dual Monarchy appeals to him because
in a picturesque way it reflects a decay which elsewhere is glossed
over by imperialist dreams, economic expansion and technological progress. The novelist's affection is very different from
the sentimental idealisation of Hofmannsthal, Bahr or Joseph
Roth, who attempted to convince their readers that foot-marches
were still appropriate to the age of the aeroplane. Musil presents
the Empire as a paradigm of European decay—and therefore,
as I shall endeavour to show, it proves an eminently suitable
milieu for the 'man without qualities'. The government, with its
inconsistency, its archaic ideology and its confusion; the people,
with their uneasy awareness of the malaise of their civilisation
and their search for a solution; and political life, with the un-
dignified mêlée of irrelevant conflicts: these features of the
Austrian scene are at once unique and representative. Musil's
reluctance to identify in his novel the cities of Vienna or Brünn,
and his invention of the name *Kakanien*, remind us that what is
enacted here is not merely the fate of this particular state. (So
too Kraus indicated the wider perspectives of *his* drama by alluding to the 'last days of mankind'.)

Musil construes Austrian *fortwursteln* as more than a sign of
political incompetence : to him it betokens a profound scepticism
with regard to conventional solutions. Like Ulrich, the hero of the
novel, the Imperial government and Civil Service appear to be
prevented from opting for any one course of action by the feeling
that they might—with equal justification and success—choose a
dozen alternatives. The Imperial authorities lack determination
and conviction because they can see no way out of a political
impasse. Ulrich goes a step further : he deduces a theory concerning the provisional nature of all experience, and contrasts his own

'sense of the possible' (*Möglichkeitssinn*) with the 'sense of reality'
(*Wirklichkeitssinn*) of so many of his contemporaries:

> He who possesses a sense of the possible does not say, for
> example, 'Here this or that has happened, will happen, must
> happen'; on the contrary he makes things up, 'Here something
> could, should, or ought to happen'; and if he is told that some-
> thing is what it is, he thinks 'Well, it could probably be very
> different'. Thus one could define the sense of possibility as the
> ability to think in terms of everything which could just as well be
> the case, and not to take what *is* any more seriously than what is
> *not*. Clearly the consequences of such a creative bent can be re-
> markable and alas, they not infrequently cause the object of other
> people's admiration to appear false, and the object of their pro-
> hibitions to seem permissible—or both to be irrelevant. Such men
> of possibility live, it is said, in a more delicate cocoon, in a web of
> haziness, phantasy, day dreams and conjunctives. (p. 16)

Ulrich points out the inadequacy of fixed, arbitrarily defined
concepts in our conventional ways of thinking about the natural
world, morality, human responsibility, the law, and politics. The
case of Moosbrugger, the schizophrenic sexual killer, illustrates
the difficulties into which traditional mental patterns can lead
in the fields of morality, psychology and jurisprudence.

How important is Ulrich's *Möglichkeitssinn* in his own life?
His ideal mode of conduct seems to be a philosophy of 'as if';
one should take decisions and act upon them, yet one should
always bear in mind that the chosen course of action is only one
of many alternatives, all equally justifiable. In brief, one
leads 'a life of provisional principles'. It is an aesthetic approach.
Life is seen not as a thing in itself, but as the raw material of an
experiment, with the sting of finality removed from experience.
One is never wholly committed to a belief, a principle, a role.
But the point is not far removed at which healthy scepticism
gives way to moral impoverishment, for the distinction between
detachment and paralysis is a fine one. Ulrich in practice errs on
the side of passivity—except in his relationship with his sister
Agathe. (An earlier hero, Törless, had relished his role as tactician
vis à vis Beineberg and Reiting. It was he who thought out the
various possibilities of a given situation, but he was incapable of
committing himself to any one suggestion.) As Musil points out,
the *Möglichkeitssinn* causes a man to become by ordinary

standards unpractical and unreliable; he lapses into lethargic indifference and Baudelairean spleen. But does not this mean that
Ulrich's remedy—the cultivation of *Möglichkeitssinn*—is a
symptom of the sickness it sets out to cure (as Kraus once wrote
of psychoanalysis)? Though more lucid and articulate, Ulrich's
response bears the hallmark of Kakanien. His indecision, apathy,
passivity and detachment result from his analysis of the confused
values of his cultural environment. Ultimately, however, he only
succeeds in making confusion worse confounded. For the man
without qualities is the man with all qualities. Since he is unable
to oppose constructively the triviality and foolishness all around
him, he himself lapses back into lukewarm conventionality and—
in the last resort—acquiesces in the foibles of his contemporaries.
In *Der Mann ohne Eigenschaften* Musil deliberately creates
a context in which his attitude of acceptance and not-so-
detached enquiry is of no great significance. Its implications had
been clearer and more urgent in the story of Törless, who tolerates
the appalling treatment of Basini on the grounds of intellectual
curiosity.

The 'confusion of values' in the Vienna of 1914 is illustrated
by the *Parallelaktion* and the characters involved in it. The
campaign is in one respect a precipitate of Austrian frustration
and helplessness. Launched in response to a German plan to
celebrate in 1918 the thirtieth anniversary of Wilhelm II's
accession, the Austrian campaign is intended to surpass the
German effort in its own commemoration in that same year of
Franz Joseph's seventieth jubilee. (Thus, ironically, even the
ultimate glorification of old Austria is an imitation of a German
idea.)[34] In effect the committee of aristocrats, civil servants, representatives of the *haut monde* and intellectuals seek a justification
for and solemn confirmation of the continued existence of their
own society. The suggestions that Franz Joseph be promoted as
a 'Peace Emperor', or that a Greater Austria be founded—its
absurdity inherent in the gratuitous German comparative—
express the desperation of a culture that is trying to perpetuate
its traditional mission long after that role is felt to be redundant.
(Similarly, Hermann Bahr dreamed of an Austria reaching as
far as Salonica—at a time when the Empire was plainly disintegrating. And Hofmannsthal tried to transfer his conception of the
'Austrian Idea' from a context in which it was no longer relevant
to the wider context of postwar Europe.) Daily the plans put

forward in the *Parallelaktion* grow more extravagant and more irrelevant, as Kakanien moves slowly towards the fateful summer of 1914.

The search for a new inspiration, for a new Idea, reflects a European tendency. The latter half of the nineteenth century, according to Musil, was an age of imitators (an echo of Nietzsche's *Bildungsphilister*). The coexistence of naturalism and preciosity, brutality and morbidity, the cult of the body and effete aestheticism, the superman and the communist—this chaotic confusion of competing faiths is symptomatic of the debility of accepted values, and of the need for a new doctrine of salvation. The inner disharmony of the age is projected into political conflicts. The nationalism that threatens the Danube Monarchy is a surrogate for religion, involving as it does the naive hope that singing the national anthem will solve every problem (again a Nietzschean echo). Graf Leinsdorf's *Parallelaktion*; Diotima's hostility towards intellectualism; Arnheim's spurious synthesis of idealism and the pursuit of power*; Hans Sepp's 'Germanic Christianity'; Feuermaul's fervid and meaningless slogan, 'Der Mensch ist gut!'; Meingast's ragout of ideas from Schopenhauer, Nietzsche and George; the General's *universale Bildung*; Schmeisser's Marxism and Moosbrugger's violence—this Vanity Fair of the mind, amusing, pathetic and deeply disquieting, mirrors a crisis of European dimensions. It is part of the pattern that Ulrich fails to find a career to satisfy him, and that the personal relationships between the characters prove inadequate. Ulrich's affairs with his various mistresses—and, in the early drafts, with Agathe—are as unsatisfactory as Clarisse's relations with her husband or Diotima's liaison with Arnheim.[35]

Ulrich perceives the truth of the situation more lucidly than his contemporaries, who are blinkered by their *Wirklichkeitssinn*. Yet he seems as much a victim of Kakanien's decline as they are. His philosophy of the 'partial solution' was anticipated by Kierkegaard as a symptom of the loss of faith :

A passionate tumultuous age will overthrow everything, pull everything down ; but a revolutionary age, that is at the same time reflective and passionless, transforms that expression of

---

* The figure owes something to Walther Rathenau; Feuermaul is a parody of Werfel, though his catch-phrase is taken from the title of an anti-war book by another Expressionist writer, Leonhard Frank.

strength into a feat of dialectics : it leaves everything standing
but cunningly empties it of significance. Instead of culminating
in a rebellion it reduces the inward reality of all relationships
by means of a reflective tension which leaves everything standing but makes the whole of life ambiguous; so that everything
continues to exist in fact whilst by a dialectical deceit, privatis-
sime, it supplies a secret interpretation of the facts—that it does
not exist.[36]

Musil was not unaware of this aspect of Ulrich's situation. He
notes that Ulrich lives in a state of 'active passivity', like a
prisoner awaiting a chance to escape. Yet when that chance
comes, in the relationship with Agathe, it is valid only for these
two individuals in this particular situation. If the escape has
any lasting meaning for Ulrich and Agathe, which is itself doubtful, it cannot offer a solution to the wider cultural dilemma
against which their story is enacted. (Nor, of course, is it intended
to do so.) Significantly, the perspective of the novel is systematically narrowed down from a European panorama to the circumscribed limits of an individual search for a personal solution. So
too Schnitzler devotes a considerable part of the first half of his
novel *Der Weg ins Freie* to an examination of anti-semitism in
Viennese society; but thereafter the novel focuses on the relationship between the hero and his mistress, and there is little attempt
to integrate the personal situation with the wider panorama. The
shortcoming is less immediately apparent in *Der Mann ohne
Eigenschaften*, given the hybrid nature of Musil's novel, but it is
particularly marked in Schnitzler's. What matters is not, to be
sure, the absence of solutions (which, one suspects, could not fail
to be facile), but the curious way in which both authors abandon
the cultural and political problems which they themselves have
raised. Here too, in Musil no less than in Schnitzler, we see a
hallmark of *fin de siècle* Vienna. Ulrich's quasi-mystical experience in his love for Agathe is not unconnected with his diagnosis
of the canker at the heart of European culture, for it is perhaps
meant to illustrate the synthesis of mind and heart which he
advocates as a means of transcending the limitations of traditional
thought. But its relevance as an illustration remains dubious.

The least problematic parts of Musil's novel are those which
present certain characters as overt representatives of Kakanien's
society and culture. The character known by the ironic pseudo-
nym Diotima is the self-appointed guardian of its cultural values.

Kakanien's heritage to her means the paintings of Velasquez and Rubens that hang in the Imperial museums; the music of Beethoven, Haydn and Mozart; the Spanish etiquette of the Court; the Burgtheater and the Stefansdom, the *haute couture* of the First District, Viennese cuisine and the gentlemanly manners of the nobility. It means, too, a fine sensibility contrasting with the 'crudeness' of the Prussians; a trace of anti-semitism; and the predominance of *Geist* and *Seele* over reason and intellect. (Her cosmopolitanism, such as it is, betrays the influence of her Western European heritage; it owes little to the culture of Dalmatia or the Bukovina.) Musil's description of her confused values catches that mingling of the true and the false, of the genuine and the spurious, of the receptive and the philistine, which is indeed characteristic of Viennese culture. Diotima's salon is designed to bring together intelligent laymen and experts from various fields, thus acting as a reservoir of ideas, a forum of interdisciplinary exchange, and a means of transmitting new knowledge to the educated public at large. But her venture is a failure. The experts ignore each other, while the laymen are baffled by the vocabulary of specialisation. What dialogue does occur is rendered meaningless by verbal imprecision.

Musil's ironic treatment of Diotima corresponds to his attitude towards many other representatives of the old Monarchy. Take, for instance, Graf Leinsdorf, the feudal Catholic aristocrat, with his sentimental illusions about the *Volk*, his distaste for bourgeois civil servants, his inability to comprehend nationalist or democratic dissension, and his fear of irresponsible agitators who bring revolutionary doctrines from abroad. (To this extent he has a parallel in the *Bezirkshauptmann* in Roth's *Radetzkymarsch* who likewise excludes the word 'revolution' from his vocabulary, recognises no 'nations', only 'peoples', and speaks not of socialists but of 'suspicious individuals'.) Despite his conservatism, Leinsdorf is in fact a landowner who has successfully adapted himself to capitalist enterprise, and this paradox is typical of his whole character. He denounces foreign capital in the Upper House, but negotiates with foreign capital when it suits him. He is religious, but acknowledges that religion has little relevance in practical affairs. He subscribes to the primacy of blue blood, yet his motto, 'property and education', is wholly middle class. Consider too the Imperial Army, one of the most respected institutions of the Monarchy. Musil lavishes affection upon General Stumm von Bordwehr as a person, but the General's career casts a dubious light on the military. And in his account of Hans Sepp's officers, Musil corrects the familiar impression that the Army was one of the two pillars of the Empire, for the officers *he* describes are indifferent to the dynasty and the official ideology. Either they are disaffected with military life or they long for a merger with the German Reich, so that the military budget may at last do justice to their requirements. Finally, Emperor Franz Joseph I himself makes a fleeting, but significant, appearance in the pages of the novel. Diotima's husband, Sektionsrat Tuzzi, relates an approach to the Emperor in connection with the *Parallelaktion*:

> The Minister sounded out His Majesty during the last audience as to what public proclamations on the occasion of the Jubilee would in the event meet with His Majesty's approval, above all, how well disposed His Majesty felt towards the plan (anticipating the tendency of the age) to accept the leadership of an international pacifist campaign ... But His Gracious Majesty in His renowned and illustrious conscientiousness and reserve, he went on, declined immediately with the sharp retort (p. 195)

And after this brilliant re-creation of bureaucratic elegance and courtly etiquette, the reader awaits the pronouncement of the object of such veneration—only to read : ' "Ah, i mag mi net vordrängen lassen." ' (' "Tut, I don't like being made to steal the limelight." ') The bathos of the Viennese dialect highlights the disparity between the majesty of the office and the homely personality that fills it—but not to Franz Joseph's discredit. There is a subtle variation of the idiom *i mag mi net vordrängen* to *i mag mi net vordrängen lassen*, which precisely illustrates the relationship between the Emperor and his advisers. Where Musil is ironically affectionate, Roth's attitude in a similar context was far more sentimental. Kraus, on the other hand, pilloried in *Die letzten Tage der Menschheit* the hypocrisy, stupidity and meanness which he believed lay beneath Franz Joseph's mask of long-suffering and dedication to duty.

It is possible to criticise Musil's re-creation of the political and cultural life of the Monarchy in its last years on the grounds of bias and distortion. It might be objected, for instance, that the majority of Imperial officers were nothing if not *kaisertreu* (though Musil distinguishes between public poses and private conviction in this respect), or that he neglects the contribution to European culture of such figures as Freud, Loos, Hofmann, Mahler, Schoenberg, Klimt or Schiele. These were 'outsiders' in their day but, for all that, products of *fin de siècle* Vienna. Musil might also be accused of underestimating or belittling the strength and value of nationalism. However, the novelist's concern is not with documentary exactitude but with 'das geistig-Typische . . . das Gespenstische des Geschehens', ('the temper of the age . . . the phantom-like nature of events').[37] (Karl Kraus wrote during the War : 'In such cases one cannot apply mathematical precision but only apocalyptic exactitude.'[38]) Incompleteness or distortion is a legitimate feature of the comic or satirical vision, whereby it conveys a fresh insight into historical realities. Musil's novel is not intended to be a substitute for objective historical analysis : rather, he seeks to elucidate the wider implications of certain historical developments and to distil something of the atmosphere of the age.

'Gently ironic' : such was Musil's own description of his attitude towards the Empire as expressed in his novel. The mellow glow of his irony may be contrasted with the asperity of Karl Kraus's satire. Musil's criticism is mitigated by his paradoxical affection for this 'most progressive' of European states, and his treatment of such figures as Feuermaul or Meingast, Diotima or Arnheim, is content to emphasise their absurdity. He barely implies the corollary of evil, pain and destruction which Kraus so devastatingly adduced. The nature of Musil's purpose accords the philosophical precedence over the political. Whereas Kraus was motivated by an outraged conscience and burning compassion, Musil is more analytic, tolerant and detached.

Kakanien and the *Parallelaktion* recede in importance after the end of the first book of *Der Mann ohne Eigenschaften*. The narrative interest concentrates increasingly on the relationship between Ulrich and Agathe. While Ulrich is still involved with Leinsdorf's campaign, however, he seizes the opportunity to lay down his own guide lines for transcending the débâcle of contemporary culture, thus taking up an important theme of Musil's essays. What Ulrich advocates in his 'World Secretariat for Exactitude and Spirit' is precisely that synthesis of *Verstand* and *Seele*, that discipline of 'art, ethics and mysticism', which Musil had first suggested in 'Das hilflose Europa'. Ulrich posits only two phases of cognition : knowledge (*Wissen*) and the intuitive anticipation of knowledge (*Ahnen*). All that lies in between—the 'certainties' which his contemporaries cherish—is a token of credulous ignorance. Ulrich's notion of the secretariat embodies his mathematical principle of the 'partial solution', of successive stages on the road to true knowledge. He envisages the quest for truth in the light of the history of science, where theories and known facts have constantly been superseded by fresh theories and new facts, that men might gradually draw nearer the truth. No one individual can achieve the final goal, just as no one system holds the key : the process is a collective effort, each individual contribution adding to the corpus of experience. Ulrich's conception of human progress is thus consistent with the emphasis on the provisional and the possible that he associates with the *Möglichkeitssinn*. Its precondition is the synthesis of two disciplines generally held to be mutually exclusive :

> The one attitude is content to be precise and sticks to the facts; the other is not content with that, but always considers the whole and deduces its knowledge from so-called great eternal truths. The one is thereby more successful, the other more comprehensive and majestic. Clearly, a pessimist could say that the results of the one approach were worthless and those of the other approach just not true. For on the Day of Judgement, when the works of men shall be weighed in the balance, what use will three papers on formic acid be—or thirty, for that matter? Conversely, what can one know about the Day of Judgement if one does not even know what can become of formic acid by that time? ! (p. 248)

In Musil's usage such terms as 'soul', 'mysticism' or the 'Day of Judgement' are devoid of transcendental connotations. His is an attempt to find an entirely immanent solution to the problem of the gulf between 'realism' (our tendency to accept the world we perceive with our senses and can articulate rationally as the only knowable, and therefore sole, reality) and our awareness that the world we 'know' is after all an 'interpretation'. It is an attempt to bridge the gap between empiricism and the cult of *Innerlichkeit* which had reft the German intellectual tradition in the nineteenth century.

Der Mann ohne Eigenschaften did not progress as far as August 1914, as was originally planned. Thus the novel does not evoke the elation and communal unity which moved Musil so intensely in the first days of the War. One wonders, however, if this experience does not impinge indirectly upon the portrayal of the mystical union enjoyed by Ulrich and Agathe. I do not wish to suggest that this mystical relationship is a direct transposition of Musil's political experience. Moreover, the personal relationship between the hero and his sister is explored more deeply, more exhaustively and above all more creatively than the political emotion. Again, the novel invokes religious and philosophical overtones in a manner barely implied by the description of national unity. Yet the nature of the two experiences is undoubtedly analogous : the escape from individuation; the intensification of one's awareness of self and the merging of the self with a greater whole; the overcoming of separation in space and succession in time; and the consummation of an emotion which the concept 'love' can only approximate. The path which Ulrich and Agathe will tread is described as one 'which in some ways was related to the world of those possessed by God . . .' (p. 761). For all its immanence, the quality of the experience is seen to be religious, it is 'mysticism in broad daylight'. Similarly, Musil called the wartime patriotic feeling a 'religious' or 'mystic' experience. There is a common denominator : the private and the national experience share a detachment from everyday life, the receding of ordinary cares and concerns, and a sense of well-being arising from disinterestedness.

The quasi-mystical mood of August 1914 was shortlived. It was followed by disenchantment—though for Musil its validity was never questioned as a consequence of what followed. Now the course which Ulrich's relationship with his sister was to take cannot be ascertained with certainty because the novel remained unfinished and we lack a definitive text. Musil's first editor, Adolf Frisé, supplied a conclusion with the aid of certain drafts and notes, according to which the relationship apparently tips over into incest and then breaks up. Frisé's interpretation of the manuscripts has been heavily criticised, in particular by Ernst Kaiser,[39] who maintains that towards the end of his life Musil was reluctant to continue the novel beyond the mystical culmination. Thereby, however, Musil surely betrayed the logic of his original scheme. Perpetual mystical communion (Ulrich at one point conjures up the image of a 'permanent vacation' from everyday reality) would be inconsistent with the theory of essayism, of the partial solution. It is also inadequate in its one-sidedness, in its utopian exclusion of evil (p. 1579). Moreover, the 'journey to the margins of possibility' is described by Ulrich himself—in a comparison echoing the 'imaginary numbers' of *Törless*—as

> a borderline case ... of limited and special validity, recalling the freedom with which mathematics sometimes makes use of the absurd to attain the truth. (p. 761)

If one takes this to mean that the truth lies beyond, rather than in, the mystical experiment, the experience is here seen as partial and provisional. And Musil's notes suggest a progression from the 'utopia' of the quasi-mystical union to a utopia 'of the inductive way of thought', that is, to the abjuring of social withdrawal.

The mystical experiment is sometimes presented as Ulrich's escape from the intolerable isolation and detachment imposed upon him by his critical insight into conventional values, and by his *Möglichkeitssinn*. His faith in the eventual triumph of the mathematical mind proves cold comfort amid the miasma of modern culture. Even though it would mean abandoning his principles, Ulrich is momentarily tempted to accept Arnheim's offer of a post in his commercial empire, such is the loneliness of the 'man without qualities'. And at the beginning of his relationship with Agathe we read:

> he sometimes longed to be involved in events, as though in a wrestling match, even if they were senseless or criminal, as long as they were authentic. Definitive, without the constant provisional quality that they have when a man remains detached from his own experience. (p. 738)

His relationship with Agathe carries escapist overtones and suggests that the real problems are being evaded, rather than tackled. This does not diminish the intrinsic value of their experience, but it limits its implication. Indeed, Frank Trommler relates all Ulrich's inconsistencies and failures to the fact that Musil treats his hero ironically throughout: the relationship with Agathe was never designed to represent more than another unsuccessful attempt to find a solution. This attempt fails as much as the effort to achieve something positive within the framework of the *Parallelaktion*.[40]

Given the analogy between the communion of the lovers and the national mood of August 1914, we have further grounds for

supposing that the mystical relationship was necessarily designed
to be something less than definitive. The religious feeling of the
first few days of the War was soon dissipated; it was extraordinary and short-lived; and despite the initial sense of liberation, the War remained—in cultural terms—an escape from an
intolerable peace, the collapse of European civilisation. Ulrich,
it is true, is not implicated in that decay as are his contemporaries : but is not his lonely detachment as intolerable in its own
way as their delusion, frustration and impotence? Both the head-
long rush into war and Ulrich's incestuous love figure as escapes
into religious experience, followed by a disastrous lapse into
everyday reality. The problem of the novel's dénouement must
remain open in the absence of a definitive text; the evidence
indicates, however, that if Kaiser is right in assuming that Ulrich
achieves in his mystical love for Agathe not merely another partial
solution but some ultimate truth, Musil thereby undertook a
major revision of the whole conception of his novel, not merely a
change of plot.

The element of escapism in the original scheme brings to mind
a similar emotion in Törless. He too occasionally wearies of his
intellectual superiority and physical passivity, and acknowledges
that his attitude is merely a pose, a 'game' to while away his
boredom. At such moments he envies his classmates who have
surrendered to their subterranean impulse :

> Then he would long to feel something definite at last; firm
> needs which distinguished between good and bad, the useful and
> the useless; to know that he was making a choice, even a wrong
> one—better that than assimilating everything in a hyper-
> receptive manner.[41]

The implications of 'even a wrong one', like those of Ulrich's
'even if they were senseless or criminal', are significant. If the
strain of excessive detachment threatens to bring about Törless's
surrender to the 'dark gods', does not Ulrich's recourse to
'mysticism' appear as simply the other side of the medal? And
do we not find a parallel, tentative though it may be, in Musil's
own curious respect for the energy, courage and determination
of the Fascist leaders?

The largely non-literary analysis to which I have subjected
Der Mann ohne Eigenschaften does not, I believe, violate its

aesthetic integrity. At the beginning of the chapter I wrote that Musil explained, where Kafka or Trakl articulated their private nightmares—and because this attempted explanation is fundamental to the novel, the critic is justified in examining the author's treatment of the historical background, and in discussing the validity of some of his arguments in non-aesthetic terms. Musil's endeavour to 'explain' leads him on occasion into a 'prosy' seriousness, and—in the later sections of the novel—to a concern which ultimately vitiates the total achievement. There, in the dialogues between Ulrich and Agathe, the novelist abandons the traditional interests of narrative fiction and concentrates upon the process of thinking, the activity of consciousness. In doing so, he tries to discover common ground between literature and psychology : but the attempt—or the very endeavour—meets with only limited success. As Heine remarked of Jean Paul, it is more a question of cerebration than of ideas. The real achievement of the novel lies in the earlier chapters, in the comedy of manners, in the critique of European culture, in the evocation of the aura of Kakanien.

9

Karl Kraus: The Absolute Satirist

Weisser Hohepriester der Wahrheit,
Kristallne Stimme, in der Gottes eisiger Odem wohnt,
Zürnender Magier,
Dem unter flammendem Mantel der blaue Panzer des Kriegers
klirrt.*

Georg Trakl

Satire is peculiarly prone to misinterpretation in one or other
of two ways: through excessive emphasis on its material or
through excessive emphasis on its literary form. The 'referential'
mode of satire and its 'imaginative' mode[1] are too interdependent
to be considered in mutual exclusion, as a recent critic[2] of Karl
Kraus's work warned. The following chapter does not pretend to
offer a balanced critical assessment of Kraus's oeuvre, for it is
confined to a specific aspect of his satire, his response to developments in national politics from 1914 to his death in 1936.
The nature and implications of that response are explored in
non-aesthetic terms, as a contribution to our understanding of the
'referential' mode of Kraus's work. Moreover, the treatment of
the 'referential' mode is itself selective. I must here concentrate
on the more significant events and the satirical response which
these evoke; I will not attempt to present a comprehensive picture
of Kraus's political writing in the two decades under review.
Frank Field has already subjected the whole of Kraus's periodical
Die Fackel to a thorough and perceptive political analysis.[3] The
present chapter, by neglecting to a large extent the historical
background and by examining certain developments in detail,

* White high-priest of truth,/Crystal voice wherein dwells God's icy
breath/Wrathful sorcerer/Beneath whose fiery mantle the warrior's blue
armour rings.

adopts an approach which Dr Field eschewed in his wider-ranging work. As a historian, he has looked at Vienna through the eyes of Karl Kraus and assessed the objective validity of Kraus's historical vision. I shall be more concerned with the subjective elements in that vision and with relating it to an intellectual tradition. A final caveat : Edward Timms has argued convincingly[4] that the figure of the Satirist which speaks through-out the pages of *Die Fackel* is not merely a mouth-piece for Kraus's personal feelings and convictions, but an imaginatively created literary persona, a satirically slanted projection of selected aspects of the author's personality. Whenever the following essay refers to 'Kraus' or to the 'satirist', the reference is to this persona —and is based on Kraus's public statements in his periodical and in his dramatic works. Any attempt to relate the ideas presented by the 'Satirist' more closely to Kraus's own thoughts must await the publication of Kraus's private papers and correspondence.

Kraus's political writing is the most extensive and the most sus-tained literary response to political developments among the Austrian writers of his time. It is the War, and the aftermath of war, which awaken—if at all—a political awareness in his con-temporaries. Kraus, however, from the first issues of *Die Fackel* in 1899, remained—among other things—a political observer. Up to about 1902 *Die Fackel* attacked incompetence, corrup-tion and nepotism in the universities, in the theatre, in the Press and in public services. In these early years Kraus still believed in his ability to remedy abuses and inefficiency through a ruth-less polemic that did not hesitate to 'name names'. Subsequently his conception of the satirist's task became more differentiated and more subtle. No longer limiting his function to the practical amelioration of society, he judged it to lie more in exposing the fundamental malaise of a civilisation and in bearing witness to the continuing validity of absolute values in a world which had apparently abandoned them. As his faith in the immediate effec-tiveness of satire diminished, so too the perspective of his satire broadened. While his themes grew more circumscribed, his analysis became more penetrating. His vision of language as a token of ethical integrity was more clearly focused, his satire be-came ever more imbued with 'aesthetic' values. Yet Kraus re-mained a 'political' writer, even when his interests seemed marginal or esoteric—because his conception of 'aestheticism' differed from the conventional meaning of the word. In 1914 his social and moral values, though never codified, though never openly linked with a political party, indicated nevertheless a political position more definitely partisan than he acknowledged.

One of the characteristic themes of Kraus's satire before the War is his campaign against the Press. He concedes that there is a basic demand for information in the modern world which the Press was originally designed to meet. What he criticises is the degeneration of the Press into a social institution of immense influence, both direct and indirect. The Press, he sees, is in effect a commercial enterprise which exists to make a profit for its owners. Yet this is the last motive which the Press itself will publicly recognise. On the contrary, newspapers have successfully sold themselves to the public as organs of Enlightenment and pillars of Culture. Kraus finds that the 'enlightenment' is selected and distorted to defend the vested interests of editors and proprietors and the social class they represent; the 'culture' content is intended to distract the readers' attention from the true nature of the Press, it again represents a class interest and, as illustrated in the *feuilleton*, it is shallow, facile and degenerate. Thus the Press neither edifies nor informs, although it persuades the public that it has a duty to do both. The twin prongs of Kraus's satire are directed at the Press's venality and hypocrisy. He criticises a style of reporting that is impressionistic, selective and sententious, instead of factual and objective. He criticises the fatuous trivialities of the 'cultural' sections. He attacks the covert connections between the Press and industry or commerce on the one hand, and between Press and government on the other. He pillories the dependence of newspapers upon advertising revenue, which creates an invidious editorial respect for the advertisers, actual or prospective, and is instrumental in blurring the distinction between 'news' and promotional material. Finally, Kraus satirises repeatedly the literary style of the Press, its insensitivity towards linguistic values, its ignorance of grammar, its perpetual clichés. Out of its own mouth it stands condemned, since this neglect of language connotes for Kraus the moral corruption upon which the Press as an institution is built.

Kraus considers the worst—because most pretentious—offender to be Vienna's leading 'serious' daily, the *Neue Freie Presse*. Just as he treats Hermann Bahr as a symbol rather than as an individual manifestation of the commercialisation of artistic

values, so too the *Neue Freie Presse*, together with its editor
Moriz Benedikt and its often distinguished contributors, is
elevated into a symbol of the hypocrisy and venality of the
Viennese Press in general. This particular newspaper proclaimed
itself to be the spokesman and champion of 'liberalism', an heir
to the sacred principles of 1848, the year of its foundation.
However, it had not escaped the decay of liberalism which
occurred in Germany and Austria in the latter half of the nineteenth century. Austria had not had a liberal government since
1879 and as a political party the liberals had ceased to be of any
importance. On the other hand, as the satirist realised, liberalism
as an ideology and way of life survived and flourished among the
Viennese bourgeoisie. Schnitzler, reflecting on the corruption
of the word 'liberalism', once compared its original meaning with
its present overtones. Previously—in 1848, for example—it
had meant 'the effort to liberate men in every sphere (to protect
them from the encroachments of those in authority, to allow
each man to seek his own salvation etc.)...'[5] Nowadays,
Schnitzler continued, the use of the word led 'directly to a
certain cheap, shallow, even sentimental attitude to life and
to the use of jargon and clichés...'[6] Kraus characteristically
added a moral dimension to Schnitzler's assessment. The satirist
was indifferent to the pristine values of liberalism: he saw
only the ideology of Benedikt and his readers—their glib faith
in progress and science, their repressive morality in sexual matters,
the ethic of industriousness, their commitment to a ruthless
economic policy, and their profession of an arbitrarily defined
'freedom' or 'democracy' whenever their social or economic
interests seemed to be threatened. Kraus perceived that the
façade of high principle concealed a soul-destroying materialism,
a patent lack of regard for anything but status and profit, and—
in their philosophy of progress—a stupidity and naivety that
verged on presumption. He expressed the link between the
ideology of liberalism and the evils of capitalism, and again the
political decline of Austria-Hungary, in an aphorism which
relates the 1848 Revolution to Austria's defeat at the hands of
Prussia in 1866 and to the economic collapse of 1873 :

> Austrian liberalism embraces with the same affection the old
> 'forty-eighters' and the veterans of '73. The result was on average
> the old contemptibles of '66.[7]

In Germany the corruption of liberalism took a more overtly political form in the National Liberals who supported Bismarck and later Wilhelm II, in return for the entrenchment and protection of their economic interests. In Austria the *Neue Freie Presse* (and the German-speaking liberal bourgeoisie) supported the government's refusal materially to amend the constitution in order to accommodate the demands of the Imperial peoples.

The values which Kraus felt to have been betrayed by the liberal ideology of a substantial section of the Viennese bourgeoisie and of its newspapers were *Natur* and *Geist*—or, put less abstractly, a respect for the mystery and majesty of the natural world, and for the spontaneous emotional development of the individual; and a devotion to things of the mind, to Art, to the classical ideal of *Bildung*.* Kraus believed that the Press had numbed the moral and intellectual alertness of its readers through its confusion of poetry and profit, and its cultivation of the cliché. Press reports, with their prefabricated reactions and instant sentiment, had gradually deprived the public of their ability to think for themselves and fully to imagine the scene or event conveyed by hackneyed phrases. The 'poverty of imagination' induced by an irresponsible Press meant that the average reader could no longer imaginatively re-create and re-live the experience distilled into the living word. Consequently the middle class had succumbed to indifference and lethargy in the face of reports of human suffering.

The Press became dangerous when the legitimate function of newspapers, the communication of factual news, was subordinated to a more ambitious aim incompatible with the capitalist

---

* Walter Benjamin once drew a parallel between Kraus and Stifter in their feeling for nature. The comparison between two such different literary *personae* seems far-fetched—until one considers Kraus's passages on animals, plants and children. Benjamin argued that in Kraus we still hear an echo of Stifter's identification of the natural law and the moral imperative. Both writers profess that secularised faith which transforms creation into a church and seeks in nature a metaphysical substitute for religion. (See the essay 'Karl Kraus' in *Illumination*, ed. Siegfried Unseld, Frankfurt a.M., 1961.) But whereas Stifter could glorify the majesty and wonder of creation and even make human life subordinate to it, Kraus laments the despoiling and ravaging of nature by economic man and himself becomes the agent of an avenging deity. Benjamin's critical analysis of Kraus's satire in its historical context is often illuminating; and it is stimulating even when his argument grows questionable.

basis of the newspaper industry. ('Capitalism' is not Kraus's own
terminology; but the economic attitude he describes is normally
described under this heading. The satirist avoids using the
specific terminology because it might imply his support for an
economic or political theory, as distinct from an ethical attitude.)
The Press became a powerful social institution—at the price of
its integrity and independence. Kraus saw a similar degeneration
in the field of technological progress. Here the original aim—to
render man's life less arduous and dangerous—had ceded to a
foolhardy race in which progress had either become an end in
itself or was exploited for commercial gain. Technological
advance had extorted too high a price from the human spirit in
terms of intellectual effort; men had lost the capacity to control
their own inventions :

> We were sufficiently complicated to build the machine and we
> are too primitive to let ourselves be served by it. We are con-
> ducting international traffic along narrow-gauge mental railways.[8]

The de-humanising process of a modern technological civilisation
was having a disastrous impact on human life. To Kraus, the
boasts accompanying the launching of the *Titanic*, and the
disaster that followed, were a terrible reminder of man's hybris
in deeming himself the master of his natural environment. The
satirist felt that modern man was incapable of keeping pace
morally with his intellectual achievements. (It was from a similar
assumption that Musil evolved his idea of the *Möglichkeitssinn*
and of the 'partial solution'.)

Kraus was not, of course, alone in his witness, as a circle of
devoted friends and disciples shows. Round about 1912 he was
drawn to a small group of Austrian aristocrats, in particular
Sidonie Nádherný von Borutin and her circle, whose way of life
bespoke a deep respect for the values he himself cherished.[9]
This *rapprochement* with aristocratic friends and audiences highlights Kraus's essentially 'conservative' sympathies in the years
1912 to 1914, and shows that his moral and social criticism
culminates in the acknowledgement of what is clearly a right-wing
political affiliation. An undercurrent of nostalgia for a pre-
capitalist, pre-liberal era is discernible in several essays during
these last two years of peace. In 'Nestroy und die Nachwelt'
(May 1912) Kraus expresses his admiration for the conservatism

of one who fought against the rule of the banal and distrusted the democratic phrase-mongers of 1848 :

> The artist takes sides so little that he sides with the lies of tradi-
> tion against the truth of deceit. Nestroy knows where the danger
> lies. He sees that knowledge brings with it the loss of faith.
> Already he can hear the ravens of freedom, black with printer's
> ink. And instead of reproaching religion with its priests, he
> prefers to reproach the enlightenment with its journalists and
> progress with its quacks.[10]

With satirical hyperbole, Kraus relates the cultural decline of Austria in recent decades to the march of democracy, and con-trasts contemporary culture with that of the *Vormärz* :

> A decade of phrase-mongering bondage has left more histrionic
> trash in the minds of the people than a century of absolutism,
> with the important distinction that creativity was encouraged
> by prohibitions as much as it is now crippled by leading
> articles.[11]

(Kraus knew full well that the harrying of Grillparzer by the Imperial censor and police had impaired the dramatist's capacity for creative work : the polemical exaggeration stresses Kraus's distaste for the 'freedom' purveyed by the *Neue Freie Presse* and defended by its subscribers.) It is therefore scarcely surprising that Kraus should write elsewhere 'that politically I have not even progressed as far as the French Revolution . . .'[12] And he cited the *Heiligenkreuzerhof*, a peaceful Barock square in the heart of Vienna, as a symbol of the Austrian culture to which *he* owed allegiance. His boyhood memories of the last great years of the Burgtheater belonged to the same pattern. As Leopold Liegler points out,[13] Kraus was a member of the generation born in the 1870s who experienced the last remnants of a once glorious culture, before these were finally swept away by a new era. In an attempt to protect a small enclave from the tide of positivism, of 'enlightenment' and intellectualism, Kraus appealed to the authoritarian tradition of Church and State, irrespective of the content of religious faith and the object of political obedience. Ultimately he was to conclude that in the Viennese 'confusion of values' there was only one incorruptible, unassailable, totally reliable authority : the authority of the German language.

Between 1912 and 1914, however, his political and cultural sympathies anticipated Hofmannsthal's conservative solution to the dilemmas of the postwar world. Before the War, Kraus's recourse to traditional authorities represented an alternative that was perhaps still possible. After the War, on the other hand, Hofmannsthal's conservatism was plainly anachronistic.

Kraus's prewar conservatism reached its apogee in the essay 'Franz Ferdinand und die Talente' of July 1914. Here the satirist interpreted the fateful assassination at Sarajevo as the responsibility of those sinister forces of 'enlightenment' and 'progress', who had feared the Archduke and could now barely disguise their relief at his death. Kraus respected Franz Ferdinand precisely because he was illiberal and reactionary and because, like Kraus himself, he set no store by popularity. (Bahr, it will be recalled, admired Franz Ferdinand's 'progressive' attitude.) Progress, Culture, the Press : these were the shadows which Kraus distinguished behind the nationalist assassins. He mourned the Archduke's passing because with him had died the last hope of those who dreamed of restoring a measure of order and discipline in the 'Austrian research institute for world destruction'.[14] And he presented Franz Ferdinand as the representative and harbinger of an older Austria of the *Vormärz*. It would be egregious to comment upon the idealised nature of his portrait of Franz Ferdinand. More important is Kraus's attraction to the Archduke's manly, militaristic qualities—an attraction foreshadowed in slightly earlier essays. An essay dated August 1912 had suggested that the military ethos of individual gallantry, discipline and determination might help to cauterise the festering wound of the age :

Let the sword which cuts to the quick take precedence over the pen which hesitates.[15]

Four months later Kraus again queried whether war might not renew contemporary culture.[16] Yet at the same period he wrote that no culture could survive war—it would simply hasten its inevitable end. For the autumn of 1912 had brought home to him the horror of the Balkan wars and of their journalistic exploitation. His savage indictment of Wilhelm II in October 1908 had already demonstrated that chauvinistic militarism in the service of national aggrandisement was totally unacceptable to him. After the War Kraus explained through the *Nörgler* (the carping critic) in *Die letzten Tage der Menschheit* that his pre-dilection for the military spirit was due partly to an illusion of war as a chivalrous combat between professionals, and partly to the belief that the banality and moral confusion of the modern age could be countered by militarist virtues. Notwithstanding the moral impulse behind his sympathies, Kraus cannot entirely escape a charge of indiscretion—or at worst of irresponsibility. In Germany writers such as Lagarde or Langbehn had advocated imperialist expansion—for purely idealistic motives, in an attempt to save Wilhelminian Germany from moral and cultural decay. In the Austrian context of the time, an undiscriminating reader must readily have associated Kraus's sentiments with those of the advocates of a preventive war against Serbia or Italy—generals and politicians who thought only of military and political advan-tage. The most outspoken of these was Hötzendorf (Chief of the General Staff); Franz Ferdinand was prepared for a preventive war with Italy, though not with Serbia; the liberal politican, Josef Redlich, also belonged to the war party, and in his diary records similar feelings among certain aristocratic circles.

The untenability of Kraus's position is illustrated by the notorious piece referring to Gerhart Hauptmann's skirmish with nationalist and militarist groups in the summer of 1913. Hauptmann, one of the leading German dramatists of the time, was commissioned by the Breslau Town Council to write a *Festspiel* in commemoration of the War of Liberation against Napoleon. He seized the opportunity to incorporate in the work itself a protest against war and jingoism. The work earned the disapproval of the bellicose Crown Prince, whereupon a storm of controversy burst upon the German Press. Liberal (Jewish) news-papers took up Hauptmann's case against a 'reactionary' censor-ship. Kraus for his part criticised the playwright for allying himself with politicians and liberal intellectuals 'with whom everything was upright and as straight as a die—except their noses',[17] and accused him of breaking faith with his patrons, who justifiably expected patriotic verse. Since Hauptmann had not had the integrity to decline such a degrading commission, Kraus argued, he should at least have delivered the goods as ordered. 'Ex-Servicemen's clubs, which when all is said and done have more right to exist than clubs for journalists, veterans who are perhaps more honourable than newspaper reviewers'[18]—they are right to protest against Hauptmann's 'progressive' piping when they are calling the tune. This piece clearly contains a good deal of satirical overstatement : but again the hyperbole is indicative of Kraus's distaste for the liberal intelligentsia. And the political effect of a piece like this is to imply support for the forces of reaction.

In July 1914 Kraus wrote that if one were to insist on attaching a political label to his views, the most appropriate designation might be 'right-wing radical'. His attacks on the Austrian establishment—notably in 'Prozess Friedjung' (December 1909) and after the death of Franz Ferdinand, when there was barely concealed satisfaction in Court circles at the elimination of the Heir Apparent—reveal that the satirist's position was not simply that of a conservative whose interest lay in preserving the status quo. The element of radicalism suggested by his own epithet evokes the concept of the 'conservative revolution', the values of which are those of a status quo ante. Kraus's views were intimated rather than argued. Nevertheless, in his own unique way, he shared the characteristic features of this particular form of conservatism : contempt for the materialism of bourgeois civilisation; hostility towards liberalism and democracy (which covered a multitude of abuses and failings in a fairly indiscriminate fashion); hatred of a decadent intelligentsia and their clichés; criticism of the Hegelian concept of the State; the opposition of *Kultur* and *Zivilisation*; and a tendency to identify the ills of modern society with some form of pernicious Jewish influence. The satirist's conservatism was modified by wartime developments and by his political realism in the postwar years, but it was never completely dissipated. At a critical juncture towards the end of his life, it was to reappear with renewed vigour.

As early as 1908 Kraus warned his public that the crisis of European civilisation might erupt into a catastrophic war.[19] He perceived the political implications of the 'confusion' and 'corruption' of values more clearly and more urgently than the majority of contemporary Viennese writers. Yet war, when it came, found him unprepared; over a year was to elapse before he finally resumed his satirical mission. As he maintained at several stages in his career, it was a shattering experience to discover that his worst fears, his most pungent satire, had been overtaken by reality, and his hyperbole outwitted by fact. In the summer of 1914 he was almost alone among Austrian writers in refusing to join in the chorus of public acclaim for the War. In November 1914 and again in February 1915 he tried to articulate his feelings and to explain his position; but not until October 1915 did his attitude harden into one of determined—and public —opposition to the War. Initially his public statements were made in order to forestall misunderstanding, to indicate that his 'silence' did not mean that he concurred in what was happening. Later, however, in the summer of 1915, his faith in his satirical mission was restored. In the early months of the War Kraus appears to have undergone a phase of paralysing doubt : he was assailed less by an ambivalence towards the War itself (though, in consequence of his respect for military virtues before the War, something of this ambiguity may have influenced him in the first weeks[20])—than by a conviction that satire had become irrelevant in what was an unprecedented situation. Before the War his work had been informed by the belief that the satirist had a duty to describe, illuminate and indict a corrupt and degenerate world, thereby testifying to the purity and intransigence of the moral imagination. Now, the tumult of war threatened to silence the voice of satire. At a basic level, Kraus felt that propaganda and popular enthusiasm had bludgeoned his audience's sensibility into a state of indifference and unreceptiveness, and that the satirist's testimony would find no echo. His first public statement[21] related the *Phantasienot* induced by the prewar Press to the outbreak of war itself, pointing out that if those who responded to or employed propaganda clichés were capable of translating them into a vision of the suffering and destruction they connoted, then war might never have been declared. (In fact, inflammatory articles in the Austro-German bourgeois Press after Sarajevo had contributed significantly to the transformation of the public mood from apathy or relief to bellicose resentment.) In the current situation, he felt that his satire would fall on deaf ears. The argument is not wholly convincing, in that Kraus had never before been deterred by the obtuseness of his public. Perhaps it betrayed his bewilderment at the enthusiasm with which war had been greeted.

At a more fundamental level, however, Kraus was faced with the problem of *Bewältigung*, of assimilating *and* re-creating in satirical form the folly of war. The horrendous events of the time, the shameless exploitation of the popular mood by journalists and literati who polluted the language in which Kraus too had to write, the spectacle of gross incompetence and wholesale corruption remaining unrequited—all this appeared at first to deny the propriety of satire and to undermine Kraus's capacity to articulate and formulate his reaction. The sheer intensity of his feeling seemed to sap the satirist's will to re-create his sense of outrage and compassion. Silence alone seemed to offer a means of protest at a time when to the public *deeds* alone were relevant. By February 1915, however, Kraus had modified his attitude; in the meantime he had realised that the wartime situation was not as unprecedented as he once felt. Now that the initial flood of patriotism had subsided, the War on the home front could be seen as an extension and exacerbation of the evils of peacetime. Kraus's prewar satire remained pertinent, for his victims were still in positions of power and influence. The transition from a repetition of satire written before 1914 to the writing of fresh satire directly related to the War was finally achieved in the autumn of 1915. With the essay 'Schweigen, Wort und Tat' of 30 October he reaffirmed his faith in the power of the satirical word. As is always the case in Kraus's work, literary creation is synonymous with *Geist*, with *Gedanke,* with commitment to a moral principle. (It was this I had in mind when I referred earlier to Kraus's 'aestheticism'.) His newfound confidence in his satirical mission implies therefore a renewed determination to proclaim the independence of the moral will in defiance of any physical or psychological pressures that might be brought to bear upon it. The voice of his satire is the voice of humanity and morality, speaking with all the authority of the German idealist tradition. In Kraus's work that tradition confronts and engages the social world instead of withdrawing from it.

Paul Schick recently published a diary entry indicating that in March 1915 Kraus was engaged upon an unofficial diplomatic mission in Italy.[22] The details of this visit are not known, although it plainly took place in the context of the German-Austrian campaign to keep Italy neutral. Schick suggests that Kraus's efforts were directed at influencing public figures in Italy to this end.[23] This mission clearly has a bearing on any discussion of the satirist's reticence during the first year of the War, but its precise significance cannot be established until further evidence has emerged. The decisive factor remains

Kraus's doubt with regard to the function and propriety of satire —and it is this factor which reappeared twenty years later, when Kraus again faced a cataclysmic political development.

In October 1915 Kraus launched his own unremitting offensive against the Austrian hinterland. The emphasis of *Die Fackel* lies less on specific events, atrocities and abuses than on the reasons for their being committed and tolerated : Kraus explained as well as attacked. He interpreted the War as an extension of the policies pursued by a materialist civilisation and as the culmination of the activities of a venal and irresponsible Press. Again and again Kraus took up the theme of *Phantasiearmut*, the blunted sensibility of his contemporaries, which blinded them to the real experience behind the language they used so glibly. (Hermann Broch was to ask : 'Are we mad, that we have not been driven mad ?'[24]) A future generation would, he claimed, learn more about the War from the fact that an actress's announcement—on stage—of 40,000 Russian casualties was greeted with thunderous applause, than from any political or military historian. To treat this defective imagination in absolute terms, as Kraus does, is scarcely a valid criterion for judging human behaviour in general: but it is highly effective as a satirical weapon, as a means of underlining the vicious vacuity of wartime editorials, speeches and propaganda *feuilletons*. Kraus was an early critic of the way in which the communication media could be used to manipulate the minds of the public—and nowhere was this criticism more justified than during the War. The Press had prepared its readers for war and had urged them on with banner headlines and emotional appeals; when hostilities broke out, it shielded its readers from a full realisation of the horrors they were perpetrating against their fellow-men. Through lies and distortions the Press could provoke a response from the enemy, or even from its own side, a response which would match the enormity of the written word. Both directly and indirectly the Press had thus fanned and fed the flames of war.

Kraus's principal target was the Viennese bourgeois Press, above all the *Neue Freie Presse* : Benedikt's jingoism provided *Die Fackel* with much material. However, the role of the Press was not confined to editorials. Kraus saw that the dubious style and manner of reporting news, which had already earned his contempt in peacetime, grew to impious proportions when its subjects were pain, mutilation and death. In the 'eye-witness'

reports of war-correspondents such as Roda-Roda or Alice
Schalek, no less than in Benedikt's malignant delight that the
corpses of hundreds of Italian sailors would by then be feeding
the fishes of the Adriatic; in the newsreels and the news-agency
bulletins, no less than in the sudden chauvinism of Hauptmann,
Dehmel, Bahr or Hofmannsthal, Kraus detected a deliberate
cloaking and evasion of reality. War was reduced to an impressionistic *feuilleton*, full of fatuous and irrelevant details. Pain and
death were subject to indecent scrutiny by 'newshounds' tracking
down a story. Horror was pillaged by intellectual scavengers.
Their lack of literary talent was matched only by their dearth
of compassion. That literati dared to profit by emulating or
describing emotions and experiences utterly foreign to them,
sealed the fate of culture at the hands of commerce. Kraus
argued that his society had betrayed both its cultural tradition—
and its very humanity. This society caused the few survivors
of a disastrous battle to reconstruct—with appropriate embellish-
ment and romantic trimmings—their terrible experience *in the
theatre*, for the delight of a bourgeois audience, without once
asking itself what it might have meant to those men to relive
their experiences. And by the same token, this society not only
tolerated but positively acclaimed a parody of Goethe's lyric
'Über allen Gipfeln'—in praise of U-boat warfare. As swords
were dipped in ink, so too pens were dipped in blood : mankind
hung crucified, while its executioners divided the spoils.

During the controversy between Kraus and the Social Democratic Party after the War, socialist critics such as Otto Bauer
accused the satirist of failing to interpret the War as a logical
outcome of the capitalist system.[25] Kraus, it is true, was too
sophisticated to reduce the catastrophe to these economic terms,
and too jealous of his intellectual integrity to employ an ideological terminology such as 'the collapse of monopoly capitalism'.
On the other hand, *Die Fackel* constantly related the War to an
attitude of mind which one may justifiably identify with the
'capitalist' (in Kraus's language, 'liberal') ethos. As a socialist
politician and ideologist, Bauer (understandably) felt frustrated at
Kraus's obstinate refusal to draw the political conclusions of his
own polemic; Kraus, the absolute satirist, understandably
refrained from associating himself overtly and explicitly with an
ideology which could only too easily decline into cliché and
unreflective abuse. Yet Kraus did offer a critique of certain

economic attitudes underlying the war-mongering of the Central Powers. He maintained that the true aims of human industry and economic activity had been forgotten, and that means had become ends. He did not criticise the economic principle of free enterprise : he attacked—for moral reasons—the way in which the 'capitalist' philosophy was now applied. 'Capitalism', no longer content with supplying a need, now created a demand in order to meet it :

> ... here life itself is at the service of the staff of life, and we consumers are its nourishment. We do not supply our own needs with the help of a trader, but *his* need for us. From such a cast of mind a world war is born, from the profound immorality of a life slipping by in an unholy mixture of sentiment and utility, lacking the courage to seek its true requirements : *these* are the causes of war, not the problem of Alsace or Galicia ... [26]

Kraus observed an unholy alliance between the War and 'capitalist' profit, between the military and industry, between patriotism and economic exploitation of the workers—a relationship which he characteristically summed up by alluding to the dual meanings of *Schild* and *Verdienst*. (The German can mean both 'shield' and 'shop sign', 'profit' and 'merit'.) Moreover, he saw a direct connection between the wretched sufferings of untold millions at the Front, and the bourgeois comforts and opulence of the profiteers and shareholders at home. Here his satire embraces an area of experience more often found in the writing of combatants (such as Owen or Sassoon in England) than in the work of civilians : the idea of the 'two nations', the prosperity and security of the one supported by the sacrifices of the other. Kraus quoted as an example of this the report of a tourist board which (in 1917) looked forward to an increase of tourism in the Tyrol after the War, as visitors flocked to war cemeteries and other memorials. The satirist exclaimed :

> If the remnants of moral decency within us do not rebel against the fulfilment of this forecast, against this expectation, the earthly remains of our dead will certainly do so ! [27]

Here again Kraus's worst fears were to be fulfilled. [28] A young Austrian writer, himself a former soldier, expressed just this betrayal in the Expressionist drama *Wunder um Verdun* (1931).

Hans von Chlumberg's play begins and ends in a war cemetery
in northern France which is visited by a group of international
tourists : and the dead indeed awake in an attempt to persuade
men to mend their ways. Yet politically, economically and on
the personal level the fallen have been written off; their memory
is forgotten, or shamelessly exploited.*

Kraus also conveyed the experience of the men at the Front
in his depiction of modern warfare as something anonymous and
remote, compared with the more personal combat of the past.
Death now came frequently unseen, and seemed particularly
fortuitous and senseless. Individual courage and endurance
counted for little where man was pitted against machine. Kraus
related this anonymity and impersonality to the world of
capitalism, to the mechanisation of industry, to a financial system
which never glimpsed the goods in which it dealt. Today the
phenomenon is not exclusive to capitalism : but it was a capitalist
system with which Kraus was familiar. Kraus indicated that the
War would be decided not by the morale, bravery, leadership
and training of the armies, but by the quality and quantity of
their equipment and armament (a judgement highly relevant to
the war of attrition). Yet the War had been ushered in and was
now being prolonged by men who spoke the language of chivalry:
it was sustained by an appeal to archaic values. The propaganda
machine made endless play of 'valour', 'glory', and 'patriotism';
emperors spoke of mailed fists, shining armour and swords—while
behind them loomed a grey backcloth of mass destruction, gas,
artillery and aerial bombardment. Language again provided the
satirist with the means of expressing this contradiction—through
the puns *chlorreich* and *technoromantisch*. (Thomas Mann once
described Bismarck's *Reich* as 'technological romanticism'.) Kraus
was aware, moreover, that a similar paradox threatened the very
existence of Germany and Austria-Hungary as imperial states.
In Joseph Roth's novel *Radetzkymarsch*, one of the characters
comments that the Habsburg Monarchy and the values upon
which it depended had no place in an age of electricity and
dynamite, and that its collapse was historically inevitable. Such
a view is 'progressive', nostalgic, and strangely consoling in its

---

* Another postwar work, *Die Wiedergeburt in Kain* (1920) by Carl
Julius Haidvogel, attacks the notion of moonlight tours of the old battlefields; here too the dead rise up to bring charity back into a heartless
world.

fatalism. Kraus by contrast stressed the *contemporaneity* of thrones and telephones as the cause of collapse—in other words, the attempt to harness out-moded political and cultural values to the chariot of economic expansion and technological advance. And *this* view poses the question of human responsibility.

Siegfried Sassoon once dreamed of leading his returning soldiers against the civilians who had prolonged and intensified the War :

> Snapping their bayonets on to charge the mob,
> Grim Fusiliers broke ranks with glint of steel,
> At last the boys had found a cushy job.
> I heard the Yellow-Pressmen grunt and squeal;
> And with my trusty bombers turned and went
> To clear those Junkers out of Parliament.
>
> ('Fight to a Finish')

Kraus too relished the thought of vengeance as early as 1915 :

> I would like for just one day to take over a command which would transfer the front into civvy street; to bomb successfully twice a day the breeding grounds of this world-wide infection, the poisonous home of hatred, the thieves' dens of bloody usury which are called by that single abominable foreign word *Redaktionen* [editorial offices]; and, with the aid of borrowed Cossacks who, to fill the cup of cruelty to the brim, would be ordered to refrain from any despoiling, to put an end to the shortage of meat and fat by a valiant raid on a Ringstrasse boulevard or on all those places where profiteers offer sacrifices to their physical welfare.[29]

Throughout the War he condemned this two-fold aspect of the hinterland, the propagandists and the profiteers. At the same time, the War seemed to him to demonstrate the degeneration of the conservative tradition. The revolutionary republicanism which he proclaimed in 1919 was anticipated by a successive distancing from the traditional social forces during the War. He had always been opposed to the Austrian government and establishment, but in the last two years of peace he had 'in self-defence' turned to the Church and to certain sections of the nobility, in the hope of finding allies in the struggle to protect threatened values. By October 1915, however, he was criticising conservative forces for their failure to oppose a senseless war which could benefit only the 'progressive' elements in society. Subsequently Kraus warned the nobility that it was selling its soul for financial gain, and was in danger of surrendering its social status to an increasingly influential bourgeoisie. He did not accuse the aristocracy of being politically responsible for the War but rather of betraying the moral and cultural values with which the satirist had once identified them. The failure of the Church to condemn chauvinism and slaughter, the inability of Pope Benedict to rouse the conscience of his priests, and the nomination of Moriz Benedikt to the Herrenhaus (the Upper House) in 1917 for his contribution to the war effort—all this helped to alienate Kraus from those very forces which before the War seemed to promise renewal and regeneration. He argued furthermore that to see the problem simply as a struggle between autocracy and democracy was to blind oneself to the actual power structure of the country; the rule of the nobility and the Crown had already given way to the rule of bureaucracy, the faceless men responsible to no visible authority except to the administrative machine itself. The assassination of the Austrian Prime Minister, Graf Stürkgh, by the young Socialist, Friedrich Adler, was thus, to Kraus, quixotic and misguided :

> There is no longer any crossbow or tyrant; there is technology and the bureaucrat. There is only the button pressed by plutocracy.[30]

Kraus here anticipated the theme of the 'banality of evil' which was to figure in his response to the Austrian crisis of 1927.

The satirist felt that the aristocracy had abdicated its power and status for material reasons, succumbing both to the temptations of 'progress' and 'liberalism' and to the allure of power-politics. When in 1922 he came to republish the essays of 1912 to 1914, he added bitter postscripts to 'Die Kinder der Zeit' and 'Sehnsucht nach aristokratischem Umgang', in which he withdrew his earlier expression of respect for the nobility and the Church and recanted his militarist sympathies. He wrote in his summing-up at the end of the War :

> The headlong rush of the conservative idea into a chaos in which it could only function as the gruesome bailiff of a philosophy utterly hostile to it, was the unparalleled realisation which this era brought home to me. In order to save our spiritual

values, ... we have no choice but to destroy completely the cloak of authoritarianism.[31]

This *Nachruf* of January 1919 conveys something of Kraus's pent-up hatred, contempt and loathing for the State, the personalities and social classes that had plunged Europe into war. It is a sustained indictment of the men responsible, delivered with the wrathful authority of an Old Testament prophet. The satirical wit and note of compassion for the victims of war transform this harrowing document into a literary achievement and a moving record of Kraus's humanity. In a sardonic parody of its own jargon, the satirist condemned the Habsburg Monarchy whose government had proved so inept and irresponsible, and scorned the familiar tenets of the imperial ideology which had been used to justify so much terror and misery :

a foul community whose claim to be allowed to plague the world with the nationalist hullaballoo was based on the divine right of the unholy shambles prevailing under Habsburg's sceptre, a sceptre whose mission appeared to be to hang over the peace of the world like the sword of Damocles; ... whose ethnic kaleidoscope produced the unity of an indefinable culture, which was forced upon the European palate as a so-called speciality—a muddy brown coffee topped with a double helping of whipped cream—and displayed in the closet of the civilised world as a tourist attraction.[32]

Free of the restraints of censorship, Kraus now destroyed the image of Franz Joseph as a venerable, shrewd, peace-loving and benevolent father of his peoples : to the satirist he appeared so mediocre as to be a 'non-person', devoid of vitality, intelligence, will-power and morality. It is a fitting verdict on his reign that it should have culminated in the disgrace of Franz Ferdinand's third-class funeral and in the effrontery of the Serbian ultimatum. In declaring war, the Habsburg Monarchy had made a final desperate attempt to rescue itself from the mire of defeat, incompetence and demoralisation : when it should have expired without fuss, it chose to involve the whole of Europe in its collapse. The Austrian obsession with prestige, Kraus maintained, had been catastrophically encouraged by a Germany obsessed with exports and power. Kraus proceeded to describe some of the atrocities committed in the name of Habsburg and

Nibelungentreue. He attacked the officer corps who were willing instruments of murder and devastation; the corruption and brutalisation of the civilian population of Vienna; the middle and upper classes who, having cheered the country into war, succeeded in evading the disease and deprivation that ravaged other sections of the community and remained basically indifferent to the plight of the workers. President Wilson, Kraus wrote, had performed an 'immortal deed' in freeing the peoples of Europe from a political nightmare : but even now, the satirist warned, the real lessons had not been learnt. Despite the republican framework the power structure of the *ancien régime* (the Press, the bureaucracy, the politicians and the bourgeoisie) survived, barely endeavouring to disguise its identity.

The operetta for which Berlin supplied the libretto and Budapest the music[33] had reached its final cacophonous bars. At first, the War had almost drowned the voice of the satirist. Thereafter, however, his testimony and indictment relayed the voice of sanity, compassion and morality in an inhumane world. As Edward Timms justly concludes, Kraus's periodical represents one of the most substantial contributions to the pacifist movement made during the First World War. What distinguishes it from the writings of other pacifists like Alfred Fried or Leonhard Frank is 'the extreme penetration of his cultural analysis and the vitality of the challenge it offers to the reader through satirical and imaginative stylisation.'[34]

Kraus is the only Austrian writer to have publicly and consistently campaigned against the War from inside Austria, braving the censorship and the military authorities, from as early as 1915. Stefan Zweig's putative pacifist drama *Jeremias* did not appear until the censorship and the powers of the military had been curtailed and a distinct war-weariness had become evident; shortly afterwards the author was safely (and officially) ensconced in Switzerland, having already served for nearly three years in the Kriegsarchiv. Hofmannsthal's depression and his idealistic gloss on the War did not develop into public protest, whereas Werfel's only outburst occurred in Switzerland in 1918 and earned him no more than a reprimand on his return to Vienna. Schnitzler remained silent. Hermann Bahr's conversion to war-weariness closely followed the trend of public opinion. And the literati of the Café Central and the Café Herrenhof (Blei, Gütersloh, Kisch, Werfel *et al.*) were careful to confine their feelings to their own circle, as they mulled over revolution during the last months of the War.

Albert Ehrenstein, it is true, published poems of protest in 1916 (*Der Mensch schreit*) and 1917 (*Die rote Zeit*), while a volume of his 'revolutionary' poems and prose (*Den ermordeten Brüdern*) appeared in Switzerland in 1918. But as Kraus himself pointed out, they were general accusations conveying the author's despair at the inhumanity of *Barbaropa* rather than attacks on specific events or individuals in his own country. During a short stay in the Kriegsarchiv as a member of the so-called *literarische Gruppe*, from June to September 1915, Ehrenstein conducted a sabotage campaign—with the aid of puns; for this he was returned to his unit. The verse of another Expressionist writer, Hugo Sonnenschein, fell foul of the censor at the end of 1914, although privately printed copies of this volume (*Erde auf Erden*) were allowed to circulate in the following year. But the patho- logical expression of decay and filth which it contains scarcely constituted an articulate attack on those responsible for the War. A periodical entitled *Der Friede* and edited by Benno Karpeles did circulate in Vienna during the War—but it did not begin publishing until January 1918, when its support for parliament- ary democracy, peace and bread, and its criticism of censorship, militarism, German nationalism and the Austrian government were not likely to incur opprobrium. (The contributors included Ehrenstein, Kisch, Alfred Polgar and Gütersloh.)

Only one voice of protest was raised with that of Kraus early in the War : the Innsbruck periodical *Der Brenner*, edited by Ludwig von Ficker. Its fourth volume ended on 15 July 1914; the first number of Volume V was promised for 1 October. In fact it did not appear until the spring of the following year, bearing the title *Brennerjahrbuch 1915* and dedicated 'in memoriam Georg Trakl'. Thereafter the magazine ceased pub- lication until October 1919. The yearbook published Trakl's last poems (including 'Grodek') and carried excerpts from Theodor Haecker's forthcoming book *Der Krieg und die Führer des Geistes* (eventually published after the War).

This protest is the only one remotely comparable with the campaign waged by *Die Fackel* : yet while Kraus continued to publish through three years of war, *Der Brenner* did not appear again until 1919. There was no great physical risk involved in speaking one's mind in Austria during the First World War,

provided that one was an established public figure. For all
Kraus's arraignment of the military and political authorities,
their activities were more restricted than was to be the case
twenty-five years later. The fact remains, however, that the
threat of official intervention sufficed to intimidate many contemporary writers. Kraus alone ignored that threat.

It might well be asked how Kraus's satire succeeded in defying
the censorship, particularly before 1917. In fact it did not
emerge entirely unscathed. Kraus could not attack the military
or the House of Habsburg directly, and several items were suppressed because they appeared too outspoken. The satirist frequently negotiated in person with the censors in order to have his
material approved. Eventually the military authorities initiated
proceedings against Kraus on a charge of defeatism but the
investigation was abruptly terminated by the collapse of October
1918.[35] The reason for the continued publication of *Die Fackel*
from 1915 to 1918 lies mainly in Kraus's satirical technique,
above all in his use of quotation. Simply by citing in the satirical
context of *Die Fackel* what the war-correspondents, the propagandists and the politicians wrote or said, Kraus was able to
draw attention to their fatuity, callousness and vicious hypocrisy.
Frequently the quotation was glossed only by an eloquent title.
At other times the use of italics in reprinting quotations, or the
telling juxtaposition of two contrasting texts conveyed both a
comment and a verdict. Brecht reminds us how unique and
inimitable this technique was.[36] For it to be effective, it assumed
a forum in which the satirist's values and attitudes were so
familiar that they could be taken for granted. The success of the
technique demonstrated the moral authority that Kraus commanded, an authority accorded him only after a career of
unimpeachable integrity which excluded any possibility of his
perspective on the quotation being misinterpreted. Alternatively
an extended *explication de texte* destroyed the intellectual and
political pretensions of the victim. Thus from newspaper reports
already printed (and therefore passed by the censor) Kraus
supplied his readers with a chronicle of the corruption and
wretchedness of life in the hinterland, demonstrating the decay of
public and private morality, the absurdities of the propaganda
and the ever increasing want and indigence. He lent authority
to his own case, and at the same time made it difficult for the

censor to object, by quoting from the classics, Rabelais, Grimmelshausen, Claudius, Goethe, Schiller, Jean Paul, Hölderlin, Schopenhauer, Nestroy, Stifter—and Bismarck. His ostensibly 'aesthetic' concern with language and a defective sensibility could be put to telling polemical effect, where his readers or audience knew of his belief in the correlation between literary style and ethical integrity. Thus most of the essay 'Der begabte Czernin' (May 1918) was devoted to the poverty of the Foreign Minister's wit, his linguistic insensitivity, the vagueness and ambiguity of his style and the shortcomings of his logic; thereby Kraus castigated his victim's intellectual and moral limitations and implied that the State must have come to a strange pass to have tolerated him as Foreign Minister.

The wartime *Fackel* numbers some two thousand pages. From October 1915 Kraus's energies did not flag, his control over a vast flood of material did not falter. Yet we do well to recall the vibrant sympathy and personal grief which informed the satirical wit.

The satire which even Kraus could not publish in wartime went into his monumental anti-war drama *Die letzten Tage der Menschheit*. The final version of the play appeared in 1922. Here the themes and subjects of the wartime *Fackel* are further elaborated. In his preface Kraus claimed that he had done little more than edit speeches, dialogues and printed documents: in fact, of course, he had done far more than that. He had stylised his material and re-created it in dramatic form. Many speeches and characters are invented, even if their language is brilliantly realistic—for example, Kommerzienrat Wahnschaffe and his family, Hofrat Schwarz-Gelber and his wife, or the officers on the *Sirck-Ecke*. There is no conventional plot, no conventional protagonist. Yet despite its enormous length and innumerable characters, the play does possess a dramatic unity and development. For the 'plot' is the War; the dramatic unity is the wartime situation. The material is bound by recurring motifs, such as the *Sirck-Ecke* scenes at the beginning of each act, the conversations between the *Nörgler* and the *Optimist* with their internal echoes and interconnections, or the balancing of the scene at the *Südbahnhof* during Franz Ferdinand's funeral (*Vorspiel*) and the scene at the *Nordbahnhof* four years later, as sick and wounded soldiers are repatriated (Act V).[37] The progress of political developments recorded by the *Feschaks* on the street corner, the modulation of the Optimist's tone from enthusiasm to weariness, from weariness to hope for the future, the growing dependence of Austria on Germany mirrored in the marked increase in Acts III and IV of scenes with German subjects, and the ever-growing deprivation and wretchedness of the Viennese streets—here lies the development of Kraus's great drama. That certain factors remain constant and unchanging : the attitude of the *Feschaks*, the tone of the editorials, the conversations of the patriotic profiteers, is, of course, a deliberate satirical device. The *Durchhalter* are petrified in their own clichés, stupidity and greed. In the last act Kraus's invention reaches mythical proportions with the animal and allegorical masks of the *Ringstrassencafé*, the giants Gog and Magog, and the appearance of newspaper vendors as corybants and maenads.[38] Finally, in the terrible cinematic images of the 'love feast at Corps Headquarters', a harrowing parody of the Last Supper, and in the grotesquely stylised visions of the epilogue, this monumental indictment of man's inhumanity reaches its awesome conclusion.

Kraus's drama, which has something of the quality of an epic poem, leads us through a moving tableau of folly, cruelty and exploitation. The victims : the oppressed, the starving, the crippled and the dying—are usually depicted as mute or humbly begging for charity. It is the tormentors who speak : the incompetent generals who pose smiling for photographs, the commanders who feast and whore while their men die, the employers who with military protection tyrannise and exploit their workmen, the priests who commandeer God for the war effort, the doctors who supply cannon-fodder according to fixed quotas. Kraus repeatedly denounces the literati, the jingoistic intellectuals, the war-correspondents, the draft-dodgers, the society snobs, and an effete or indifferent aristocracy. He exposes atrocities against civilians, drumhead courts-martial, bestial field-punishments, the torturing (by electric therapy) of men suffering from nervous disorders, the appalling treatment of rankers and prisoners in general. He depicts a society dominated by an attitude of mind that calls a woman *das Mensch** : in the Army, in the offices of

---

* A slang term meaning 'wench', in which the word for a human being (*der Mensch*) is reduced to an impersonal, neuter gender; the grammatical change conveys the brutal disrespect and arrogant indifference to human feeling involved.

the bureaucrats and in hospitals, human beings are stripped of their basic humanity and regarded as no more than 'human material' or '(factory) hands', as objects of consumption, the content of administrative files or the extension of industrial plant. This process of de-humanisation is the logical outcome of that *Phantasiearmut* which Kraus had for so long attacked—and is a prominent theme in the Expressionist literature and art of a world thrown out of joint by the cataclysm of 1914.

Die letzten Tage der Menschheit is the tragedy of mankind. But it is also the personal tragedy of the two least stylised, least caricatured characters in the play, whose dialogues punctuate the action and comment obliquely on it : the *Nörgler* and the *Optimist*. The dramatic significance of these scenes is the individual conflict between the two observers. In Timm's words,

> these two characters, apparently so antithetical in their position, are in reality profoundly dependent upon each other for their salvation. The *Optimist* seeks of the *Nörgler* enlightenment as to the true condition of man; hence the insistence of his questions. The *Nörgler*'s need, unacknowledged but implicit in his whole situation, is to emerge from the isolation to which his prophetic vision has condemned him and re-establish communication with mankind : hence the urgency of his replies.[39]

The *Optimist*, the average, intelligent, level-headed observer, fails to come to terms with the War or to perceive the reality of the situation. The tragedy of the *Nörgler*, on the other hand, is 'that of the seer condemned by the intensity of his moral vision to isolation and failure.'[40]

Their arguments range over the fundamental causes of the War—the decay of culture and morality—with which readers of *Die Fackel* were already familiar. The dialogue also touches upon the contrast between England and Germany in their approach to politics. The *Nörgler* sees in England a strict separation of the spheres of politics and culture, of capitalism and *Geist*, of war and creative art; whereas the confusion and intermingling of these two spheres has wrought havoc in Germany and Austria. Musil showed through the figure of Arnheim that the alliance of *Leben* and *Geist* could prove a spurious synthesis, serving merely to conceal and embellish a ruthless practical ambition. Similarly, the *Nörgler* claims that evil thrives best when masked by idealism. He maintains that England makes no pretence about its motives for going to war : the protection of its political and commercial interests. Germany, however, decks out its material aims in idealistic guise. In Germany lavatory paper is adorned with quotations from the classics, and generals are honoured with university degrees. During the War, the *Nörgler* asserts, both sides were guilty of bombing civilians :

> the difference is that the Germans were not content simply to drop bombs but sent witticisms along with them, and even conveyed 'Christmas Greetings' to the inhabitants of Nancy in a wrapping of steel and explosive.[41]

In short, the *Nörgler* criticises a characteristic development of recent German history : the confusion of idealism and *Realpolitik*. Kraus's satire on Wilhelm II, 'Ein Kantianer und Kant', is directed against the same abuse. The *Nörgler*'s remedy is to appeal for a strict separation of philosophy and politics.

We are here concerned with one of the implications of the 'non-political' attitude. Kraus attacks those who exploit and manipulate pseudo-philosophical precepts for a political purpose. But what of those well-meaning idealists who endorse a mundane political programme from high-minded motives? In modern Germany the ideas of poets and thinkers have been intimately bound up with political ambitions and developments. Their ideas are the visions of dreamers and philosophers, not the pragmatic thinking of men of affairs; yet they have been accepted as the hard currency of national politics. I refer not to the attempt to put a recognisable *political* programme into practice, but to the desire to achieve through political agencies certain *moral* or *cultural* goals.* There is a danger that, as Max Weber warned, the sheer uncompromising nature of the moral or philosophical purpose may clash with and override mature and proper political

---

* To quote at random one instance among thousands: Ferdinand Kürnberger, himself an Austrian but also a Pan-German, described the Franco-Prussian War thus—'Few wars contain in their gladiatorial bodies a soul, the cosmic spirit [*Weltgeist*] grants few wars the privilege of expressing an Idea and a Truth ... This is the lasting beauty and uniqueness of the War of 1870: it has a meaning. It is a rational creation. It realises Truth and Justice.

'The truth it conveys is the age-old truth that the Teutons are the leaders of Europe, and the justice it proclaims is the renewed acknowledgment of this truth.' ('Eine hundertjährige vollkommene Ohrfeige'.)

considerations, subordinating all to the realisation of the ideal, and justifying every means by reference to the *geistig* end. It was of this that Heine had spoken :

> Kantians will make their appearance who know no piety in the world of phenomena either, who will mercilessly churn up the ground of European life with sword and axe, to extirpate the last roots of the past. Armed disciples of Fichte will appear, their fanaticism impervious to fear and egoism alike; for they walk in the spirit, they defy matter ... the nature philosopher for his part will strike terror in men's hearts because he will join with the primitive forces of nature and conjure up the demonic powers of Germanic pantheism, and because there awakes in him an aggression which we find in the Germans of old, an instinct which fights not in order to destroy or to triumph, but merely for the lust of battle . . . .[42]

This 'idealism' may, of course, amount to little more than a vulgarised and confused compendium of diverse concepts, or a desire to defend and preserve German 'culture' and the German 'spirit'. But there is here an immense store of emotional and spiritual energy upon which the *Realpolitiker* can draw. Such idealism is evinced in Langbehn's *Rembrandt als Erzieher* (1890), Mann's *Betrachtungen eines Unpolitischen* (1918) and Grimm's *Volk ohne Raum* (1926) (to take some random examples). It is seen in the reaction of Zweig and Bahr to the outbreak of war, and in Kraus's suggestion (in 1912) that militarism might provide an antidote for the moral ills of German civilisation. It is also implicit in the Habsburg ideology of supranationalism. The *Nörgler*'s appeal for a strict separation of *Geist* and *Politik* appears to supply a pertinent criticism of this tradition.

On the other hand, the *Nörgler*'s criticism is strangely involved in the very tradition it attacks. What the *Nörgler* would restore is precisely that situation in which an ill-starred confusion of philosophy, ethics and politics could arise. The overlapping of these spheres is *preceded* by an endeavour to maintain a rigid distinction between them. The writers who have supplied recent German history with its 'ideological superstructure' were themselves imbued with disdain for the socio-political dimension; their ostensible concern lay exclusively with *Geist* and *Innerlichkeit*. Their lack of creative interest in the social and political sphere leads to political ingenuousness, which in turn produces those dangerously intransigent moral visions and overriding philosophical abstractions. The separation of *Geist* and *Politik* would indeed provide a valid solution, if it could be rigidly maintained. However, it is a matter of historical fact that such a distinction is prone to break down, giving way to a perilous form of fusion. A more realistic solution may therefore be found not in separation but by positing a responsible and clearsighted relationship between the two spheres, in which the limitations of each are recognised and respected.

At the end of *Die letzten Tage der Menschheit*, the Universe resolves to destroy mankind because it is an affront to the rest of creation. After the Apocalypse, silence. And finally the Voice of God is heard, pronouncing with helpless sorrow : 'Ich habe es nicht gewollt.' ('It was not my wish.') These last words, a bitter parody of Wilhelm II's self-exoneration, imply not tragic catharsis but despair. Nonetheless, the satirist's own feelings at the end of the War were compounded of grief and anger *and* qualified hope. But unlike Musil or Werfel, he did not succumb to the euphoria of the armistice period. He knew full well that the legacy of the War remained despite the silencing of the guns; he knew too that the majority of his contemporaries had failed to assimilate the lesson of their wartime experience. Kraus's drama is more than an indictment of the past—it is a presage of the future. It is not fortuitous that the final scene closes on a cosmic wasteland.

Kraus's attitude towards the Habsburg Empire *after* the War is consistent with the critical position adopted in his 'Nachruf' and with various polemical passages in *Die letzten Tage der Menschheit*. He felt that Franz Joseph's culpable behaviour had revealed the perils of a hereditary monarchy, and as late as 1924 he still found it necessary to satirise an attempt to whitewash the old Emperor. Neither did he spare the hapless Karl up to the latter's death in 1922. While lending full support to the Republic in the early postwar years, Kraus perceived that there was little deep-rooted support for it in the country at large. (In January 1919 he observed that the Viennese love of spectacle alone would guarantee the exiled Karl an enthusiastic welcome, should he decide to return.) As we have seen, several contemporary Austrian writers—notably Franz Werfel and Joseph Roth—who were indifferent to the Empire in the immediate postwar period, grew appreciably nostalgic at a later date, under the pressure of political developments in the 1930s. Kraus, however, did not undergo any significant change of heart. Yet in some of his later essays he conjured up the memory of Empire in order to drive home a polemical point. In 'Der Hort der Republik' (October 1927) he emphasised the mediocrity, stupidity and inhumanity of Seipel's government by recalling the *ancien régime*—albeit of a period prior to 1914 :

> I am almost afraid that it might be interpreted as a confession of monarchism, if I remind the reader that the old era had personalities at its disposal who—long before the decision of influential zombies to usher in the dance of death—had too much red blood in their veins to taste that of their subjects, and too much human dignity to offend that of their charges as evidence of their power ... even socialist quarters could not deny that under the Monarchy the very desire for popularity and mania for saluting on the part of the head of state offered a certain amount of protection against bureaucratic excesses.[43]

Subsequently (in 1934) Kraus described the Imperial censors as civilised beings compared with the National Socialists and the Social Democrat intellectuals now in exile. He also implied that the decision of the Entente to support the dismemberment of the Habsburg Monarchy offered no real political solution to the problems of Central Europe. He drew his most radical analogy with the Empire in his final denunciation of that social democracy which (as we shall see) he once so ardently supported :

> The Social Democratic Party is responsible—and it is the author of *The Last Days of Mankind* who says so—for the fact that by comparison with a democracy which encourages every excrescence of the prewar world to grow to tropical dimensions, life in the state which released the curse appears rehabilitated; that we are seized by a cultural homesickness for that super-annuated monstrosity, and that political liberty, violated and ridiculed by those very people who pay lip service to it, has ceased to be a matter worthy of intellectual concern.[44]

This, of course, is not nostalgia for the Imperial past. While it stresses that the moral and cultural values which the Social

Democrats had apparently rescued in 1919 no longer repose on the republican Left, the wheel never quite turns full circle, for in the crisis at the beginning of the thirties Kraus looks not to Otto von Habsburg but to Dollfuss, the authoritarian Austrian Chancellor.

The satirist wrote in 1934 that *Die Fackel* had sought before the War to combat the corruption of the 'conservative idea'; after 1918, however, it attempted to forestall the corruption of the 'revolutionary idea'.[45] Since Kraus was concerned to defend certain moral, cultural and intellectual values, he saw no paradox in his change of political allegiance. To him the old world was by 1918 hopelessly compromised through its unhappy marriage with the new, and in order to restore and conserve the purity and integrity of traditional values, he opted for the Republic, for parliamentary democracy and for the Social Democratic Party:

> The democratic tendency must be supported in the struggle against its own consequences, and the aristocratic cause deserted in its own interest.[46]

So too in Germany Thomas Mann and his fellow 'conservatives' Max Weber, Walther Rathenau, Ernst Troeltsch, Friedrich Meinecke and Friedrich Naumann swung behind the Weimar Republic. In his address 'Von Deutscher Republik' (1922) Mann related his republicanism to the conservative-revolutionary thesis of *Betrachtungen eines Unpolitischen* (1918). He admits that he remains a conservative by nature—but not in the sense of one who clings to the past for its own sake (which would merely be 'reactionary'). He claims that he is a conservative for the sake of the future, since he would preserve what is valuable in the legacy of the past to enable the new age to orientate itself by clear landmarks. Mann argues that change must be controlled and canalised lest it destroy indiscriminately all vestiges of the past. His increasing sympathy with socialism leads him later to suggest 'an alliance and pact between the conservative idea of culture and the revolutionary idea of society'. This notion springs from a moral impulse which hopes for the realisation of a more just social and economic framework. Now, Mann's reaction to the postwar world is akin to that of Karl Kraus. But the Viennese satirist enters the political arena at an earlier date, and the history, though not the origin, of his socialist sympathies follows a very different path.

What precisely was Kraus's position *vis-à-vis* the Social Democrats in 1918 and 1919? A recent commentator drew attention to the distinction which Kraus always made between his loyalty to 'the cause of the working class' and his relationship with the Social Democratic Party.[47] From his election appeal on behalf of the Social Democrats in February 1919, it is clear that Kraus's alliance with the Party was tactical. He advocated a protest vote against the bourgeois parties rather than a positive commitment to the socialist ideology. He reminded his listeners of the débâcle of international socialism in 1914: but he also pointed out that the socialists bore the least burden of responsibility for the War. He frankly dissociated himself from Marxist philosophy (in fact he rejected its materialism)—but this, he felt, was at present irrelevant. In the forthcoming elections, the first of the postwar era, it was simply a question of affirming or abjuring the slaughter of the past four years. The socialists could be justly proud of the fact that chauvinism was alien to their tradition and that they had refrained from rationalising support for the War in ideological terms. Kraus's favourable attitude towards the Party was thus conditional from the outset. During the War the campaign of the *Arbeiterzeitung* against the jurisdiction and sentences of Austrian courts-martial, and against the hardships inflicted upon the civilian population, had enlisted his respect; but here again his criticism of certain editorials, his warning that the socialist organ was 'a newspaper like any other', exposed to the same corruption as the bourgeois Press, anticipated later developments.

Kraus's attitude towards Communism was less ambiguous. He abhorred the terrorism which seemed inseparable from its accession to power, and protested against the atrocities committed by Communists in Munich and Budapest. This violence was for him a corollary of the movement's origins in a repressive, reactionary environment. At the same time he considered that its extremism was bound to produce an equally violent response—as in Hungary, where the soviet government of Béla Kun was replaced by Horthy's reactionary terror. The satirist criticised the Viennese Social Democrats in 1919 for their reluctance to suppress an impending Communist coup. Nevertheless, he was so incensed by evidence of the way in which the bourgeoisie and upper

classes remained unrepentant after the War that he commended
the idealism inherent in the Communist faith of a figure like
Rosa Luxemburg:

> My own opinion—and here I intend to speak frankly to this
> inhuman breed of bloodstained men of property and their
> hangers-on, because I consider the World War to be an un-
> equivocal fact and the age which has reduced human life to a
> muck heap to be an inexorable watershed—my own opinion is
> this: Communism as a reality is merely the reflection of their
> own life-defiling ideology, though blessed with a purer idealistic
> origin, a perverse vaccine for a purer idealistic purpose—Devil
> take its practice but God preserve it as a constant threat over the
> heads of the propertied classes who to protect their wealth would
> like to drive everybody else into the frontline of famine and
> patriotic honour—comforted with the words that man cannot
> live by bread alone.[48]

(Heine expressed similar feelings in the Preface (1855) to
Lutetia.)

Events of the early postwar years showed Kraus the circumscribed limits of the social and political revolution initiated in
November 1918. Austria, the land where the right conclusions
were never drawn, had apparently learnt nothing from the War.
Former Imperial generals were given pensions by the Republic,
while the Viennese middle class considered itself unfairly victim-
ised by the minimal economic measures of the Socialist city
council. The bourgeois protagonists of Kraus's comedy *Wolken-
kuckucksheim* (1923) complain only of the drabness of Vienna,
of rising wages, the organisation of labour, social welfare
measures, controlled rents, taxation—and the loss of their investment in war loans. Kraus saw that the bourgeoisie associated its
present grievances and the economic collapse of the country with
the Republic and the increased power of the Socialists: hence
the sentimental nostalgia for the Habsburgs (and the Hohen-
zollerns), hence the electoral victory of the Austrian bourgeois
parties in the 1920 elections, and the swing to the Right in
Hungary. The indifference of the middle class towards their
responsibility for a disastrous war was indicative of a fundamental ethical defect: the prosperity of bourgeois society had
always depended (Kraus argued) upon the deprivation of others,
and it tolerated without qualms the coexistence of want and

Nationalists remove the Imperial Eagle from the Police Headquarters in Prague, 28 October 1918

The Palace of Justice, Vienna, in flames on 15 July 1927

Members of the Heimwehr

A Schutzbund exercise in a Viennese
suburb in 1933

Wien, XXI. Schlingerhof

Civil War, February 1934: in front of a shell-damaged block of workers' flats, two corpses lie in the gutter while government forces patrol the street

SA men on parade on the Heldenplatz, Vienna

Vienna, March 1938. Members of the Fatherland Front try to whip up support for Schuschnigg and an independent Austria shortly before the plebiscite called by the Chancellor was due to be held

Anschluss: German troops receive a welcome from the people of Linz

plenty. However, the satirist's attitude towards the bourgeoisie was also influenced by a cultural consideration. He felt that the bourgeois regarded art as yet another commodity, as a barren status symbol, as the privilege of the 'happy few' who could afford to enjoy it. In the working class, on the other hand, Kraus believed that he had found a social group at once more tolerant of the artist's creative freedom and more receptive to the urgent message of his own satire. (It is the frustration of this hope which accounts for Kraus's feud with the cultural section of the Social Democratic Party later in the twenties.)

Kraus's disillusionment with a society which ignored the terrible lesson of the War was intensified by the actions of the victorious Entente. Their failure to relieve the agony of Central Europe, together with the vicious terms of the Peace Treaties, demonstrated that France had donned the mantle of Prussia, and Czechoslovakia the mantle of Austria-Hungary. Kraus, like Musil, was now bitterly critical of President Wilson for condoning the revanchist feeling of his allies, especially since his former idealistic pronouncements had sounded so encouraging.

Years later Kraus related the rise of National Socialism to the lost opportunities of 1919. He referred to the unpreparedness of the German public for news of military defeat in 1918; he cited the failure of the Social Democrats in Austria and particularly in Germany to revolutionise their society; and he asserted that a misguided attempt to claim financial compensation for the evils of the War was not only unpractical but also foolish, in that it strengthened Germany's desire for revenge. The political débâcle was accompanied by a cultural disaster, for the phenomena which Kraus had satirically illuminated during the War were permitted to thrive. (Yet the twenties were *also* the age of Benn, Brecht, Kafka, Mann, Rilke and others. Kraus would have argued that the achievements of these individuals could not compensate for the abysmally low level of culture in general. And yet, was the general level of culture any higher in Kraus's beloved *Alt-Wien*?) Wartime clichés which had invoked drawn swords to symbolise gas and high explosive implied obtuseness towards the significance and overtones of language, and a corresponding insensitivity to the experience of one's fellows; there, the cliché had been *contradicted* by reality. The next step, according to Kraus, was the *subordination* of reality to cliché : with a new awareness of the primitive meaning of idiom and metaphor, the Nazis translated language into reality, while remaining impervious to the human experience involved. Again : during the War the Central Powers had attempted to preserve an archaic social and political structure with the aid of modern technology and the rationalisation of their economy. A similar paradox characterised the National Socialist state, where the benefits and destructive power of advanced technology existed side by side with—and indeed fostered—a recourse to medieval bestiality, to tribalism and irrationality. Kraus perceived that the War had solved little and that it had bequeathed to the new era a legacy of chauvinism, callousness and violence.

At the end of the War he turned to the Austrian working class and the Social Democratic Party as the only possible guarantors of the values he cherished. Only in the Party did he see any hope of restoring a correct relationship between means and ends in public life; here alone he observed a proper respect for the rights of the individual and a true insight into the function and limitations of politics. By 1923, however, Kraus was already in conflict with the Party.[49] The estrangement grew steadily until 1927, when the satirist entered into litigation with the *Arbeiterzeitung*. After the July riots of that year, he concluded an armistice with the Party in an attempt to bring the Chief of Police, Johannes Schober, to book for the massacre of nearly a hundred demonstrators and bystanders.

Kraus's essay 'Der Hort der Republik' (October 1927) begins with an anthology of quotations from the socialist and bourgeois Press, from foreign sources and the report of the City Council's commission of enquiry, from letters, speeches, testimonies, and his own poster demanding Schober's resignation. He then proceeds to analyse the implications of the events of 15 July. Although he acknowledges that the demonstrators included a certain number of fire-raisers, looters and stone-throwers, he argues that the provocation of a small minority called forth a completely disproportionate response from the police, whose victims were principally the defenceless, the unsuspecting and the innocent. For all its excesses and foolhardiness, the demonstration itself was a spontaneous and sincere protest in a just cause. That Seipel's government and the Austrian middle class could acclaim, approve and commend the actions of the police, illustrates the hideous nature of a society composed of avaricious bourgeois and 'professional' Christians. Kraus denounces the social system which made such atrocities possible, a religion which denied mercy and charity to the victims, a republic which pinned medals on the breast of murderers. Kraus relates the absence of remorse and atonement to the War, to the defective sensibility of his contemporaries and the anonymous irresponsibility of the bureaucratic machine. Perhaps his most perceptive insight is precisely this theme of the 'banality of evil', of the dutiful, ruthless competence of an unthinking functionary:

> Was it not the technoromantic charm of that 'momentous' time, that accountants were transformed into Attilas and Attilas turned back again into accountants? ... in a world which has no Albas, merely functionaries, men capable of committing deeds because they are incapable of imagining their consequences, one must realise that it is an anonymous force of irresponsibility which places even these helpless subordinates at the mercy of the power they themselves wield, and which does such nameless damage to their souls.[50]

Schober's actions and the attitude of the Seipel government hastened Kraus's disenchantment with Austrian democracy. Democratic liberties, he felt, had conjured up a tragi-comic situation, creating a society which was uncouth, which could barely conceal its rapaciousness beneath a veneer of *Gemütlichkeit* and whose horizons extended no further than the parish pump. If it was oppressive in the old days to be ruled by an anointed imbecile, at least—up to the last years of peace—the idiocy was confined to the highest circles. At all events it was more palatable than a republic in which every cretin regarded himself king. Here Kraus commits the error of which he had accused the bourgeoisie immediately after the War: he implies a causal connection between present ills or malpractices and a political system which is in fact morally neutral. A republic and a parliamentary democracy do not necessarily produce a Seipel and a Schober. Yet the argument is echoed by many of his contemporaries. Of course, Kraus does not indulge in political theorising. But if he is not in fact condemning the democratic system as such, if his criticism is pertinent only to this particular democracy, then he fails to make the distinction clear. In a historical context where parliamentary democracy was uncritically identified with this particular system, and where the whole democratic principle was falling increasingly into disrepute, the effect of Kraus's remarks must have been to suggest a sweeping attack on the basic issues of democracy.

For a year after the Palace of Justice riot, Kraus suppressed his criticism of the Social Democratic Party in order to preserve a common front against a common enemy. Yet he received no more support from the party hierarchy in his campaign against Schober than in his crusade against the blackmailer Bekessy between 1924 and 1926. Thereafter the breach between Kraus and the Party could no longer be healed. It was not a question of the 'god that failed', since he had never subscribed to the socialist ideology. Just as his concern with the cause of the working class was a moral commitment, so too his estrangement from the Party was motivated on his side by an outraged conscience. His opposition rested in the first instance upon moral intransigence : he attacked hypocrisy and compromise, rather than political ineptitude or miscalculation. This first stage is recorded in his 'Rechenschaftsbericht' of 1928, an essay which effectively sums up his charges against the Party in the 1920s. Personal rancour, perhaps, accounted for his criticism of the bourgeois morality of party members who disliked his enlightened views on sexuality; and an element of vanity may, perhaps, be detected in his resentment at the attitude of the party hierarchy towards his publicistic activities. (Kraus refused to subordinate his pen to any external considerations.) Possibly he was unrealistic in castigating the *Arbeiterzeitung* for accepting capitalist advertisements, or in denouncing the *Kunststelle* for its patronage of a worthless operetta-culture. Nevertheless, the essence of his charges —corruption within the hierarchy, and the dead hand of *embourgeoisement*—was not so easily dismissed. The Austrian Social Democrats were a nominally revolutionary party which had chosen to work within a democratic framework, which had built up an extensive bureaucratic apparatus and achieved valuable, if not radical, social aims. Yet in the postwar republic it seemed doomed to perpetual opposition. Clearly it would have risked much in seeking to realise its revolutionary programme; thus it tended to cling to the limited power it already enjoyed, even at the cost of betraying its original principles. Kraus asserted that in order to safeguard their privileges and influence, the socialist leaders had succumbed to compromise and corruption. They allowed themselves to be blackmailed by Bekessy, they condoned various financial scandals, and tried to stifle the voice

of protest. Worst of all, the abuses of the old world were permitted to thrive more vigorously than ever before.

At this point Kraus still hoped for a reform of the Party
from within. There followed the rise of the National Socialists
in Germany and the degeneration of Austrian political debate
into sterile vituperation and open violence. Kraus's attitude
grew increasingly intransigent—and increasingly 'political'.
Confronted with the threat from Germany, he now refused to
conclude another tactical alliance with the 'bad representatives
of a good cause.'[51] To the ethical indictment of the Social
Democratic leadership he now added an attack on the criminal
obtuseness of their politicking, which threatened to leave Austria
defenceless against the enemy without :

> And were this world all Nazis o'er*—in the creation of whom
> social democracy here and in Germany has played the greatest
> role—we must be clear in our minds that, ever since humanity
> has allowed itself to be deceived by politics, there has never
> been a greater failure than the activities of this party, and that
> the defiling of every single ideal which it has utilised in order
> to share with the bourgeoisie, is now complete.[52]

Thus began the searing essay 'Hüben und Drüben' (October
1932). The Social Democrats, Kraus wrote, might not be quite as
corrupt as the bourgeois parties : but they surpassed their rivals in
hypocrisy. They condemned capitalism—yet accepted the
revenue from its advertisements. Party propaganda denounced
the bourgeois parties and the Fascists—yet the socialist leaders
cultivated 'tactical' links with their own opponents in secret.
They thought in one way and acted in another, polemicised in
one direction and manoeuvred in another. Publicly they supported the Anschluss, while requesting protection against the
Heimwehr from foreign governments who were opposed to the
Anschluss; but they also preached Austrian independence, while
dreaming in their hearts of union with Germany. This fundamental dishonesty, born of cowardice and weakness, had borne
fruit in the form of the ultimate betrayal : the Party had co-
operated with the Schober government and thus dishonoured

---

* Kraus parodies a line from Luther's hymn 'Ein' feste Burg ist unser
Gott'. In Carlyle's translation the original runs: 'And were this world
all devils o'er,/And watching to devour us,/We lay it not to heart so
sore;/Not they can overpower us.'

the memory of the victims of 15 July. In Germany the Social
Democrats were attempting to channel for their own ends the
rising tide of chauvinism. But *Sozialnationalismus*, a hybrid
growth fed by Karl Marx and Vater Jahn, bore the same stigma
as the *Nationalsozialismus* with which it was trying to compete.
The nationalist clichés of the Socialists, with their talk of 'French
vassals', 'German' liberty and 'German' democracy would be
tragic if they were sincerely meant : but as it is, their hypocrisy
was merely nauseating. Kraus's essay marked the final parting of
the ways. Discounting the hope of reform from within, he proclaimed that the only answer was to abandon the Party altogether.

The satirist was under no illusion as to the political ambitions
of the Christian Socialists, but found them at least sincere in
their antagonism towards a Nazi Germany. It is not altogether
surprising, therefore, that in the Austrian crisis of February 1934,
Kraus sided with the Dollfuss regime against the Social Democrats. He had saddened or angered many of his readers by
remaining silent when Hitler acceded to power. After the issue
of December 1932, *Die Fackel* did not appear again until
October 1933, when it carried an obituary for the architect
Adolf Loos, and the following poem :

> Man frage nicht, was all die Zeit ich machte.
> Ich bleibe stumm;
> und sage nicht, warum.
> Und Stille gibt es, da die Erde krachte.
> Kein Wort, das traf;
> man spricht nur aus dem Schlaf.
> Und träumt von einer Sonne, welche lachte.
> Es geht vorbei;
> Nachher war's einerlei.
> Das Wort entschlief, als jene Welt erwachte.
>
> (Let no one ask how all this time I've spent.
> I hold my peace;
> and give no reason why.
> And stillness reigns where once the earth was rent.
> No word struck home;
> One speaks in sleep alone.
> And dreams of sunshine that once laughed.
> But it will pass;
> It won't make any difference—then.
> Words died away when that world came to life.)[53]

The next number appeared in July 1934. In the meanwhile Brecht was one of the few who comprehended or respected the significance of Kraus's silence :

> Als der 'Beredte sich entschuldigte
> dass seine Stimme versage
> trat das Schweigen vor den Richtertisch
> nahm das Tuch vom Antlitz und
> gab sich zu erkennen als Zeuge.

> (When the man of many words apologised
> for words having failed him,
> his silence appeared before the Court,
> removed the veil from its face and
> revealed itself as a witness.)[54]

When in February 1934 Kraus supported Dollfuss, he alienated his socialist public by what they felt to be his double betrayal.[55] Social Democrat leaders and intellectuals in exile, together with their Czech hosts, poured abuse upon his head until the satirist was provoked to justify his position in a long essay entitled 'Warum die "Fackel" nicht erscheint' (July 1934).

It might indeed be asked why Kraus now refused to sink his differences with the Social Democrats as he had done in 1927. The point is that the two situations were by no means similar. The massacre of July 1927 had cost the lives of demonstrators and onlookers who, for the most part, were entirely innocent of the excesses perpetrated by a small minority. The demonstration —to Kraus—was just, the slaughter of the demonstrators unpardonable, The State never in danger. At that time the satirist saw a clear-cut moral choice between approving of murder or bringing the murderers to justice. In 1934, on the other hand, the position was far more complex. An armed rebellion against the legitimate government of the State had occurred, ill-prepared and ill-timed, but still premeditated. The *Republikanischer Schutzbund* (socialist militia) itself chose to make a desperate stand in workers' housing blocks, thereby exposing innocent civilians to death and injury. And now the shadow of Hitler loomed over the whole tragic affair. By challenging Dollfuss's authority, so Kraus believed, the Austrian Social Democrats were in danger of sabotaging the only effective and practical defence against Nazi tyranny.

Die Fackel of July 1934 repeated the satirist's ethical indictment of the Social Democratic Party, but compounded these
charges by referring to its political culpability in the February
conflict. The socialist leaders merged with the ghosts of Schober
and the Seipel government of 1927; with the unrepentant
bourgeoisie of 1919 and 1920; with the politicians, journalists
and patriots of the war years. Kraus denounced their callous indifference to the suffering that they had inflicted, the defective
sensibility mirrored in their clichés, their incapacity to perceive
the measure of their responsibility, and their glib jargon. In the
suppressed essay *Die dritte Walpurgisnacht*—which predates the
sections of 'Warum die "Fackel" . . . ' directed against the Social
Democrats—Kraus had stressed the emptiness of the metaphors
of violence employed by the socialists at a time when all their
fighting spirit appeared to be dissipated. Thus the abortive rising
of February 1934 must have incensed him all the more for being the disastrous attempt of weak men to live up to the blood-
thirstiness of their own clichés. (Kraus was perhaps reminded of
Austria's concern with 'prestige' and 'honour' in July 1914.) The
Party (he felt) could not even plead a misplaced enthusiasm in
its own defence, since the leaders *knew* that the rising would fail,
yet persisted in sending the *Schutzbund* and the innocent victims
of the fighting to their deaths. The argument of 'defending our
principles' in the mouths of those who (in his opinion) had sullied
and betrayed every principle they professed—this awoke no
sympathetic echo in the satirist.

Kraus turned finally and irrevocably against the parliamentary
democracy which the Social Democrats claimed to represent. He
agreed with Dollfuss:

> that against the resurrection of Wotan parliamentarianism was
> ineffective, that against the mysteries of *Blut und Boden* demo-
> cracy was helpless, and that the predestination of gangsters was
> not to be thwarted by universal suffrage.[56]

He assailed the impotent phrase-mongering of the parliament-
arians and the rationalistic, legalistic foundation of parliamentary
theory. By a similar token, he asserted that the Catholic resistance to National Socialist infamy was more courageous, constant
and hopeful than that of atheistic marxist forces. In 1927 he had
attacked Austrian Catholics for their lack of charity; then, he

assailed the *Bodenständigkeit* of the Christian Socialists, calling them 'peasants let loose on the town'.[57] In the present crisis, however, he revised his assessment of Catholicism, and criticised the socialist leaders for being a rootless urban intelligentsia, enjoying a false sense of superiority over the provinces which they treated with unjustified contempt.

Frank Field maintains that Kraus shared Dollfuss's dream of 'a Catholic Austria that would regenerate Christendom',[58] but this seems unwarranted. Certainly he was susceptible to the moral and cultural values for which Dollfuss appeared to stand. Nonetheless, Kraus's admiration and support were inspired primarily by defensive considerations, in a way which anticipates Thomas Mann's qualified support of German Communism after 1945. In *Die dritte Walpurgisnacht*, prior to the Civil War, Kraus referred sceptically to the cultural ambitions of contemporary Austria, with its questionable 'Christian-Germanic' ideals of beauty. He also criticised the kith-and-kin argument of the government press which lamented German hostility towards Austria, and he disapproved of the official slogan that Austria's prime role was that of 'mediator'. Even *after* February 1934 he publicly dissociated himself from the ideology of the government and the *Vaterländische Front*.[59]

Yet Kraus believed that he had found in Dollfuss a personification of that conservative tradition which he had defended before the War. At the same time he considered the *Vaterländische Front* to have regenerated the 'revolutionary idea' for which he had fought since 1918. Thus he remained consistent both in his commitment to 'conservative' values *and* in his loyalty to the cause of the working class. He attacked the socialist leaders and ideologists rather than the rank and file. While he expressed his admiration for the courage of the *Schutzbündler* and his compassion for their suffering, he claimed that they had been misled and betrayed by the party leadership. His declared aim was to free the workers from the clutches of 'politicians' and intellectual parasites, the men who made a living out of the relief of misery and who traded in hardship. The socialist achievements in Vienna, he argued,—better housing, education, labour legislation and social welfare schemes—owed less to the intrinsic merits of the party bureaucracy than to the sheer urgency of the need; any 'relatively decent democracy' would have taken similar measures.

The interests of the workers, whom Kraus called 'the most valuable, deprived, inadequately compensated section of humanity—
who work for others and are oppressed even by their liberators',[60]
were better served by Dollfuss than by those who would send
them to their deaths. (The *christlicher Ständestaat*, after all,
corresponded to the anti-capitalist, syndicalist socialism of the
'conservative revolution'; Dollfuss's Fatherland Front, it could
be argued, was not so obviously tainted by capitalism as, say, the
Grossdeutschen.) Kraus repudiated the frenzied accusations that
the Christian Socialists were 'assassins of the workers' and
'Christians who spoke through the muzzles of guns' : he rejoined
that the government was justified in defending the State from
armed attack. He had nothing but scorn and contempt for those
exiled socialists who compared Dollfuss with Hitler. In a situation
where Austria was struggling to maintain her independence, the
satirist—who was never in favour of the Anschluss—appealed
that the authoritarianism of the Austrian chancellor be recognised as the lesser evil.*

Kraus's arguments in 1934 often recall those of an earlier
period : the years 1912 to 1914, when he was sympathetic to the
cause of the 'conservative revolution'. (The historical context is,
of course, entirely different and his ideas have evolved accordingly.) Then *Die Fackel* opposed the 'democracy' and 'freedom'
championed by a decadent liberalism; now it opposes the parlia-
mentarianism of a corrupted Social Democracy. Then it attacked
the materialistic outlook of a bourgeoisie which had subordinated
ends to means and disguised its avarice behind a pseudo-culture;
now *Die Fackel* attacks the dishonesty, hypocrisy and shameful
compromise of a party which is prepared to pay any price to
protect its vested interests and privileges, and has subordinated
considerations of humanity to those of politics, while mouthing
high-minded clichés. Then, as now, Kraus denounced an unscrupulous intelligentsia which thrived on the moral and intellectual lethargy of the public. Then, as now, the values that he
prized were *Geist* and *Natur*—and the antidotes which he pre-
scribed against the poisons of the age were authority, integrity,

---

* In 1938 his appeal was heeded. In the plebiscite campaign organised by
Schuschnigg to try to forestall the German annexation, the leaders of the
socialist underground and the free trade unions advised their followers to
vote for an independent Austria, not in support of Schuschnigg but *against*
Hitler.

discipline and courage. In 1914 Kraus wrote of the late heir to
the throne that Franz Ferdinand seemed in an age of universal
tribulation to have the stature of a real man.[61] Twenty years
later—to the month—Kraus wrote that in Dollfuss's case he
reserved his right to make an exception and regard a politician
as a 'real man'. In 1914 and in 1934 the only hope for the future
lay in a single heroic personality who in Kraus's view bore the
stamp of *Altösterreich*. And a grim irony decreed that both the
potential saviours of Austria should have been assassinated as
the preliminary to political catastrophe.

One's sense of *déjà-vu* is most powerfully endorsed by the
analogy between Kraus's 'silence' in August 1914 and his 'silence'
in 1933. His response to Hitler's accession to power was anticipated by a short speech of November 1930. Confronted by the
moral and political bankruptcy of the Social Democrats and by
the ineluctability of a 'revolt of the troglodytes' in Germany,
Kraus again expressed a shattering scepticism with regard to the
power of satire :

> the material surpasses the satire that formed it, putting the
> imagination to shame, mocking the inability to encompass this
> fresh experience.[62]

What Paul Schick terms 'an expression of pessimism' may in
1930 still have been satirical hyperbole. It still has an echo in the
poem of October 1933, 'Das Wort entschlief, als jene Welt
erwachte.' And in the first half of 'Warum die "Fackel" nicht
erscheint' Kraus explores and analyses the reasons for his 'silence'.
His arguments are in several respects familiar from the apologia
of 1914–15 : the ineffectiveness of protest—of *his* form of protest
—in a world where the proper relationship between language and
reality no longer obtains, and where reigns a truth more appalling
than Kraus's satirical fiction; the problems of assimilating this
horrendous reality and of re-creating it in an adequate satirical
form. These objections, these obstacles were relevant in 1914,
but they were overcome. Why then was Kraus's self-doubt so
much more corrosive in 1933 and 1934? The satirist's fear of
provoking reprisals against innocent victims inside Germany
speaks more for his humanity than for his political realism—
and is in any case (of itself) an inadequate explanation. A more
fundamental reason lies in the nature and extent of the Nazi

terror which rendered the problem of satirical *Bewältigung* so much more difficult. We know that Kraus did apply his well-tried satirical method to National Socialism : *Die dritte Walpurgisnacht* was originally envisaged as an issue of *Die Fackel*. Yet he chose to withhold publication at the proof stage. Instead there appeared a confession of helplessness and resignation.

The suppressed essay opens with the statement : 'Mir fällt zu Hitler nichts ein' (I have no bright ideas about Hitler). Did Kraus remember an earlier aphorism in which he had employed the same construction?

> Es ist halt ein Unglück, dass mir zu jedem Lumpen etwas einfällt. Aber ich glaube, dass es sich immer auf einen abwesenden König bezieht.

> (It is my misfortune that every rogue I come across gives me ideas. But I believe that this always relates to an absent king.'[63]

It is the increasing remoteness and irrelevance of the absent monarch which helps to account for Kraus's self-doubt. At the end of a long career spent in an unremitting struggle against folly, mediocrity, obtuseness, irresponsibility and corruption, he was faced with an evil greater than the world had ever known. Up to now his satire had rested upon the tacit assumption that the framework of morality and sanity within which it operated represented the only valid scheme for the age, however much his satirical targets appeared to deviate from those values. With the rise of National Socialism, Kraus's own faith in those values was not shaken : but after 1933 Germany constructed its own world, which irrevocably abjured Kraus's values and opposed them with a completely alien frame of reference. To read certain sections of *Die dritte Walpurgisnacht* is to enter a Kafkaesque nightmare of perverted logic and inverted causality on a scale which Kraus had never before met. The difference between the First World War and the age of Hitler is precisely the distinction between a 'scoundrel' (*Lumpen*) and conscious criminality; between the insensitive use of the cliché, and a deliberately literal application of the metaphors of violence and cruelty; between the ultimately unwitting, deluded actions of a Berchtold or a Czernin, and the calculated infliction of horror; between those who knew not what they did, and those who were fully aware of the implications of their policies. In this unprecedented situation Kraus reiterated his familiar theme of *Phantasiearmut* inculcated by journalism, claiming that

> if one had in good time ordained beatings for the professional despoilers of values and words, an innocent humanity would not have been flogged with steel rods in concentration camps.[64]

Yet his own emphasis on the reawakening of the inherent cruelty of certain common metaphors (e.g. 'Salz in offene Wunden streuen', 'mit harter Faust durchgreifen' etc.) points to the fact that he was now faced with a different phenomenon. Of course the Nazis could not imaginatively *feel* the suffering of their victims—but they were quite capable of imagining the *effects* of their methods. In the course of *Die dritte Walpurgisnacht* Kraus commented that perhaps after all in the course of these reflections he did have something to say about Hitler: he did indeed perceive the self-contradictions, the cruelty, the naked evil of National Socialism, as his analysis reveals. Here, however, the satirist was a witness and recorder of reality. He no longer felt himself to be master of his material, no longer the confident manipulator of satirical symbols. Ultimately the sheer enormity of Hitlerism eluded satirical *Bewältigung*.[65]

Kraus's satire was in any case ill-suited to such a task.[66] His oeuvre was founded upon the 'pre-established harmony of word and world', upon the correlation of a man's language with his sensibility and therefore (he claimed) with his moral worth. For him the cardinal sin was *Phantasiearmut*, the defective imagination. There was no place in his satirical scheme for the active and knowing will to do evil. Though Kraus realised that the Nazi terror lay outside the frame of reference of his own satire, it seems unlikely that he ever became fully aware of the implication of this for his 'vision of language'.

Die dritte Walpurgisnacht ended with allusions to and quotations from *Macbeth*. The note of vengeance followed Kraus's observation of frustration and discontent among the SA; he suggested that Hitler would reap a whirlwind of violence and bloodshed. The public statement 'Warum die "Fackel". . .' was a good deal more fatalistic.[67] At one point Kraus implied that Hitler could have been defeated politically, if men of courage and determination had been prepared to speak the only language that the Nazis understood: 'About turn! Quick march!' Since this political responsibility had been evaded, nature must be left to take its course : National Socialism would collapse when it could no longer satisfy the appetites it had whetted. At times Kraus wrote of National Socialism in elemental rather than in political or moral terms : it was an 'elemental occurrence', a 'whirlwind', an 'avalanche', a 'volcano' and a force of nature 'which no power could defeat, except itself'. This resignation implied despair— *now* surely understandable—of mere political measures.

Kraus's response to the political developments of his time is more sustained, more perceptive, more urgent and more direct than that of any contemporary Austrian writer. He descends into the political arena in a way completely alien to his fellow writers. It is possible to quote many instances of Kraus's contempt for and condemnation of 'politics' as a degrading and immoral human activity, and he frequently takes pride in declaring his indifference to political issues. He warns that his concern lies with the form of his satirical statements rather than with their content. Charges of 'aestheticism' were levelled against him during his lifetime, and echoed recently by Dr Frank Field in the context of Kraus's change of political allegiance in the early thirties.

Let us say all that can be said against this undertaking of a lifetime and its tragic ending : his vision of language is permeated with the aura of *fin de siècle* Vienna, positing as it does the life of the imagination and the literary sensibility as the ultimate, absolute value. His political reaction, though on occasion pragmatic, is shot through with a mixture of moral intransigence, and insouciance. His political judgements may be influenced by narrowly 'aesthetic' impressions, as in his attitude towards the trial of Graf Moltke before the First World War, or towards an audience of naval officers at Pola in November 1913.[68] The most notorious example of the quicksand into which Kraus's 'aestheticism' could lead is his admiration for a stylistic stroke in the Imperial manifesto issued at the outbreak of war : 'Ich habe alles reiflich erwogen.' ('I have given everything due and proper consideration.') In fact Kraus consistently misquotes this particular phrase[69]—but even his version is scarcely less of a bureaucratic cliché than the original. Yet Kraus felt that it conveyed the experience and the majesty of a lifetime of conscientious public service. His essay 'In dieser grossen Zeit' cites the mani-

festo as a 'sublime proclamation', a 'poem'; although he later had
to admit that the admired sentence did not correspond to Franz
Joseph's true conduct, he refused to retract his praise. He resolved
the dilemma by declaring the words to be those of an Austrian
civil servant who had indeed reflected fully upon the significance
and implications of the decision which he was formulating. (Egon
Erwin Kisch identifies the writer as Maurus Bloch, a Prague
journalist employed in the Austrian *Ministerratspräsidium*).
Here, as elsewhere, Kraus 'discounts the possibility that a "concern with language" may turn out to be in practice nothing
more substantial than a concern for language'.[70] The same criticism can be levelled against Kraus's commendation of the style
of Fürst Starhemberg's anti-Hitler speech, or his praise for Dollfuss's use of the words 'Um Gottes willen . . .' or for the message
which greeted a Nazi minister at Aspern airfield, that his visit was
'undesirable'. These last examples may again appear to be
clichés. However, it is not the 'literary' quality of the expression
that matters to Kraus but the human experience which appears
to him to inform the language.

The abdication of satire before Hitler signals a withdrawal into
language. And this withdrawal constitutes Kraus's most severe
'aestheticism', his greatest 'irresponsibility'. Having confessed
his impotence and defeat, he finds a haven of refuge from an
intolerable reality in the very vision of language which had
ultimately proved only partially valid. At the nadir of his satirical
career, he escapes into a world of inwardness and secure cultural
values, of linguistic treatises and seminars—into a vision whose
limitations and irrelevance in *this* particular situation he openly
concedes. At the last Kraus remained tragically enmeshed in the
literary and intellectual tradition of Vienna.

And now, when all this has been said against Kraus's unparalleled undertaking, we must *also* acknowledge that in his
work the limitations of the Viennese tradition are largely overcome. At critical moments in Austrian history from 1914 to
1934 he became a 'political' writer; at such moments he did not
shrink from concerning himself with political issues or from seeking political support for his cause. Of course, his commitment
springs from his loyalty to certain moral and cultural values; it
eschews ideology; it is entered upon reluctantly and with reservations; and it is always accompanied by the implicit qualification that politics is a subordinate sphere, a means to an end.

Were he to think otherwise, he would not be an independent intellectual, a creative artist, but a politician. It is only with such reservations that the intellectual can embark upon political activity, while remaining true to his propensities, his training and his social function. The point is that in 1915, in 1919, in 1927 and again in 1934, Kraus publicly opts for *das kleinere Übel*, publicly allies himself with a political tendency or party. And he reveals an insight into the relationship between 'art' and 'life', between creative activity and politics, which is unparalleled in the work of his Austrian contemporaries, and in Germany is matched only by Thomas Mann* and Bert Brecht. Kraus's observations on this theme deserve to be quoted at length because—for all their hyperbole—they describe and *judge* (by implication) a whole cultural tradition : the cult of *Innerlichkeit*, the legacy of German idealism on the one hand and—at one remove—of prolonged political authoritarianism on the other.

> Outside my door a quarrel has broken out in which my life is at stake. I must interrupt my work to take sides, for the outcome threatens to disturb me even more. I support the man who seeks to preserve my life and thereby everything else of consequence ... I want to rush out into the street and call on everyone to help because all our lives are at stake. (1920)

> But the meaning of art is only fulfilled when the meaning of life is not being extinguished; symphonies cannot be written when a life wounded unto death is groaning for mercy nearby. That which influences life is itself dependent upon life. Aesthetes who perceive the disruption may blame the noise that causes it. In fact, however, the mystery from which we wrest the creative work encompasses this enigmatic harmony with every living thing, so that the diminishment of life also diminishes the mind that creates ... The decision to clothe the nakedness of a freezing human being with a Rembrandt canvas would in my opinion be a constructive action in a barren age. For although the mind is greater than the man, man is greater than the product of the mind—and that individual could himself be another Rembrandt. (1919)

---

* Eg. 'Kultur und Politik' (1939). Mann's insight, however, is conveyed on a far less distinguished *artistic* level. When his artistically significant writing is politically relevant, it is invariably 'conservative' and 'ironic'; when his publicistic work is overtly liberal or socialist in intent, it is of little artistic interest.

I am not concerned about the world of the mind—I can take
care of that myself! What is at issue is the securing of the very
basis of life. (1933)[71]

It is not only Kraus's commitment to social and political realities
that is impressive but also the nature of that commitment:
critical, humane, antithetical to established powers but realistically acknowledging the need for tactical alliances with existing
political forces. In the period 1914 to 1938 the majority of
creative writers in Austria merely grope their way towards a
similar insight.

One way and another, Kraus dominates any study of the
politics of Austrian literature during this period. For all his
involvement in the Viennese environment, there is something
profoundly un-Viennese about his sheer intransigence and the
absoluteness of his ethical and cultural values; he manifests none
of that fickleness, inconsistency, arbitrariness, easy-going com-
plaisance and mental slovenliness for which, like Kürnberger
before him, he castigated his fellow citizens. One way and
another, Brecht's verdict is brilliantly apposite: 'Als die Zeit
Hand an sich legte, war er diese Hand.' ('When the age laid
violent hands on itself, *he* was its chosen instrument.')[72]

Coda

The writers with whom I have been dealing show great variations within the broad limits imposed by my theme. It is not easy to indicate one or more common denominators in their reaction to political developments. More fruitful, perhaps, is Wittgenstein's concept of 'family likenesses'—that is, characteristic features which occur in different combinations among individual members of a family. No two members are identical, but they are clearly related to one another. We then find that these writers do share certain characteristic responses, though not all occur in the work of each and every one, and some authors display traits peculiar to themselves. There remains a sufficient overlap to enable us to identify most of them as belonging to the same 'family'.

One of the first things that strikes us is the widespread indifference towards the problems of the Habsburg Monarchy in the years before the First World War, particularly among the more introspective, impressionistic writers such as Hofmannsthal, Zweig, Schnitzler or Musil. Only those whose work was by its very nature closely bound up with contemporary events—Bahr's journalism and Kraus's satire—exhibited any noticeable interest in the specific political and social pressures assailing their society. And even Kraus passed through a period of ostensible 'aestheticism' round about 1905. Of the younger generation of writers, Werfel, the only one who had launched out on a literary career by 1914, was openly hostile to what he felt to be the crude horse-trading and demagogy of political affairs. Reading the work of these writers in the prewar years, we form little impression of the problems their society faced: the claims of Slav nationalism, the rise of organised mass parties, and the continental ambitions of Germany and Russia. Where a disquieting insight is glimpsed, as in *Leutnant Gustl* or *Die Verwirrungen des jungen Törless*, the full social implications are not drawn. It seems reasonable to argue that the introversion, the 'aestheticism', the endeavour to distinguish between social or cultural problems on the one hand, and political issues on the other, are connected with that loss of self-confidence and political purpose among the Austrian bourgeoisie and upper classes which several of these writers themselves criticised in retrospect. Before 1914 it was not, of course, difficult to disregard or overlook the urgency of the political dilemmas facing Vienna; the city had lived with them for so long that there appeared to be no particular cause for alarm. Although the image of an irresponsible, feckless society dancing on a volcano is dear to the moralist, we do well to recall the powerful sense of security and stability which pervaded that world. The Imperial administration and the Austrian economy continued to function with relative smoothness from day to day, irrespective of the inkpots being hurled in Parliament and the absence of any coherent, viable long-term strategy. Thus it is not until about 1912 that we find Hofmannsthal expressing his sense of foreboding and pessimism, or Kraus echoing the hopes of the war party, or the young Jewish intellectuals in Prague attempting to bridge the gulf between the German and Czech cultures of the city. In the passing references of Zweig or Hofmannsthal to politics, or in Schnitzler's portrayal of political situations, or in Musil's essays, we see how politics had been totally discredited in their eyes by the stagnation, obstructionism, endless manoeuvring and occasional eruptions of crude *Realpolitik* of the last decades.

In August 1914 there was an almost universal clamour for war in Vienna. It was joined by Hofmannsthal, Zweig, Bahr and Musil; although Kraus and Schnitzler remained silent, the latter too shared for a time the enthusiasm of his fellow citizens, while it is not certain that even Kraus was entirely impervious to the popular mood. Two other factors stand out. First, there is a strong feeling of national revival, of an emergence from the doldrums of recent years, of a new confidence and vigour conveyed by writers who had hitherto been indifferent to the political situation; secondly, this feeling is allied to a sense of identification with Germany, with their 'kith and kin', with the culture to which they believed they fundamentally owed allegiance. In a moment of supreme crisis when the conflict threatened to develop into a racial struggle between German, Slav and Latin, the Viennese instinctively looked to their powerful protectors to the north. We see here a harbinger of the Anschluss fever of 1918–19 and of the enthusiasm which greeted the invading Germans of 1938. As the War dragged on, the pendulum swung back again. Hofmannsthal and Bahr began to emphasise the separateness of Austria and the differences between her and the Reich. Hofmannsthal opposed the Anschluss proposals of 1918–19 while Bahr clung to a belief in Austria's unique historical mission even in his last novel. This fluctuation can be seen in the context of the protracted debate about the national identity of Austria, the problem of the precise relationship between the Austro-Germans and the Germans of the Reich. The same problem ultimately underlay the argument of 'cultural symbiosis' as advanced by Hofmannsthal, Bahr, Werfel, Roth and even Doderer. The argument was originally adduced as an instrument of unity in the struggle against Napoleon. In the later nineteenth century it was used to justify a continuance of the Imperial framework in the face of nationalist pressures. From the First World War onwards, however, it was invoked primarily to distinguish between Austrian and German culture. The supranational consciousness, the mediation between east and west, was seen as Austria's special contribution to European cultural history and a justification of her cultural and political independence from Germany. Where the notion was put forward, the real differences between the two cultures were overlooked in favour of the vague idea of a cultural synthesis between Vienna and the nationalities of the nineteenth-century empire. What we find on examining this relationship more closely is less a synthesis than a largely one-sided colonial relationship. Yet the cultural myth has persisted to this day. It is a classic example of an ideology in the Marxist sense—a false consciousness originally created in a particular historical context as an instrument of politics which then becomes autonomous and all-pervading, so that it is accepted uncritically by those brought up in its ambience.

The problem of national identity is at least as old as Austria's exclusion from the German League in 1866. The generation of Grillparzer and Bauernfeld still felt themselves to be Germans, albeit citizens of a multi-national empire. For them there was no tension between cultural identity and political loyalty, since German culture still reigned supreme within the Empire and the Habsburg Monarchy played a leading role among German states.

After Bismarck's victory in 1866 Austria was compelled to turn
her attention away from Germany and to seek her destiny in
south-eastern Europe. So too her intellectuals were faced with
the problem of re-defining and justifying their cultural allegiance.
Henceforth there existed a latent conflict between culture and
politics which was to have far-reaching consequences. The official
'Habsburg' culture and the supranational ethos were confined
during the last decades of the Empire to the Hofburg, the aristocracy and the officer corps; the nationalities went their separate
ways, the Austro-Germans remaining in varying degrees *deutsch-
national*, pledged to German hegemony but loyal to the Habsburg crown. With the exception of the Pan-German fanatics
centred around the politician George von Schönerer, the Austro-
Germans acquiesced in their separate political identity from the
Reich. During the Franco-Prussian War the Viennese upper
classes and the masses were united in their support for France
and their hostility towards Prussia: the wounds of Königgrätz
smarted more painfully than those of Solferino. Yet as we have
seen, in 1914 many intellectuals saw the impending conflict in
purely German terms, a measure of the way any 'Austrian'
consciousness had been eroded. At the end of the War, once the
imperial mission and with it most of Austria's economic resources had disappeared, there again arose a powerful popular
desire for union with Germany which Musil, for example, shared.
Instead the Allies decreed the preservation of a separate republic.
As Karl Stadler has recently shown,[1] this state signally failed to
instil any true sense of national identity in its citizens. Even the
Austrian fascists of the thirties lacked the strident nationalism
of their counterparts elsewhere. It took the German occupation
and the consequences of being shackled to Hitler's yoke to create
for the first time a popular and deeply-felt Austrian patriotism.
That development is prefigured in the growing appreciation of
the old Empire among the writers of the thirties.

The disintegration of the Austro-Hungarian Empire was
initially mourned by only one of the authors under review,
Hofmannsthal. To Kraus the collapse was a just retribution for
the wrongs of the past. To Werfel it was a welcome manifestation of the destruction of a corrupt order. To Musil it was the
inevitable outcome of decay and disorientation. Zweig remained
indifferent while Roth publicly opposed those who dreamed of
a Habsburg restoration. Thirty-five years later Doderer still

contrived to see the fall of the Habsburgs in a positive light, in that it had preserved the unique flavour of Austrian culture. The Monarchy and its attendant problems rarely captured the attention of these writers in the first postwar decade; if they did describe the old Empire, it was in a spirit of critical or ironic detachment. It took the threat of National Socialism and the general brutalisation of political life in the thirties to bring about a revaluation of the Habsburg state. Now it was seen by Roth and Werfel in particular as a haven of culture and civilised life in sharp contrast to a barbaric and contemptible present. Since in the case of both writers their revived interest in the Empire was connected with a new awareness of the Jewish problem, perhaps the traditional tolerance shown by the Habsburgs to the Jews played some part in this development. But in a sense, any prewar social and political structure would have served the same purpose, for what we have here is a nostalgia for the 'good old days' which in retrospect seemed so far removed from the complexities and burdens of modern society. The revaluation was determined less by the intrinsic virtues of the Habsburg Empire than by the ever more urgent pressures of the 1930s. The change of attitude did not produce any creative tension in Roth or Werfel; Roth's openly partisan *Kapuzinergruft* was inferior to his earlier, more objective novel *Radetzkymarsch*. Ironically, the two supreme literary achievements inspired by the Empire were the work of writers who repudiated it as a political and cultural ideal—Musil's *Der Mann ohne Eigenschaften* and the satire of Karl Kraus.

The War effectively put an end to the attitude of withdrawal from political affairs that had been a legacy of the *fin de siècle*. It compelled attention in one way or another, just as the Revolution of 1848 had done in an earlier age. Schnitzler alone virtually ignored the experiences of those four years and their aftermath in his postwar work. The involuntary involvement of his fellow writers led after 1918 to a far greater degree of political awareness on their part than could ever have been thought possible before the War. Although several retained their suspicion or open condemnation of activism, Roth and Werfel at least overcame this antipathy under the pressure of events, and Hofmannsthal endeavoured to reconcile politics and ethics. Nevertheless, the resistance to politics proved stubborn and few were aware of the true nature of their political position.

Schnitzler, Zweig and Musil appeared to ignore the fact that non-involvement was also a political decision. Musil misinterpreted the kind of freedom which literature requires. Hofmannsthal, in his attempt to preserve certain moral and cultural values in a non-partisan, non-political fashion, remained woefully blind to the political implications of his later writing, whereas Doderer was led by a similar concern to perform a literary and intellectual sleight of hand.

The absence of any writing comparable with the work of the English poets of the First World War has already been noted. Although the Habsburg Empire produced two classical examples of the literature of war in the form of Kraus's *Die letzten Tage der Menschheit* and Hašek's *The Good Soldier Schweik*, in general wartime experiences rarely impinged directly upon the Austro-German writing of this period. This is in marked contrast to the situation in the Weimar Republic where the theme of the *Kriegserlebnis* was of central importance in right-wing thinking.[2] There the War bred a new generation of nationalists who hailed the conflict as a cosmic or biological phenomenon, a ritual of suffering and purification. They celebrated the spirit of comradeship in the trenches (the *Frontgeist*) and the blood-sacrifice of the fallen and pledged themselves to the regeneration of the German people. Their resentment at the military defeat and political humiliation inflicted upon Germany, their bitterness at what they felt to be the treason of defeatist politicians who had stabbed the army in the back, were potent political factors in the Weimar years for they totally alienated a militant section of society from the new republic. In Austria, on the other hand, the alienation was less aggressive and due not to nationalist antipathy but to the problem of national identity. Here the defeat was so crushing, the consequences so disastrous that the preconditions for the nationalist revival in the Reich—a state still strong and largely intact, apparently oppressed and exploited by jealous or vengeful neighbours—were lacking. The First Austrian Republic was too preoccupied with the struggle for survival to afford much opportunity for dreaming of *revanche* or regeneration.

There was an absence too of Marxist literature such as was written in Germany (or in exile) by Brecht, Becher, Seghers, Wolf and Renn. Instead of the 'committed' theatre of Piscator we find the escapist spectacles of Max Reinhardt. For a brief

time at the end of the War, diaries or publicistic pieces reflected
a mood of euphoria as plans for the refashioning of Europe were
discussed, but these wild hopes were rapidly dispelled. The
Viennese 'revolution' was far less radical and bloody than contemporary events in Germany. The tangible social achievements
of the early twenties, particulary in Vienna itself, tended to be
overlooked by our writers. What we find are Hofmannsthal's
forebodings of revolutionary violence, Werfel's bitter disenchantment, Roth's weary resignation and Kraus's sustained indictment of the Socialists for betraying revolutionary values.

The creative response to specific developments in postwar
Austrian politics was sporadic—again with the notable exception
of Kraus's satire. Of the crises which might have left their mark
—the July riot of 1927, the Civil War and the murder of
Dollfuss in 1934, the abortive struggle to preserve Austria's independence—the July events and the Anschluss featured in only
two works and the Civil War not at all. Ironically the developments of the thirties impinged more upon German writing (for
example, Anna Seghers's novel *Der Weg durch den Februar*
and Friedrich Wolf's drama *Floridsdorf*) and upon committed
English writers (for instance, the poems of John Lehmann,
Stephen Spender's extended poem *Vienna* and his story 'Two
Deaths', and Christopher Isherwood's *Prater Violet*).[3] Those
Austrian writers who might have responded to the events of the
thirties tended to see them as part of a wider European pattern
and it was this which engaged their attention, above all the
threat from Germany.

Schnitzler's uncompromising individualism and scepticism at
one extreme and Kraus's reluctant, critical involvement at another represent the poles between which Austrian writers of this
period move. Both bore the hallmark of *fin de siècle* Vienna.
The satirist, however, succeeded in transcending the limitations
of that environment. The decline of the House of Habsburg had
been accompanied by the progressive withdrawal of Austrian
writers from the world of public affairs; the catastrophic culmination of its reign wrenched them out of their indifference or
contempt; but in one mode or another their lives thereafter were
lived out in the shadow of the broken Imperial eagle.

Appendix

An Outline of Austrian History 1914–1938

1914

28 June	Assassination of Archduke Franz Ferdinand at Sarajevo.
23 July	Austrian ultimatum to Serbia, delivered with the agreement and support of Germany.
25 July	Serbia's conciliatory answer repudiated by Austria-Hungary.
28 July	Austria declares war on Serbia; bombardment of Belgrade on 29 July.
	Russian mobilisation on Austrian frontier.
	Austro-Hungarian Reichsrat, prorogued in March, now suspended together with provincial assemblies.
31 July	Russia's general mobilisation makes negotiations proposed by Sir Edward Grey and belatedly supported by Germany impossible.
1 August	Italy declares her neutrality.
	Germany announces general mobilisation and declares war on Russia.
	France announces general mobilisation.
4 August	German troops enter Belgium.
	England declares war on Germany.
6 August	Austria-Hungary declares war on Russia.
	Initial German-Austrian gains in the East soon reversed.
	Serbs repulse Austrian invasion.
2 September	Fall of Lemberg.
	Russians occupy Galicia and the Bukovina, even penetrate into Hungary.
	Second Austrian attack on Serbia fails.
2 December	Austrians capture Belgrade in third offensive but are soon driven out again.

1915

22 March	Przemysl surrenders to Russians.
April	Desertion of large part of Czech regiment to Russians.
23 May	Italy declares war on Austria-Hungary after Treaty of London promises her territorial gains in Tyrol and along the Adriatic coast.
	German-Austrian forces break through Russian lines at Gorlice.
August	Warsaw occupied by Central Powers. Russians now cleared from almost all of Galicia, the Bukovina and Russian Poland.
October	German-Austrian troops capture Belgrade.
	Bulgaria enters the war on side of Central Powers and presses into southern Serbia. Serbia and Montenegro occupied until 1918, but make no appreciable contribution to food supplies in Austria.
	Shortage of foodstuffs and raw materials grows more acute.

1916

January	Austrians enter Albania.
May	Austrians attack eastwards of River Adige and seize Asiago plateau.
	Demonstration against food shortages in Vienna, repeated in September.
4 June	Brusilov offensive launched. Russians retake the Bukovina and again threaten Hungary. Troops transferred from Italian Front to meet this danger. Italians recover half of the territory lost in May.
July	Cesare Battisti, Socialist deputy from South Tyrol, is hanged by Austrians for treason, after serving with Italian Army.
August	Italian offensive in Isonzo sector leads to evacuation of important Austrian base at Gorizia, but fails to open route to Trieste.
27 August	Encouraged by success of Brusilov offensive, Rumania enters the war on side of Entente and attacks Transylvania. German, Austrian, Turkish and Bulgarian troops counter-attack and on 6 December capture Bucharest. Substantial parts of Rumania occupied but do not yield anticipated supplies of food and oil.

21 October	Austrian Prime Minister Stürgkh assassinated by radical Socialist, Friedrich Adler, in an attempt to swing party leaders against the war.
21 November	Death of Franz Joseph; he is succeeded by Karl.

1917

January	The Entente announces its intentions with regard to Danube Monarchy: liberation of Italians, Rumanians, Slavs and Czechoslovaks. Despite its vagueness, the declaration is interpreted as a policy of dismemberment.
1 February	Germany renews unrestricted U-boat warfare.
24 March	Secret letter from Karl to Prince Sixtus of Bourbon who was sounding French government's attitude to a peace settlement. Karl does not indicate intention to conclude separate peace—but he does promise in the event of peace negotiations to obtain for France a 'settlement of her just claims in Alsace-Lorraine' and he approves of French views on Belgium and Serbia. Karl's Foreign Minister Czernin has no exact knowledge of this letter.
2 April	America enters the war.
1 May	Socialist peace demonstration in Vienna.
30 May	Reichsrat reconvened.
	Authority of the military curtailed, easing of censorship, amnesty for civilians convicted by courts-martial (2 July).
	Increasing war-weariness.
	In Reichsrat Slav deputies attack dualist structure of the Empire, but plans for constitutional reforms meet with opposition from German nationalists and the Hungarian ruling class.
July	Kerensky offensive catches Central Powers by surprise; Russians occupy eastern Galicia. Under counter-attack the now exhausted Russian armies crumble.
August	Italian gains on Isonzo.
2 October	Czernin's Budapest speech denies that Austria-Hungary has territorial ambitions, urges return to frontiers of 1914, freedom of the seas, and limitation on armaments.
25 October	German-Austrian breakthrough at Caporetto captures Udine, drives Italians back to River Piave, only a day's march from Venice. Gorizia retaken. Lack of agreement between Germans and Austrians

on priorities, and inadequate transport result in wasted opportunity. Anglo-French reinforcements bolster Italian resistance.

Bolsheviks win power, Lenin stops fighting.

9 December Armistice between Central Powers and Rumania.
20 December Peace negotiations between Russia and Central Powers at Brest-Litovsk. Russians refuse to accept German demands, talks break down, fighting resumes.

Terrible winter in Austrian cities. Widespread starvation and disease. Virtual breakdown of supply system.

Prisoners of war returning from Russia (including Otto Bauer) begin to spread Marxist propaganda, especially in transit camps and army units.

1918
6 January   Czech politicians issue Epiphany Resolution demanding freedom, and censuring Czernin's conduct of negotiations at Brest-Litovsk.

8 January   Wilson's Fourteen Points. With regard to Austria-Hungary, he did not demand dismemberment but autonomous development for the nationalities, the evacuation of occupied territory and the creation of an independent Poland.

18 January At Pola sailors and workers protest against food shortages.
Strikes and demonstrations in Vienna and Wiener Neustadt.

3 March   Treaty of Brest-Litovsk. The exceptionally harsh terms imposed upon a helpless Russia cost Austria-Hungary what good-will she could still muster among the Entente. Separate treaty with Ukrainian nationalists sets up an independent Ukrainian Republic in the teeth of Soviet protests, and alienates pro-Habsburg Poles.
Central Powers occupy Ukraine and try to divert grain supplies to Germany and Austria. The task pins down ten Habsburg divisions alone, but grain is not forthcoming in anticipated quantities.

March–   Ludendorff's four offensives in the West. Total
July   effort fails.
2 April   Czernin refers to peace feelers from Clemenceau.

Latter ripostes that it was Vienna which had made
bid for separate peace, and he reveals terms of
Sixtus letter. Major scandal. Karl assures Berlin
that the section referring to Alsace-Lorraine is a
forgery. Residual Austrian prestige in the Reich
is undermined.

Czernin resigns.

Congress of Oppressed Nationalities meets in
Rome.

Faced with threat of imminent transfer of 40
German divisions from Russia to the Western
Front, and urged on by exiled Slav nationalists,
the Entente concentrates its propaganda on stirring up nationalist feeling in the hinterland and
among Habsburg troops at the front.

1 May	Crowd of 70,000 demonstrates in Prague against the Habsburgs, calling for food, peace and independence.
7 May	Peace Treaty with Rumania; again severe conditions imposed. Conference between Germany and Austria-Hungary at Spa consolidates military and economic alliance.
14 June	Habsburg armies launch another major offensive on Italian Front, but it fails. The news triggers off riots in Vienna. Throughout the summer, disturbances, strikes and mutinies occur in the Czech provinces, while Czech deputies in the Reichsrat grow ever more self-assertive. Local disorders in Bosnia and Dalmatia.
	Entente governments come out publicly in sympathy with the aspirations of the Czechoslovaks and South Slavs.
	Recognition of Czech government-in-exile.
September	Penetration of German front in the West. Bulgaria collapses, leaving south-east flank exposed to Allied thrust.
4 October	Vienna and Berlin sue for armistice on basis of Fourteen Points.
16 October	Karl belatedly announces that Austria (though not Hungary) will be reconstructed on federal lines. National Diets are to be summoned for this purpose.
20 October	Wilson replies that commitments to the Czechoslovaks and the Yugoslavs had superseded Point

Ten of his address, which had advocated merely autonomous development.

21 October   Provisional National Assembly of *Deutschösterreich* set up.

Hungarian troops begin to withdraw from Italian Front on the orders of the Károlyi government.

24 October   Allied attack in Piave sector. Habsburg armies fight back for five days.

29 October   Czech troops mutiny and the Front rapidly collapses.

28–29 October   Habsburg authority in Bohemia and Moravia handed over to nationalists. Czechoslovakia claims Slovak and Ruthenian areas from Hungary; Czech troops begin to trek homewards from the Italian Front.

National Council in Agram (Zagreb) declares its independence from Hungary, announces that Croatia and Dalmatia will unite with Serbia.

Rumania claims Transylvania and the Banat of Temesvár from Hungary.

An independent Poland is proclaimed.

Inside Austria, the Social Democrats join a coalition government. Pressure grows in favour of a Republic and the Anschluss.

3 November   Austria signs armistice.

11 November   Karl renounces participation in state affairs.

12 November   Provisional National Assembly declares that *Deutschösterreich* is a constituent part of the German Republic.

Outside Parliament, deputies proclaim birth of the Republic of *Deutschösterreich*. Members of the Red Guard, believing that they are being attacked, fire into the Parliament building, but withdraw after being pacified by Social Democrats. 31 casualties, most injured in panic-stricken flight of the crowd. A Red Guard pamphlet is printed on the presses of the *Neue Freie Presse*.

1919

Secessionist movements in Tyrol and Vorarlberg, and Yugoslav attempts to annexe parts of Carinthia, threaten the very existence of the new Austria. The central government eventually restores its limited authority; the Yugoslavs do not finally withdraw until October 1920, after two years of sporadic fighting and a plebiscite. *Deutschwestungarn* (Burgenland) is ceded to Austria under the Peace Treaty, but Hungary is reluctant to yield; Austrian sovereignty is not asserted there until November 1921.

During the first half of 1919 workers' and soldiers' councils play an influential part in Austrian politics. But the great obstacle to social revolution and the dictatorship of the proletariat is a politically aware and experienced peasantry, already committed to the support of right-wing parties. No cooperation between peasants and revolutionary proletariat is possible; in terms of political power, rural population and industrial workers are more or less equally balanced.

Important social reforms introduced between 1919 and 1921. In Vienna, the Socialist city council is progressive in the field of welfare, housing, education and taxation. There are substantial constitutional and administrative changes, but no fundamental reform of the established social order. Attempts to nationalise key industries or to change property relationships are defeated.

16 February	National elections for a Constituent Assembly, with women voting for the first time. Social Democrats win 72 seats, Christian Socialists 69; there are 26 German nationalist deputies of various loyalties.
	Coalition government of Social Democrats, Christian Socialists and civil servants is formed, with Karl Renner, the Socialist leader, as Chancellor.
21 March	Soviet republic declared in Budapest.
7 April	Soviet republic declared in Munich.
17 April	Communist-inspired demonstrations in Vienna. Hungarian agitators continue to foment discontent. The Entente warns that it will cut off supplies to Austria if a soviet republic is declared there.
2 June	First part of peace conditions handed to Austrian delegation, headed by Renner, at St Germain.
15 June	Attempted Communist putsch in Vienna fails. Thereafter the Austrian Communist Party is of little significance until the Social Democrats are driven underground or into exile in 1934. It was the policy of the Social Democratic Party to keep

radicals and moderates under one roof, thus preventing the split in the socialist camp that proved so disastrous in Germany.

10 September   Austrian Peace Treaty accepted by Parliament.
Anschluss is forbidden under the terms of the Treaty, except under the auspices of the League of Nations. The name *Deutschösterreich* is abandoned. The Social Democrats, especially the radical Bauer faction, cling to the hope of a union with a socialist Germany. The Grossdeutsche Volkspartei which emerged in September 1920 from the union of seventeen national and provincial groups, also supports Anschluss. The Christian Socialists remain divided on this point.

19 October   Second coalition government (Christian Socialists and Social Democrats).

1920
12 May   *Heimatwehr* founded in Tyrol. Similar provincial organisations in Carinthia, Styria and Upper Austria. Originally they were local self-defence forces set up in the chaos at the end of the war to preserve law and order or to repel foreign invaders. Later tolerated by the authorities as a form of auxiliary police. Once the threat of anarchy and the need for military action passed, these organisations became political weapons directed against strikes, demonstrations and any other form of insurrection inspired by the Socialists. They were led by former junior officers, and armed and financed by small sections of industry and the banking world; also subventions from foreign governments, especially Italy. After July 1927 they were reformed on a national, federal basis. Played key role in Civil War crisis.

June   Coalition collapses.
10 October   Klagenfurt plebiscite; southern Carinthia, claimed by Yugoslavia, remains Austrian.

November   New elections: Christian Socialists win 79 seats, Social Democrats 62, Grossdeutsche (Pan-Germans) 18, 1 independent (Czernin).
Socialists go into opposition, where they remain for the duration of the First Republic.
New cabinet of Christian Socialists and civil ser-

vants. Grossdeutsche can in general be relied upon to support the government; in 1921 they enter a new cabinet under Schober.

1921

April | Ex-Emperor Karl returns to Hungary in an attempt to recover the Hungarian throne, but is out-manoeuvred by the Regent, Admiral Horthy. On the return journey through Austria, Karl's train is besieged by angry railway workers.

October | Karl again attempts a putsch in Hungary and again fails.
Austria in the grip of inflation.

1 December | Workers riot in Vienna, party leaders have no control over them.
Ödenburg (Sopron) plebiscite; capital of Burgenland stays Hungarian, after the rest of the province has been transferred to Austria.

1922

1 April | Karl dies in Madeira, aged 35; his son Otto becomes Pretender.

31 May | First government of Ignaz Seipel, a coalition of Christian Socialists and Grossdeutschen. Seipel, a Catholic prelate, dreamed of a regenerated Austria, which would be a source of inspiration to the suffering peoples of Central Europe. He envisaged union with Germany in the wider context of European unity. He aimed at a coalition of all non-Marxist parties.
Inflation reaches its height: the Krone is worth only 1/15,000 of its nominal gold value.

4 October | Seipel negotiates Geneva Protocols, a major diplomatic achievement:

    (i) Britain, France, Italy and Czechoslovakia guarantee Austrian independence. Austria pledges to maintain her independence for 20 years.

    (ii) Signatories guarantee a League of Nations credit of 650 million gold crowns to stabilise the Austrian currency. A new unit is introduced, the Schilling. Credit to be spent under the supervision of a League of Nations commissar.

(iii)   Austria pledges to balance her budget within
        two years, to preserve law and order, and to
        mortgage customs and excise duties and
        income from State tobacco monopoly as
        guarantee.

The currency is thus stabilised at the cost of heavy
unemployment and severe economic restraint.
Seipel commands the support of most of the bourgeoisie and the peasantry, including the Grossdeutschen, but is fiercely opposed by the Socialists.

1923

A nationally organised *Republikanischer Schutzbund* is formed out of local *Arbeiterwehr* formations; later the Socialist militia reaches a peak of
80,000 men, and in 1934 still numbers some
60,000. (Compare Austrian Army, with a ceiling
of 30,000; police and gendarmerie muster about
15,000 men each.)
After the mass unemployment of the first postwar years, the level never falls below 10 per cent
of the working population even in the relatively
prosperous years between 1924 and 1929.

October   New elections : Christian Socialists win 82 seats,
          Social Democrats 68, Grossdeutsche 10, Landbund
          (peasant party) 5.
          Coalition as before.

1924
November   Railway strike. Seipel resigns, having already run
           into opposition within his own party over the
           attempt to persuade the Länder to introduce
           administrative and economic reforms. New govern-
           ment under Ramek continues coalition of Christian
           Socialists and Grossdeutschen.

1925

Anschluss idea begins to gain popularity in 'non-
political' spheres—economic and cultural. Notion
of a customs union with Germany born.

1926
30 June   Departure of League of Nations commissar marks
          the end of the process of stabilisation.

Collapse of the Central Savings Bank (Zentralbank der deutschen Sparkassen) due to incompetence and speculation. Christian Socialist politicians involved : for political ends, they had made large sums available from the Post Office Savings Bank. Latter also on the verge of folding up. 187.5 million Schilling required from public funds to keep both banks solvent.

The scandal eventually brings down the Ramek government.

16 October — Second Seipel administration : completes economic recovery, but public expenditure still strictly controlled.

3 November — Linz congress of the Social Democratic Party repudiates violence and affirms its faith in democracy; but it also maintains that force would be justified in meeting counter-revolution.

1927
24 April — New elections bring Socialist gains—they now muster 42 per cent of the vote : Christian Socialists 73 seats, Social Democrats 71, Grossdeutsche 12, Landbund 9.

Weak coalition government of bourgeois parties.

15 July — Workers' protest in Vienna against the acquittal of members of the *Frontkämpfer* organisation who had been accused of participating in a shooting fracas in which an old man and a boy had been killed. An inflammatory editorial in the *Arbeiterzeitung* helps to spark off a demonstration. The Social Democrat leadership is taken by surprise, no units of the *Schutzbund* are detailed for crowd control, and the demonstration rapidly gets out of hand. The police had accepted the party leaders' assurance that no official demonstration was planned, therefore there is only a small force on alert. The crowd sets fire to the Palace of Justice and prevents the approach of fire engines, despite appeals from the Socialist mayor of Vienna. Latter refuses to call in the Army, as Schober, now Chief of Police, demands. Schober therefore obtains permission direct from the Federal government to arm his men with carbines. Police open fire on demonstrators, mounted police charge with drawn sabres.

Dum-dum type bullets used. Wanton violence results in heavy toll of death and injury. 89 killed, including 4 policemen. An attempt to call a general strike fails; in Tyrol and Carinthia the *Heimwehr* intervenes to break transport strike.

The riot reinforces the position of the *Heimwehr* by conjuring up the bogey of violence and anarchy; the *Heimwehr* is now reorganised into a federal force and stages frequent parades etc. Even liberal sections of the bourgeoisie now estranged from the Social Democrats. Seipel moves closer to the *Heimwehr,* partly to ensure their support in a crisis, partly in order to be able to control them more effectively. Having failed to build a stable bourgeois coalition, and confronted with increasing political violence, Seipel despairs of a workable parliamentary democracy.

Opposition between the working class and the bourgeoisie grows ever more pronounced.

In the autumn a Social Democratic Party conference reaffirms that violence might be justified in meeting counter-revolution, but deplores the violence employed by the workers on 15 July. The *Schutzbund* is strengthened as much for internal discipline as for protection against outside forces.

Renner advocates a bid to enter the coalition; Bauer is opposed to the idea.

1929

Seipel resigns.

The *Heimwehr* grows in strength, its threats against Parliament become vociferous, it begins to demand a state modelled on Italian fascism.

Unrest spreads.

September   Schober becomes Chancellor, heading a government of Christian Socialists, Grossdeutschen, a nominal *Heimwehr* representative and distinguished lay experts.

Imminent collapse of the Bodencreditanstalt is prevented by the intervention of the Creditanstalt bank : latter forced by the government to take over the Bodencreditanstalt's commitments.

7 December   A new constitution comes into force. Instead of making it more authoritarian, as the *Heimwehr*

had expected, Schober in fact strengthens it without destroying its democratic basis; in this he is aided by the Social Democrats. Increased powers for the President (hitherto a largely ceremonial office); government given greater freedom of action to make it less susceptible to parliamentary pressure.

Heimwehr alienated by this buttressing of the legal democratic system.

1930

Growing economic crisis and unemployment.

In Germany Parliament is dissolved and the President rules by decree. In the September elections the National Socialists become the second largest party in the Reichstag.

18 May   A national rally of the *Heimwehr* denounces the existing state and proclaims a fascist programme (this is the occasion when the Korneuburg Oath was taken). It repudiates parliamentary democracy and advocates a corporative state. It also announces that the *Heimwehr* will contest the next election as an independent party.

Schober loses support of Christian Socialist ministers.

2 September   New cabinet of *Heimwehr* and Christian Socialists under Vaugoin. Starhemberg, one of the national leaders of the *Heimwehr*, is Minister of the Interior. Friction ensues within the coalition. Government has no majority in the Nationalrat; Parliament is therefore dissolved.

10 November   New elections: Social Democrats win 72 seats, Christian Socialists 66, Grossdeutsche (or Nationaler Wirtschaftsblock) 10, Landbund 9, Heimatblock (the political arm of the *Heimwehr*) 8.

National Socialist vote in Austria is about 200,000, so distributed that they fail to win representation. This is the last national election under the First Republic. Government of Grossdeutschen and Christian Socialists.

The *Heimwehr* goes into opposition.

The economic crisis grows more urgent.

1931

March   Dollfuss enters cabinet as Minister of Agriculture.

News leaks out of negotiations over a Customs
Union between Austria and Germany. Outcry from
France and the Little Entente who see this as the
first step towards *Anschluss*. After the International
Court of Justice has passed judgement, Austria and
Germany are compelled to announce in September
that they will not pursue the matter.

In the months of internal crisis that follow, Seipel
makes overtures to the Social Democrats with a
view to forming a coalition, but the Socialists
refuse.

June

At the beginning of the month the Creditanstalt
closes its doors. A month earlier it showed a debt
of 140 million Schilling, blamed upon the takeover
of the Bodencreditanstalt in 1929. All reserves plus
most of the share capital have been dissipated.
Government decides to put in 100 million Schilling
from public funds, leaving the National Bank and
the House of Rothschild to find 30 million each.
It is a devastating blow to the Austrian economy.
Economic chaos threatens Central Europe. Crisis
of confidence at home and abroad. Bank of England
steps in to stave off the worst effects.

Government is forced to resign.

New cabinet formed: Christian Socialists, Grossdeutsche and Landbund; with support of Social
Democrats it introduces drastic measures for right-
ing the economy.

13 September

A *Heimwehr* putsch in Styria fails to win support
of the *Heimwehr* in neighbouring *Länder* and
collapses.

1932

Grossdeutsche leave the government. Schuschnigg
made Minister of Justice, Dollfuss continues as
Minister of Agriculture.

6–8 April

London conference discusses Tardieu Plan for the
economic integration of Central Europe (Austria,
Hungary, Czechoslovakia, Yugoslavia and
Rumania) under French aegis. Centred in Prague,
the block would help thwart German and Italian
ambitions. The plan founders on the opposition of
Germany and Italy; it is also opposed by the

	Austrian Social Democrats who still hope for union with a Socialist Germany.
24 April	In elections to State Legislatures (the last provincial elections under the First Republic) the Social Democrats make gains, there is an upsurge in the strength of the Austrian Nazis, and smaller parties are almost wiped out. All parties except the Christian Socialists press for a general election. The government refuses, but soon has to resign.
20 May	Dollfuss heads a government of Christian Socialists, Landbund and Heimatblock. Fey, another *Heimwehr* leader, is Minister of Security. This government commands a majority of only one seat. In Styria the *Heimwehr* joins with the Nazis. The obstructionism of the Social Democrats, now the most powerful single political force in the country, drives Dollfuss further into the *Heimwehr* camp; they urge a final showdown with the Socialists.
15 July	Protocol of Lausanne. Austria obtains League of Nations credits in return for a renunciation of the Anschluss for another ten years. The agreement is violently opposed by the Social Democrats and the Grossdeutschen. In the course of the year Dollfuss consults Otto Bauer about the possibility of a 'black-red' coalition.

1933

30 January	In Germany Hitler becomes Chancellor; political terrorism reigns as Germany prepares for new elections.
4 March	Austrian Parliament suspends itself amid total confusion.
15 March	Government uses police to prevent a sitting of the Lower House which it claims is illegal. Social Democrats refrain from protesting through extra-parliamentary action, for fear of being crushed by a combination of the government and the National Socialists. Dollfuss orders the *Schutzbund* to be disbanded; it goes underground. The Constitutional Court is suspended, and press censorship imposed.

Dollfuss's increasing authoritarianism is based on a 'War-economy Enabling Act' of 1917.

26 May   Austrian Communist Party banned.

28 May   Hitler imposes a tax of 1000 marks on German citizens intending to visit Austria, thus dealing a severe blow to the tourist industry.

Dollfuss launches the would-be 'non-partisan' Fatherland Front.

Austrian Nazis begin a terrorist campaign.

19 June   National Socialist movement in Austria is outlawed; hard-core Nazis flee to Bavaria, where they form the Austrian Legion of nearly 15,000 men. Detention camps set up in Austria.

Total membership of the movement at this point is some 43,000, compared with only 4,500 in 1928. German radio stations and aircraft bombard Austria with Nazi propaganda.

September   Cabinet reshuffle : 'non-party' administration.

11 September   Dollfuss outlines plans for the reshaping of the State on corporate lines (*auf berufsständischer Grundlage*). He himself fully believed in the concept—but it was in any case a condition imposed by Mussolini (at Riccione on 19/20 August) in return for Italian support for continued Austrian independence.

The major problem is the integration of the Socialists in the Fatherland Front. Feelers are put out on both sides in the search for compromise solutions—even up to 7 February 1934, a few days before the Civil War. Nazi terror intensifies.

1934
January   Mussolini presses for decisive anti-parliamentary measures, especially the destruction of the Social Democratic Party.

2–9 February   The *Heimwehr* resorts to intimidation of the authorities in the federal states.

10 February   The Socialist mayor of Vienna is stripped of his control of the police.

11 February   Fey announces : 'Tomorrow we will get to work and make a good job of it . . .'

12 February   The Civil War breaks out.

It begins in Linz, where the *Schutzbund*, acting on their own initiative, offer armed resistance to police searching for arms. Faced with a *fait accompli*, the Party executive in Vienna declares a general strike. The Socialist militia lacks any overall strategy and detailed instructions; many weapon caches have already been confiscated and many leaders arrested in police raids. Confusion and improvisation result. There is fighting in the Viennese suburbs (where the government has to rely heavily on Fey's *Heimwehr* units), in Graz, in the industrial area of Upper Styria, in Steyr and Sankt Pölten. Isolated pockets of the *Schutzbund* are pitted against the police, gendarmerie, Federal Army and the *Heimwehr*. In Vienna artillery is called in to cut short resistance. The Socialists fight desperately from the modern municipal housing blocks. The general strike fails to materialise, there is no mass uprising. The government asserts control, the Socialist leaders are arrested or driven into exile, the Party and the trade unions are outlawed.

There are 128 fatal casualties on the government side and 193 civilian dead.

17 March   The Rome Protocols on cooperation and consultation between Italy, Hungary and Austria are signed.

1 May   A new constitution envisages a corporative state; parties are to be replaced by professional or occupational bodies in which the class struggle is resolved. Various advisory councils are to be set up to comment upon legislation proposed by the government; a *Bundesrat* elected from these councils would have the right of veto but no power to initiate legislation and scarcely any right of debate.

This machinery is never put into effect. The government continues to rule by decree.

From May to July the Nazis unleash a new wave of terror.

25 July   A Nazi putsch in Vienna fails, but Dollfuss is murdered.

Mussolini discourages German intervention by massing Italian divisions on the Brenner.

Hitler, seeing that he has been misled by Austrian

Nazis, now becomes more conciliatory and sends von Papen to Vienna as his special envoy. Schuschnigg becomes Chancellor.

1936

Collapse of the Phoenix insurance company rocks Austria.

14 May   Starhemberg is dropped from the cabinet and replaced as leader of the Fatherland Front. The *Heimwehr*, its political influence no longer significant, is absorbed into the Federal Army.

11 July   German-Austrian agreement is signed. (Italy is now embroiled in Africa and moving closer to Germany, thus no longer a reliable guarantor of Austrian independence.) In return for German recognition of Austrian independence and a pledge of non-intervention, Austria agrees to grant an amnesty to all but the gravest Nazi offenders and to accept two members of the quasi-Nazi 'National Opposition' into the cabinet.

November   New cabinet no longer has any *Heimwehr* members.

1938

Austria now diplomatically isolated.

12 February   Schuschnigg is summoned to Berchtesgaden to meet Hitler. He is browbeaten into promising concessions which would reduce Austria to the status of a German satellite.
              On his return he tries to out-manoeuvre Hitler by holding a plebiscite.

9 March   Schuschnigg announces a referendum on the Anschluss for 13 March.

11 March   Under pressure from Goering, Schuschnigg resigns. Germany demands a government under Seyss-Inquart, the legalisation of the National Socialist movement and permission for the Austrian Legion to return. President Miklas refuses to yield except to force. As confused negotiations continue in Vienna, Nazis occupy key posts in the provinces. Hitler obtains an assurance from Mussolini that Italy will take no action, and orders the German Army to enter Austria on 12 March.

Notes

INTRODUCTION

1. Arthur J. May, *The Passing of the Hbsburg Monarchy 1914–1918*, Philadelphia, 1966, devotes a short section to the wartime activities of various Austro-German writers but the account is sketchy and inaccurate (Volume I, 'Life Flows On'). Similarly the few pages devoted to the same subject by Albert Fuchs in his otherwise admirable *Geistige Strömungen in Österreich 1867–1918*, Vienna, 1949 (pp. 270–75) are uninformative and unreliable.

2. Magris' study ranges over the whole field of Austrian literature from the late eighteenth century and goes beyond specific political themes. The book stirred up a good deal of resentment and criticism among Austrian scholars, much of it determined by the very attitude that Magris set out to expose. The most cogent critique came from Walter Weiss in his essay 'Österreichische Literatur—eine Gefangene des Habsburgischen Mythos?', now to be found in *Geschichte in der österreichischen Literatur des 19. und 20. Jahrhunderts*, published by the Institut für Österreichkunde (Vienna, 1970). Weiss argued that Magris had substituted one ideology for another, thus giving rise to a narrow and over-simplified treatment of his examples.

3. 'Kultur und Politik' (1939), *Reden und Aufsätze 4*, Frankfurt a.M., 1960, p. 853. For a sociologist's view of the problem, see Ralf Dahrendorf, *Society and Democracy in Germany*, London, 1968.

4. Otto Rommel has edited an excellent anthology of these texts in *Der österreichische Vormärz*, DLER, Reihe Politische Dichtung, Volume 4, Leipzig, 1931; I am indebted to his lucid and objective introduction.

5. Ilsa Barea, *Vienna. Legend and Reality*, London, 1966, p. 207, a fascinating, thought-provoking survey of Viennese social and cultural history.

6. Ibid., pp. 366, 324, 323.

7. Hermann Broch, *Hofmannsthal und seine Zeit*, Munich, 1964, p. 82. E. H. Buschbeck finds that the characteristics of this society, its lack of concern with public affairs and its great literary and artistic understanding, were a development of the *Biedermeier* tradition; see *Austria*, London, 1949, p. 92.

8. C. E. Schorske, 'Politics and the psyche in *fin de siècle* Vienna', *American Historical Review*, Vol. LXVI (1961). See also the same author's 'The Transformation of the Garden: Ideal and Society in

Austrian Literature', a paper presented to the Twelfth International Congress of Historical Sciences, Vienna, September 1965.

9. Barea, op. cit., p. 215.

CHAPTER I : HOFMANNSTHAL

1. *Hugo von Hofmannsthal—Eberhard von Bodenhausen. Briefe der Freundschaft*, ed. Dora Freifrau von Bodenhausen, Berlin, 1953, letter of 30 April 1912.

2. *Hugo von Hofmannsthal—Leopold von Andrian. Briefwechsel*, ed. Walter H. Perl, Frankfurt a.M., 1968, letter of 24 August 1913.

3. Letter to Bodenhausen of 7 October 1914. He had expressed similar elation at the time of the partial mobilisation of 1909 when in a letter to Harry Graf Kessler he remarked upon the quiet determination of the Austrian people and the cessation of political squabbling.

4. For a detailed discussion see Z. A. B. Zeman, *The Break Up of the Habsburg Empire 1914–1918*, Oxford, 1961.

5. Letter to Bodenhausen of 7 October 1914.

6. *Briefe der Freundschaft*, op. cit., pp. 235–36. There is evidence that the philosopher Rudolf Pannwitz helped to bring about this change of heart by giving Hofmannsthal moral encouragement.

7. Ibid., letter of 30 April 1912.

8. Letter of 28 November 1928, in 'Hugo von Hofmannsthals Briefe an Josef Redlich,' *Forum* (Vienna), III. Jahr, Heft 31/32 (July/August 1956). See also letter of 6 December 1925 in *Hugo von Hofmannsthal—Carl J. Burckhardt. Briefwechsel*, ed. Carl J. Burckhardt, Frankfurt a.M., 1957.

9. Letter to Redlich of 13 January 1919 (cf. n. 8).

10. Letter to Hoyos, 27 October 1916, in *Hugo von Hofmannsthal—Josef Redlich. Briefwechsel*, ed. Helga Fussgänger, Frankfurt a.M., 1971, p. 149.

11. Cf. Kurt Sontheimer, *Antidemokratisches Denken in der Weimarer Republik*, Munich, 1962, p. 308.

12. Hugo von Hofmannsthal, *Gesammelte Werke in Einzelausgaben*, ed. Herbert Steiner, *Prosa IV*, Frankfurt a.M., 1955, pp. 7–8. This is the standard edition of H.'s works.

13. *Prosa III*, Frankfurt a.M., 1952, p. 444.

14. 'Das Schrifttum als geistiger Raum der Nation', *Prosa IV*, p. 413.

15. Klemens von Klemperer, *Germany's New Conservatism. Its History and Dilemma in the Twentieth Century*, Princeton, 1957, p. 11, n. 16.

16. *Prosa IV*, p. 472.

17. Both in the article 'Europäische Revue' and in a letter to Redlich on 8 November 1928. In 1924 Rohan founded an international federation for cultural cooperation and Hofmannsthal helped to chair its annual conference in Vienna in 1926.

18. Sontheimer, op. cit., p. 116, n. 2 and pp. 242–43. Rohan's essays were collected under the title *Umbruch der Zeit 1923–1930*, Berlin, 1930.

19. Letter to Redlich on 8 November 1928.
20. Letter to Redlich of 9 November 1926. Schmitt's *Die Diktatur* (1921) and his *Politische Theologie* (1922) were in Hofmannsthal's library.
21. Sontheimer, pp. 94–98, 195–98, 277, 328–31.
22. *After Strange Gods. A Primer of Modern Heresy*, London, 1934, pp. 18–19.
23. Especially 'Das Publikum der Salzburger Festspiele', 'Zum Programm der Salzburger Festspiele 1928', 'Das Salzburger grosse Welttheater' (1925). In 1936 32 per cent of the working population in Austria was employed on the land as against 6 per cent in England.
24. Sontheimer, p. 155.
25. Jacques Droz, *Le romantisme allemand et l'Etat. Résistance et collaboration dans l'Allemagne napoléonienne,* Paris, 1966; also Magris, op. cit.
26. K. R. Stadler, 'Austria' in *European Fascism*, ed. S. J. Woolf, London, 1968, p. 96–97, p. 105.
27. *Lustspiele II*, Frankfurt a.M., 1965, p. 230.
28. *Aufzeichnungen*, Frankfurt a.M., 1959, p. 202.
29. *Dramen IV*, Frankfurt a.M., 1958, pp. 200–1.
30. See for instance Emil Staiger, *Goethe*, Vol. 1, Zurich, 1952, pp. 298–99.

CHAPTER 2 : BAHR

1. See 'Gruss an Bahr und Hofmannsthal' (May 1916), reprinted in Karl Kraus, *Weltgericht*, ed. H. Fischer, Munich/Vienna, n.d. and *Die letzten Tage der Menschheit*, Act I, Scene 19.
2. *Österreich und dessen Zukunft,* quoted in *Der österreichische Vormärz*, op. cit., pp. 83–84. See also Eduard Bauernfeld, *Erinnerungen aus Alt-Wien* (1872), Vienna, 1923, p. 137; and Ferdinand Kürnberger, 'Politischer Allerseelentag' (1871) in *Siegelringe,* Munich, 1910.
3. *Dalmatinische Reise*, Berlin, 1909, p. 52.
4. *Hugo von Hofmannsthal—Harry Graf Kessler. Briefwechsel 1898–1929*, ed. Hilde Burger, Frankfurt a.M., 1968, letter of 14 October 1908 and Kessler's reply.
5. Herbert Cysarz, *Zur Geistesgeschichte des Weltkriegs. Die dichterischen Wandlungen des deutschen Kriegsbilds 1910–1930,* Halle/Saale, 1931, pp. 113–16.
6. *Schwarzgelb*, Berlin, 1917, p. 18.
7. Fuchs, *Geistige Strömungen . . .*, p. 70.
8. *Die Rotte Korahs* (1918), Vienna, 1948, pp. 487–89.
9. *Tagebuch 1918*, Innsbruck/Vienna/Munich, 1919, entry for 21 October.
10. *Schicksalsjahre Österreichs 1908–1919. Das politische Tagebuch Josef Redlichs*, ed. Fritz Fellner, 2 vols, Graz/Cologne, 1953, entries for 11 April and 20 August 1917.
11. See *Die Fackel*, Nr. 514–18 (July 1919), 'Proteste'.

12. For Luxemburg, see *Liebe der Lebenden: Tagebücher 1921–23,* Hildesheim, n.d., entry for 15 February 1921 (apropos her letters from prison); for Hungarian Revolution, ibid., entry for 18 February 1923.

CHAPTER 3 : SCHNITZLER

1. Karl Kraus, *Worte in Versen,* ed. Heinrich Fischer, Munich, 1959, p. 134.
2. *Komödie der Worte* (1915), *Fink und Fliederbusch* (1917), *Doktor Gräsler, Badearzt* (1917).
3. 'Und einmal wird der Friede kommen...' in *Arthur Schnitzler: Aphorismen und Betrachtungen,* ed. Robert O. Weiss, Frankfurt a.M., 1967, pp. 187–96.
4. 'Kriegsgeschichte', *Literatur und Kritik,* Heft 13 (April 1967).
5. *Die letzten Tage der Menschheit,* ed. H. Fischer, Munich, 1957, p. 160 (Act I, Scene 22): the Nörgler speaks.
6. J. P. Stern, 'Karl Kraus's Vision of Language', *The Modern Language Review,* Vol. LXI, No. 1 (January 1966), p. 83.
7. *Aphorismen ...,* p. 203.
8. Letter of 2 August 1918 in *Georg Brandes und Arthur Schnitzler: Ein Briefwechsel,* ed. Kurt Bergel, Berkeley and Los Angeles, 1956; 'Bemerkungen zur Politik', *Forum,* IX Jahr, Heft 108 (December 1962).
9. *Jugend in Wien. Eine Autobiographie,* ed. Theresa Nickl and Heinrich Schnitzler, Vienna, 1968, pp. 96–97.
10. Bernard Blume, *Das nihilistische Weltbild Arthur Schnitzlers,* Stuttgart, 1936, pp. 6, 26.
11. Arthur Schnitzler, *Die dramatischen Werke,* 2. Band, Frankfurt a.M., 1962, p. 960.
12. See Christa Melchinger, *Illusion und Wirklichkeit im dramatischen Werk Arthur Schnitzlers,* Heidelberg, 1968, pp. 117–19, 125.
13. Martin Swales, *Arthur Schnitzler: A Critical Study,* Oxford, 1971, p. 277.
14. *Der Weg ins Freie,* Berlin, 1918, pp. 131–32, 316.
15. *Liebelei. Leutnant Gustl. Die letzten Masken,* edited with an Introduction by J. P. Stern, Cambridge, 1966, p. 26.
16. Such an argument has now been advanced in Swales's study of Schnitzler, esp. pp. 58–68.
17. Letter to Liese Steinruck on 22 December 1914.

CHAPTER 4 : WERFEL

1. 'Aphorismus zu diesem Jahr', *Die Aktion,* 4. Jhg., Nr. 48–9 (5 December 1914).
2. *Austria as it is,* [anon.], London, 1828, p. 91.
3. For accounts of the Germans in Prague, see e.g.:
    Max Brod, *Der Prager Kreis,* Stuttgart etc., 1966;

Peter Demetz, *Rene Rilkes Prager Jahre*, Düsseldorf, 1953;
Pavel Eisner, *Franz Kafka and Prague*, New York, 1950;
Eduard Goldstücker, 'Zum Profil der Prager deutschen Dichtung um 1900', *Philologica Pragensia*, V. Jhg., Heft 3 (1962); (ed.) *Weltfreunde: Konferenz über die Prager deutsche Dichtung*, Berlin/ Neuwied, 1967;
Egon Erwin Kisch, *Marktplatz der Sensationen*, Vienna, 1947;
Kurt Krolop, 'Zur Geschichte der Prager deutschen Literatur', *Literatur und Kritik*, Nr. 2 (May 1966).

4. 'Glosse zu einer Wedekind-Feier', *Prager Tagblatt*, Nr. 105/xxxix (18 April 1914), quoted in Kurt Krolop, 'Ein Manifest der "Prager Schule"', *Philologica Pragensia*, VII. Jhg., Heft 4 (1964), p. 334.

5. Max Brod, *Streitbares Leben: Autobiographie*, Munich, 1960, p. 143.

6. *Zeit-Echo. Ein Kriegstagebuch der Künstler 1914–15*, Munich/ Berlin, 1915, Heft 3, p. 26. Unaccountably the most recent study of Werfel's life and work—Lore B. Foltin, *Franz Werfel*, Stuttgart, 1972—calls this piece a 'satirical sketch'.

7. 'Die christliche Sendung. Ein offener Brief an Kurt Hiller', *Die neue Rundschau*, Jhg. XXVIII (January 1917), p. 103.

8. Quoted in Adolf D. Klarmann, 'Franz Werfel's Eschatology and Cosmogony', *Modern Language Quarterly*, Vol. VII (1946), p. 391.

9. *Weltfreunde*, ed. Goldstücker, op. cit., p. 71.

10. Klarmann, loc. cit. Subsequent commentators such as Lore B. Foltin and Josef Pfeifer ('F. W. und die politischen Umwälzungen des Jahres 1918 in Wien', *Etudes Germaniques* 26 [1971], pp. 194–207) have followed this interpretation.

11. For details see L'udovít Šulc, 'Über den entscheidenden Abschnitt im Leben E. E. Kischs (1917–1919)', *Weltfreunde*, ed. Goldstücker.

12. Franz Blei, *Erzählung eines Lebens*, Leipzig, 1930, pp. 473–80.

13. *Barbara oder die Frömmigkeit*, Frankfurt a.M./Hamburg, 1953, pp. 428–29.

14. Quoted in Anton Kuh, *Von Goethe abwärts*, Vienna/Hanover/ Berne, 1963, p. 96.

15. See W. A. Berendsohn, *Die humanistische Front. Einführung in die deutsche Emigranten-Literatur*, Zurich, 1946, p. 146; Foltin, op. cit., pp. 73f, 78–79; Klaus Mann, *Der Wendepunkt: Ein Bericht*, Berlin/Frankfurt, 1958, pp. 343–44.

16. Magris, *Der Habsburgische Mythos...*, p. 266.

17. *Der Abituriententag*, Fischer Bücherei Nr. 268, Frankfurt a.M./ Hamburg, 1959, p. 38.

18. Werfel, *Erzählungen aus zwei Welten*, 2. Band, ed. Adolf D. Klarmann, [Vienna] 1952, pp. 181–82.

19. Werfel, *Twilight of a World*, London, 1937, p. 12; I have slightly altered the original translation by H. T. Lowe-Porter.

20. See Foltin, op. cit., p. 96 and Lore B. Foltin and John M. Spalek, 'Franz Werfel's Essays: A Survey', *German Quarterly*, Vol. XLII (1969), pp. 172–203.

21. *Twilight of a World,* pp. 29–30.
22. See Imanuel Geiss, *Juli 1914. Die europäische Krise und der Ausbruch des Ersten Weltkriegs,* DTV, Munich, 1965.
23. *Erzählungen aus zwei Welten,* 2. Band, p. 385. Klarmann there supplies a German translation of the commentaries on individual stories which I have re-translated into English. The only published version of the introductory essay is Lowe-Porter's English translation of 1937. The German MS is now in the possession of the S. Fischer Verlag.
24. *Erzählungen aus zwei Welten,* 3. Band, ed. Adolf D. Klarmann, Frankfurt a.M., 1954, pp. 461–64.

CHAPTER 5 : ROTH

1. Joseph Roth, *Briefe 1911–1939,* ed. Hermann Kesten, Cologne/Berlin, 1970—letter to a cousin on 24 August 1917.
2. See David Bronsen, 'Phantasie und Wirklichkeit. Geburtsort und Vaterschaft im Leben Joseph Roths', *Neue Rundschau* 79 (1968), pp. 494–505; 'Joseph Roths Kriegsdienst', *Schweizer Monatshefte* 49 (1969), pp. 569–81; 'Die journalistischen Anfänge Joseph Roths, Wien 1918–1920', *Literatur und Kritik* 5 (1970), pp. 37–54.
3. Joseph Roth, *Werke in drei Bänden,* ed. H. Kesten, Cologne/Berlin, 1956, Vol. II, p. 470.
4. *Der stumme Prophet,* ed. Werner Lengning, Cologne/Berlin, 1965, p. 213.
5. *Briefe,* letter to Herbert Ihering, 17 September 1922.
6. Bronsen, 'Die journalistischen Anfänge . . .' p. 46.
7. Joseph Roth, *Der neue Tag. Unbekannte politische Arbeiten 1919–1927, Wien, Berlin, Moskau,* edited with an introduction by Ingeborg Sültemeyer, Cologne/Berlin, 1970.
8. *Werke II,* p. 398.
9. Ibid., pp. 623–24.
10. Anton Böhm, 'Das grosse schwarze Gesetz. Notizen zu Joseph Roths Gesamtwerk', *Wort und Wahrheit,* Vol. XIV (1959). Böhm does not take the argument far enough.
11. *Briefe,* letter to Benno Reifenberg, 30 August 1925 and letter to Brentano on 31 July 1927.
12. See Leo Rosten, *The Joys of Yiddish.* Harmondsworth, 1971, pp. 94–95.
13. *Der stumme Prophet,* pp. 267–68.
14. 'Nachruf' (January 1919), in *Weltgericht,* ed. Heinrich Fischer, Munich/Vienna, n.d., p. 306.
15. *Werke I,* p. 282.
16. Geiss, *Juli 1914,* op. cit., p. 31.
17. Barea, *Vienna,* op. cit., p. 259.
18. *Hofmannsthal und seine Zeit,* op. cit., p. 73.
19. *Werke I,* p. 357.

20. See eg. Walter Goldinger, *Geschichte der Republik Österreich,* Vienna, 1962, p. 66 and Gordon Brook-Shepherd, *Anschluss: The Rape of Austria,* London, 1963, pp. 111–17; also Roth's letter of 28 April 1933 to Stefan Zweig.

CHAPTER 6: ZWEIG

1. Herbert Luethy, 'The Folly and the Crime. Thoughts on 1914', *Encounter* (March 1965), p. 12.
2. See *Die Welt von Gestern: Erinnerungen eines Europäers,* London/ Stockholm, 1941, Chapters IX–XI; Friderike Zweig, *Stefan Zweig,* Transl. Erna McArthur, London, 1946, p. 63; Randolph J. Klawiter, *Stefan Zweig: A Bibliography,* Chapel Hill, 1965, introductory essay (based uncritically on the autobiography); and Erwin Rieger, *Stefan Zweig: Der Mann und das Werk,* Berlin, 1928, p. 62. While Prater in *European of Yesterday: A Biography of Stefan Zweig,* Oxford, 1972, rightly corrects the impression given by the earlier sources that Zweig was opposed to the War from the outset, Zweig's military record-sheet and the history of the 'literarische Gruppe' seems to have escaped his attention. Prater's account of the war years is thus still incomplete and occasionally misleading. Above all, it is not critical enough of Zweig's attitude and of the subsequent attempts by the author and his wife to obscure the extent of his involvement with the government propaganda machine.
3. Kurt Peball, 'Literarische Publikationen des Kriegsarchivs im Weltkrieg 1914 bis 1918', *Mitteilungen des Österreichischen Staatsarchivs,* 14. Band (1961).
4. Prater, p. 101.
5. Friderike Zweig, op. cit., p. 84; she assumes (wrongly) that Moriz Benedikt was dead at this time and that she dealt with his son Ernst. Prater repeats this mistake. See also *Stefan Zweig-Friderike Zweig: Briefwechsel 1912–1942,* ed. Friderike Maria Zweig von Winternitz, Berne, 1951, pp. 82–83.
6. *Die Fackel,* Nr. 484–498 (October 1918), p. 127.
7. 'Vom "österreichischen" Dichter: Ein Wort zur Zeit', *Das Literarische Echo* (1 December 1914).
8. *Neue Freie Presse,* 6 August 1914.
9. *Berliner Tageblatt* (Abend-Ausgabe), 19 September 1914.
10. See *Die Welt von Gestern,* Chapter X and Romain Rolland, *Journal des Années de Guerre 1914–1919,* ed. Marie Romain Rolland, Paris, 1962, p. 63.
11. Prater, op. cit., p. 72 (letter to Kippenberg, undated but clearly written in the autumn of 1914).
12. Prater, p. 80.
13. Rolland, *Journal,* entry for 20 November 1917. Prater notes (p. 250) that if Erasmus represented Zweig as he really was, Castellio, the hero of another historical study of 1936 who showed himself more heroic and aggressive in his stand against fanaticism,

was a portrait of Zweig as he would have liked to be.
14. Prater, p. 174.
15. This was a judgement on Taine which Zweig himself quoted in his thesis in 1904. Prater observes (p. 25) that it expresses 'something of Zweig's own approach in his successful historical studies of later years'.
16. Joseph Roth, *Briefe 1911–1939*, ed. Kesten, Cologne/Berlin, 1970, letters of 26 March 1933 and 7 November 1933.
17. Prater, p. 216.
18. See Klaus Mann, *Der Wendepunkt. Ein Bericht*, Berlin/Frankfurt, 1958, p. 267; also Prater, pp. 193–94.
19. Published in the *Festschrift zum 50. Geburtstag für Max Brod*, ed. Felix Weltsch, Mährisch-Ostrau, 1934, quoted in Berendsohn, op. cit., pp. 149–50.
20. The remark, which dates from 1901, is quoted by Harry Zohn, 'The World of Arthur Schnitzler', *The Jewish Quarterly*, Vol. X, No. 1 (1963), p. 27.

CHAPTER 7 : DODERER

1. *Das Geheimnis des Reichs,* Vienna, 1930, p. 48.
2. Introduction to *Österreich: Bilder seiner Landschaft und Kultur,* Zurich, 1958.
3. Stefan Zweig, *Europäisches Erbe,* ed. Richard Friedenthal, Frankfurt a.M., 1960, p. 184.
4. This argument was included in a lecture given to the Greek PEN Club in Athens on 8 May 1964. A copy of the typescript was given to me by the author in the course of an interview in 1966. Doderer himself drew my attention to the argument. In other respects the address was a straightforward translation into French of the introductory essay in *Österreich*.
5. *Die Dämonen: Nach der Chronik des Sektionsrates Geyrenhoff,* 2 vols., Munich, 1967, p. 21; *The Demons,* transl. by Richard and Clara Winston, New York, 1961, p. 17.
6. Ibid., p. 624; transl., p. 637.
7. E.g, *Tangenten. Tagebuch eines Schriftstellers 1940–1950*, Munich, 1964, pp. 368, 397–98, 387.
8. 'Mass und Wert', *Reden und Aufsätze 4,* Frankfurt a.M., 1960, p. 805.
9. The contrast is remarked on by H. M. Waidson, 'Heimito von Doderer's Demons', *German Life and Letters*, Vol. XI (1957–58), p. 222; and by Frank Trommler, *Roman und Wirklichkeit*, Stuttgart etc., 1966, p. 147.
10. Charles A. Gulick, *Austria from Habsburg to Hitler*, Vol. I, Berkeley and Los Angeles, 1948, p. 744. For the impressions of an English eye witness, see G. E. R. Gedye, *Fallen Bastions*, London, 1939, pp. 26–38.

11. *Die Dämonen*, pp. 348–49; transl. p. 354. The translators omit the phrase in square brackets.
12. *Österreich*, op. cit., p. 10.
13. See 'Nicht alle zogen nach Berlin. Die zwanziger Jahre in Wien', *Magnum* (Cologne), 9 Jhg., Heft 35 (April 1961), and *Tangenten*, op. cit., p. 351.
14. *Die Dämonen*, pp. 252–53; transl. pp. 256–57. Again the English version omits a significant phrase. The mood recalls a passage from *Das Geheimnis des Reichs* where the narrator describes how after the Bolshevik Revolution Russia was sealed off from the West:

> Auch war deutscher Tüchtigkeit sowie jüdischer Gelenkigkeit zunächst jeder kaufmännische Zutritt durch die Unsicherheit des Eigentumes verwehrt, sie konnten also nicht (ähnlich wie sie es während des Krieges daheim getrieben hatten) die Ecksteine des aufwachsenden Schicksalsbaues hundsgleich bepissen, sie konnten nicht das schwer ringende Russland behend verwerten, und sie konnten nicht hinter der Front des Geschehens—unter dem blendenden Titel äusserster ökonomischer Notwendigkeit—Anteilsscheine ausgeben auf kommerzielle Nebenprodukte der Weltgeschichte, vielmehr wüteten Hunger und Mangel frei, wie das Schicksal sie wollte. (op. cit., p. 46)

CHAPTER 8 : MUSIL

1. Reprinted in *Robert Musil: Leben, Werk, Wirkung*, ed. Karl Dinklage, Zurich/Leipzig/Vienna, 1960.
2. Biographical details in Dinklage, ibid., 'Musils Herkunft und Lebensgeschichte'.
3. *Tagebücher, Aphorismen, Essays und Reden* (Gesammelte Werke in Einzelausgaben, zweiter Band), ed. Adolf Frisé, Hamburg, 1955, p. 442. Henceforth this volume is referred to thus: II p. 442. See also *Der Mann ohne Eigenschaften: Roman* (Gesammelte Werke in Einzelausgaben), ed. Adolf Frisé, 35.–40. Tausend, Hamburg, 1965, pp. 1495–96. Subsequent page references in the text are taken from this edition.
4. 'Europäertum, Krieg, Deutschtum' (September 1914) in II.
5. See 'Die Nation als Ideal und Wirklichkeit' (1921), II pp. 608, 617–18; also notebook entries II pp. 217, 218.
6. Frisé's dating of an essay fragment in II pp. 855–59.
7. II pp. 620, 627 and notebook entries II p. 219 (1919–20) and II p. 295 (after 1921).
8. Especially in 'Das hilflose Europa oder Reise vom Hundertsten ins Tausendste' (1922).
9. II p. 618, II p. 636, II p. 858, II p. 225.
10. The image is twice used by Musil—in II p. 590 (referring to the

lack of ideological conviction) and in II p. 603 (referring to slow economic expansion).

11. 'Der Anschluss an Deutschland' (1919), II p. 603.
12. Ibid., II p. 604.
13. Karl Kraus, *Weltgericht*, op. cit., p. 277.
14. Barea, op. cit., pp. 19–20.
15. Eduard Bauernfeld, *Erinnerungen aus Alt-Wien*, ed. Josef Bindtner, Vienna, 1923, p. 137.
16. Friedrich Funder, *Vom Gestern ins Heute. Aus dem Kaiserreich in die Republik*, 2 Vienna/Munich, 1953, pp. 373–74.
17. Barea, op. cit., pp. 37–8.
18. Buschbeck, op. cit., p. 76.
19. 'Der Anschluss an Deutschland.'
20. Cf. Wolfgang Rothe (ed.), *Der Aktivismus 1915–1920*, DTV Munich, 1969.
21. II p. 609 and II p. 598.
22. Robert Musil, *Briefe nach Prag*, ed. Barbara Köpplová and Kurt Krolop, Reinbek bei Hamburg, 1971, letter of 23 April 1921.
23. II p. 418.
24. II p. 497 (notebook entry which Frisé dates 1938–41).
25. 'Vortrag in Paris' (1935) and 'Der Dichter und diese Zeit' (1936).
26. II p. 638.
27. II p. 640.
28. Hofmannsthal, *Prosa II*, ed. H. Steiner, Frankfurt a.M., 1951, p. 18.
29. Musil, *Prosa, Dramen, späte Briefe* (Gesammelte Werke in Einzelausgaben, dritter Band), Adolf Frisé, Hamburg, 1957, p. 144.
30. II p. 590.
31. II p. 605.
32. Diary entry (1940), II p. 477.
33. I have taken as an example the passage 'Dort in Kakanien ... vor der Zeit unterbrochen worden wäre', op. cit., pp. 32–34.
34. W. Grenzmann, 'Der Mann ohne Eigenschaften. Zur Problematik der Romangestalt' in Dinklage, op. cit., p. 52.
35. Frank Kermode, 'A Short View of Musil', *Puzzles and Epiphanies*, London, 1963.
36. Soren Aabye Kierkegaard, *The Present Age*, transl. A. Dru and W. Lowrie, London, 1940, p. 15.
37. In an interview with Oskar Maurus Fontane, *Die literarische Welt*, 30 April 1926, reprinted in Dinklage, op. cit.
38. *Die Fackel*, Nr. 462–71 (October 1917), p. 171.
39. Ernst Kaiser, 'Der Mann ohne Eigenschaften: ein Problem der Wirklichkeit', *Merkur XI*, Heft 7 (July 1957). See also the exhaustive criticism of Frisé's reading of the manuscripts in Wilhelm Bausinger, *Studien zu einer historisch-kritischen Ausgabe von Robert Musils Roman 'Der Mann ohne Eigenschaften'*, Reinbek bei Hamburg, 1964. A new critical edition of the novel is in preparation.
40. Frank Trommler, *Roman und Wirklichkeit*, Stuttgart etc., 1966, pp. 87f.
41. III p. 49.

CHAPTER 9 : KRAUS

1. I have borrowed these terms from the excellent study by E. F. Timms, *Language and the Satirist in the Work of Karl Kraus*, PhD dissertation, typ., Cambridge.
2. Paul Schick, *Karl Kraus*, Reinbek bei Hamburg, 1965, p. 139.
3. Frank Field, *The Last Days of Mankind: Karl Kraus and his Vienna*, London, 1967.
4. Timms, op. cit., esp. p. 73.
5. Arthur Schnitzler, 'Bemerkungen zur Politik', *Forum* (Wien), IX. Jahr, Heft 108 (December 1962), p. 499.
6. Ibid., p. 500.
7. Karl Kraus, *Beim Wort genommen*, ed. Heinrich Fischer, Munich, 1965, p. 273.
8. Karl Kraus, *Untergang der Welt durch schwarze Magie*, ed. H. Fischer, Munich, 1960, p. 11 ('Apokalypse', October 1908).
9. Ibid., pp. 343–44 ('Sehnsucht nach aristokratischem Umgang', July 1914).
10. Ibid., p. 238.
11. Ibid., p. 240.
12. *Die Fackel*, Nr. 400, p. 92, quoted by Timms, op. cit., p. 255, note 1. References from *Die Fackel* are henceforth noted thus : F. 400.
13. Leopold Liegler, *Karl Kraus und sein Werk*, Vienna, 1920, p. 62.
14. *Untergang der Welt . . .*, p. 418.
15. Ibid., p. 361 ('Die Kinder der Zeit', August 1912).
16. Ibid., p. 444 ('Untergang der Welt durch schwarze Magie', December 1912).
17. Ibid., p. 251 ('Und Hauptmann dankt', July 1913).
18. Ibid., p. 253.
19. Ibid., p. 11 and p. 14 ('Apokalypse').
20. Caroline Kohn suggests that initially at least he may have hoped for a swift conflict which would bring about the moral and cultural regeneration of his society. See her *Karl Kraus*, Stuttgart, 1966, p. 84.
21. 'In dieser grossen Zeit', read on 19 November 1914.
22. Schick, op. cit., pp. 77–78.
23. The suggestion is confirmed by Kraus himself in a rare reference to his Italian visit—which Schick omits to cite: see 'Verbroigter Loibusch' (December 1924) in *Widerschein der Fackel. Glossen*, ed. H. Fischer, Munich, 1956, p. 390.
24. Hermann Broch, *Die Schlafwandler*, Part III, '1918. Huguenau oder die Sachlichkeit', Zurich, n.d., p. 443.
25. Field, op. cit., p. 103.
26. *Weltgericht*, p. 41 ('Die Schönheit im Dienste des Kaufmanns').
27. Ibid., p. 158 ('Eine prinzipielle Erklärung', read on 11 November 1917).
28. See 'Reklamefahrten zur Hölle', F. 577–82.
29. F. 413–17, p. 27 ('Schweigen, Wort und Tat', 30 October 1915).
30. F. 462–71 (October 1917), p. 171 ('Verwandlungen').

31. *Weltgericht.* pp. 283–84.

32. Ibid., p. 277.

33. Ibid., p. 214.

34. Timms, op. cit., p. 374.

35. See 'Ad Acta' (April 1919) in *Weltgericht*. It was the Viennese police under Johannes Schober who supported Kraus in his protest against the Army's attempt to intimidate witnesses. Kraus commended Schober for his courage and independence during the War. In 1927 he campaigned for Schrober's resignation—see pp. 220–21.

36. B.B., *Gesammelte Werke 19, Schriften zur Literatur und Kunst 2* (Werkausgabe, edition suhrkamp), Frankfurt a.M., 1967, pp. 430–31. 'Kein Wort hilft diesen Schreibern oder Rednern über die wahrhaft tödliche Stille hinweg, die ihren Auslassungen folgt, ohne Urteil werden sie abgeführt. Eine leere Stelle auf dem Papier lyncht sie. Sie haben sich um ihren Hals geredet, und man hat sie nicht unterbrochen.'

37. See Franz H. Mautner, 'Die letzten Tage der Menschheit' in *Das deutsche Drama vom Barock bis zur Gegenwart. Interpretationen,* ed. Benno von Wiese, Band II, Düsseldorf, 1958, p. 380.

38. Walter Muschg relates this progression to Döblin's *Berlin Alexanderplatz* and Barlach's 'Der gestohlene Mond'—see his *Von Trakl zu Brecht. Dichter des Expressionismus,* Munich, 1961, p. 193.

39. Timms, op. cit., p. 394.

40. Ibid., p. 401.

41. *Die letzten Tage der Menschheit,* ed. Heinrich Fischer, Munich, 1957, p. 215.

42. In *Zur Geschichte der Religion und Philosophie in Deutschland* (1834).

43. F. 766–70 (October 1927), p. 64.

44. F. 876–84 (October 1932), p. 7.

45. F. 890–905 (July 1934), p. 181.

46. Quoted by Leopold Liegler, op. cit., p. 389.

47. Friedrich Jenaczek, *Zeittafeln zur 'Fackel'. Themen—Ziele—Probleme,* Gräfelfing bei München, 1965, p. 59.

48. F. 554–56 (November 1920), p. 8.

49. For a detailed account of the relationship between them, see Field, op. cit., Chapter V.

50. F. 766–70, pp. 63–64.

51. F. 845–46 (November 1930), quoted by Jenaczek, p. 69.

52. F. 876–84 (October 1932), p. 1.

53. F. 888 (October 1933), p. 4.

54. Bertolt Brecht, 'Über die Bedeutung des zehnzeiligen Gedichts in der 888. Nummer der Fackel (Oktober 1933)', quoted in full by Kurt Krolop, 'Bertolt Brecht und Karl Kraus', *Philologica Pragensia,* IV. Jhg., Heft 2/4, pp. 219–20.

55. Even Brecht was now disillusioned—see 'Über den schnellen Fall des guten Unwissenden', also quoted by Krolop, loc. cit., pp. 226–27. To this day Kraus's decision still rankles, even among sympathetic admirers of his work like Hans Weigel who recently

NOTES273

criticised the satirist's affirmation of Austrian independence as being too cryptic. Kraus's support for Dollfuss should have been phrased more clearly and succinctly, he argues. Instead of an extended polemic against the Social Democratic leadership, Kraus should have issued a ringing appeal for national unity. See H.W., *Karl Kraus oder Die Macht der Ohnmacht*, DTV, Munich, 1972, p. 336.

56. F. 890–905, pp. 276–77.
57. F. 766–70, p. 65.
58. Field, op. cit., p. 227.
59. F. 890–905, p. 177.
60. Ibid., p. 213.
61. *Untergang der Welt* . . ., p. 418.
62. Schick, op. cit., p. 124.
63. *Beim Wort genommen,* op. cit., p. 290.
64. F. 890–905, pp. 60–61.
65. Werner Kraft has suggested that Kraus's work at this time was permeated with an intuition of his own impending death. Cf. 'Es war einmal ein Mann . . . Uber die "Dritte Walpurgisnacht" von K.K.', *Merkur* 22 (1968), p. 930.
66. J. P. Stern, 'Karl Kraus's Vision of Language', *The Modern Language Review,* Vol. LXI, No. 1 (January 1966).
67. The earliest parts of the essay are dated 'January 1934', the last 'Early July'; could the purge of June 30 which consolidated Hitler's position have increased Kraus's pessimism?
68. Instances cited by Timms, op. cit., pp. 257–59.
69. Timms points out that the actual phrase read 'Ich habe alles geprüft und erwogen' (op. cit., p. 261). Joseph Roth too admired this manifesto and called it 'ein literarischer Einfall'.
70. Timms, p. 267.
71. (a) 'Klarstellung' (F. 554), quoted in W. Kraft, *Karl Kraus: Beiträge zum Verständnis seines Werkes,* Salzburg, 1956, pp. 117–18.
    (b) F. 514–18 (August 1919), pp. 47–48.
    (c) *Die dritte Walpurgisnacht,* ed. Heinrich Fischer, Munich, 1952, p. 217.
72. Quoted by Walter Benjamin, *Illuminationen,* ed. Siegfried Unseld, Frankfurt a.M., 1961, p. 388.

CODA

1. In *Austria*, London, 1971. Stadler also shows that the Allied veto against the *Anschluss* in 1919 came as a great relief to the German government (p. 111).
2. See e.g. Kurt Sontheimer, *Antidemokratisches Denken*, op. cit., Chapter V.
3 See Horst Jarka, 'British Writers and the Austria of the Thirties' in *Österreich und die angelsächsische Welt*, 2. Band, ed. Otto Hietsch, Vienna/Stuttgart, 1968. Referring to a show-piece of post-

war municipal housing in Vienna which was also one of the centres of Schutzbund resistance in 1934, an Austrian historian has written of a 'Karl-Marx-Hof mystique' among English left-wing circles in the thirties.

Select Bibliography

This is a brief list of books relating to the historical and cultural background.

BAREA, Ilsa, *Vienna. Legend and Reality*, London and New York, 1966
BASIL, Otto, 'Panorama vom Untergang Kakaniens' in *Das grosse Erbe*, Graz/Vienna, 1962
BROCH, Hermann, *Hofmannsthal und seine Zeit*, Munich, 1964
BROOK-SHEPHERD, Gordon, *Dollfuss*, London, 1961
——, *Anschluss: The Rape of Austria*, London, 1963
CRAIG, G. H., 'Engagement and Neutrality in Weimar Germany', *Journal of Contemporary History*, Vol. II, No. 2 (April 1967)
CRANKSHAW, Edward, *The Fall of the House of Habsburg*, London, 1963 and New York, 1971
DAHRENDORF, Ralf, *Society and Democracy in Germany*, London, 1968 and New York, 1969
DEAK, Istvan, *Weimar Germany's Left-Wing Intellectuals*, Berkeley and Los Angeles, 1968
DROZ, Jacques, *Le Romantisme allemand et l'état: Résistance et collaboration dans l'Allemagne napoléonienne*, Paris, 1966
FIELD, Frank, *The Last Days of Mankind: Karl Kraus and his Vienna*, London and Mystic, Conn., 1967
FISCHER, Ernst, *Von Grillparzer zu Kafka: Sechs Essays*, Vienna, 1962.
FUCHS, Albert, *Geistige Strömungen in Österreich 1867–1918*, Vienna, 1949
GEDYE, G. E. R., *Fallen Bastions: The Central European Tragedy*, London, 1938
GEIGER, Theodor, *Aufgaben und Stellung der Intelligenz in der Gesellschaft*, Stuttgart, 1949
GEISS, Imanuel (ed.), *July 1914: Outbreak of the First World War. Selected Documents*, London, 1967
GOLDINGER, Walter, *Geschichte der Republik Österreich*, Vienna, 1962
GRIMM, Reinhold and Jost Hermand (eds.), *Exil und Innere Emigration*, Frankfurt, 1972
KLEMPERER, Klemens von, *Germany's New Conservatism: Its History and Dilemma in the Twentieth Century*, Princeton, 1957
KOHN, Hans, *Karl Kraus, Arthur Schnitzler, Otto Weininger: Aus dem jüdischen Wien der Jahrhundertwende*, Tübingen, 1962

LESER, Norbert, 'Austro-Marxism: A Reappraisal', *Journal of Contemporary History*, Vol. I, No. 2 (April 1966)

LOEWY, Ernst, *Literatur unterm Hakenkreuz: Das Dritte Reich und seine Dichtung: eine Dokumentation*, Frankfurt/Hamburg, 1969

MACARTNEY, C. A., *The Habsburg Empire 1790–1918*, London, 1968 and New York, 1969

MAGRIS, Claudio, *Der Habsburgische Mythos in der österreichischen Literatur*, Salzburg, 1966

MAY, Arthur J., *The Passing of the Hapsburg Monarchy 1914–1918*, Philadelphia, 1966

MOSSE, George L., *The Crisis of German Ideology*, New York 1964 and London, 1966

Österreich am Vorabend des Weltkrieges, publ. Institut für Österreichkunde, Graz/Vienna, 1964

REDLICH, Josef, *Austrian War Government*, New Haven, 1929

——, *Schicksalsjahre Österreichs 1908–1919: Das politische Tagebuch Josef Redlichs*, ed. Fritz Fellner, Graz/Cologne, 1953

REIMANN, Paul, *Von Herder bis Kisch. Studien zur Geschichte der deutsch-österreichisch-tschechischen Literaturbeziehungen*, Berlin, 1961

ROMMEL, Otto (ed.), *Der österreichische Vormärz*, DLER, Reihe politische Dichtung, Band 4, Leipzig, 1931

SCHORSKE, C. E., 'Politics and the psyche in *fin de siècle* Vienna', *American Historical Review*, Vol. LXVI (1961)

SONTHEIMER, Kurt, *Antidemokratisches Denken in der Weimarer Republik*, Munich, 1962.

——, *Thomas Mann und die Deutschen*, Fischer Bücherei 650, Frankfurt a.M./Hamburg, 1965

STADLER, K. R., 'Austria' in *European Fascism*, ed. S. J. Woolf, London, 1968

——, *Austria*, London and New York, 1971

STERN, Fritz, *The Politics of Cultural Despair: A Study in the Rise of the Germanic Ideology*, Berkeley and Los Angeles, 1961

STERN, J. P., *Reinterpretations: Seven Studies in 19th Century German Literature*, London and New York, 1964

TAYLOR, A. J. P., *The Habsburg Monarchy 1809–1918*, London and New York, 1964

ZEMAN, Z. A. B., *The Break Up of the Habsburg Empire 1914–1918*, London, 1961

Index

278 THE BROKEN EAGLE

Czechoslovakia, vii, 61, 65, 70, 71, 219, 248, 251, 256
Czernin, Ottokar Graf, 121, 209, 230, 245, 246, 250

Doderer, Heimito von, xi, xii, 132–47, 169, 238, 241, 268–9; *Das Geheimnis des Reichs*, 133–5; *Die Strudlhofstiege*, 133, 136, 144; *Die Dämonen*, 133, 136, 137–47; *Der Grenzwald* 135
Dollfuss, Engelbert, 19, 111, 127, 216, 224, 225, 226, 227, 228, 229, 233, 242, 255, 256, 257, 258, 259, 273,
Donauland, 115
Dostoyevsky, 69, 135, 147, 162
Dvořák, 64, 157

Ebner-Eschenbach, Marie von, 62
Ehrenstein, Albert, 70, 207
Eliot, T. S., 6, 14, 15–16, 17, 95
European movement 2, 7, 8, 118, 124, 126, 130

Fascism (*see also Italy*), 14, 15, 100, 167, 185, 223; in Austria, 80, 139, 239, 255; in Germany, 93, 100, 241; struggle against, 80, 101, 126
Fatherland Front, 227, 228, 258, 260
Federalism, 39, 42, 108, 247
Ficker, Ludwig von, 207
Fontane, Theodor, 148
Franz Ferdinand, Archduke, 36, 44, 65, 82, 105, 113, 194, 195, 196, 205, 209, 229, 243
Franz Joseph I, Emperor, 81, 82, 84, 88, 100–101, 102, 103, 104, 106, 107, 136, 176, 180, 205, 214, 233, 245
Franzos, Karl Emil, 159
Freud, Sigmund, 20, 46, 91, 113, 150, 152, 181
Fried, Alfred, 126, 206
Funder, Friedrich, 159

Ginzkey, Franz Karl, 45, 114
Goethe, Johann Wolfgang von, 20, 30, 158, 171, 200, 209
Grillparzer, Franz, xvii, xx–xxi, 1, 9, 30, 109, 145, 158, 162, 238

Grün, Anastasius, xvi, xvii, xviii, xx, 159
Gütersloh, Albert Paris, 71, 206, 207

Habsburg, Otto von, 41, 87, 88, 110, 111, 216, 251
Habsburg Myth (*see also* Supranationalism), xii, 80, 81, 83, 144, 155, 238, 261
Haecker, Theodor, 207
Hartmann, Moritz, xvi, 159
Hašek, Jaroslav (and Schweik), 10, 82, 241
Hauptmann, Gerhart, 96, 195–6, 200
Heimwehr, 18, 110, 111, 137, 223, 250, 254, 255, 256, 257, 258, 259, 260
Heine, Heinrich, 129, 186, 213, 218
Herzl, Theodor, 102, 128
Hiller, Kurt, 69, 70, 79, 163–4
Hitler, Adolf, xiv, 21, 77, 84, 89, 93, 100, 101, 110, 111, 127, 136, 166, 167, 225, 228, 229, 230, 231, 233, 239, 257, 258, 259, 260, 273
Hofmannsthal, Hugo von, vii, xi, xx, 1–32, 33, 37, 41, 45, 46, 48, 59, 64, 66, 81, 84, 86, 96, 99, 103, 109, 115, 130, 149, 152, 154, 162, 174, 176, 194, 200, 206, 236, 237, 238, 239, 241, 242, 262–3; *Christinas Heimreise*, 1; *Jedermann*, 1, 8, 26; Scandinavian addresses, 5–8, 19, 27; *Das Salzburger grosse Welttheater*, 6, 26–8, 32; 'Der Dichter und diese Zeit', 6, 19; 'Die Österreichische Idee', 7; 'Briefe des Zurückgekehrten', 8, 152; *Der Rosenkavalier*, 8, 10, 21, 25; *Der Schwierige*, 10, 21–5, 144; *Der Turm*, 10, 13, 14, 28–32, 79, 159; *Arabella*, 25–6, 159; *Die Frau ohne Schatten*, 3, 10; 'Ein Brief', 19, 152, 170–1; 'Das Schrifttum als geistiger Raum der Nation', 11–12, 21; Österreichische Bibliothek, 37, 64
Holy Roman Empire, 4, 5, 18, 40, 84, 101, 110
Horváth, Ödön von, 92
Hungarian (*see also* Revolution and Magyar), 156, 159, 160, 248, 249, 251; independent policies, 42, 85–6, 109, 153, 245, 247; antipathy to Franz Ferdinand, 105; music, 157
Hungary, 71, 85, 249, 251